KERYGMA
the BIBLE in DEPTH

Revised Edition

LEADER'S GUIDE
edited by John E. Mehl

ISBN 1-882236-00-9

The Scripture quotations contained herein are from the New Revised Standard Version of the Bible, copyrighted 1989 by the Division of Christian Education of the National Council of the Churches of Christ in the United States of America, and are used by permission. All rights reserved.

Kerygma Program Study Resources are published and distributed by The Kerygma Program, 300 Mt. Lebanon Boulevard, Pittsburgh, PA 15234. Phone 800/537-9462. Fax 412/344-1823.

the KERYGMA
program

300 Mt. Lebanon Blvd.   Pittsburgh, Pennsylvania 15234

CONTENTS

Foreword

This revision of the *Leader's Guide* has been prepared as a companion for the new edition of the *Resource Book*. Dr. Walther has thoroughly revised the material in the "Notes from the Author." We have also reviewed all of the activities in the "Session Plans" and revised previous suggestions or added new ones to correspond to changes in the *Resource Book*. In addition, we have enlarged the type size and opened up the format so the material can be read more easily.

The work of revision was begun in 1990 by Barbara Minges, who wrote a substantial portion of the original *Leader's Guide*. Following her untimely death in the fall of 1991, Dr. Byron Jackson, Associate Professor of Christian Education at Pittsburgh Theological Seminary, and Dr. Bardarah McCandless, Professor of Religion at Westminster College in New Wilmington, PA., picked up the task. Dr. D. Campbell Wyckoff, General Editor of The Kerygma Program, and Dr. Donald L. Griggs, Education Editor, reviewed the manuscript and made numerous suggestions. We are also grateful to Raymond F. Luber, Director of Seminary Relations at Pittsburgh Seminary and Patricia Heidebrecht, Assistant Manager of the United Church of Canada Bookroom, for proofreading the text and checking the biblical references. Elizabeth Modispacher, "wonder" typist at the Kerygma office, entered the copy into her Macintosh and patiently made last minute changes requested by the editorial staff.

We trust you will find this *Leader's Guide* useful as you prepare to lead *Kerygma: The Bible in Depth*. We also hope it will encourage you to create your own session plans and activities for your unique group. Over the years, several leaders have sent us suggestions for the *Guide*. Some of them are contained in this edition. Others, because of length or other considerations, have not been included. They all, however, provide evidence of the creativity of the Kerygma community.

John E. Mehl

Preparing to Lead *Kerygma: The Bible in Depth*

by Donald L. Griggs

Introduction

In this section we will be working with some of the information and skills that you as a leader will find helpful as you prepare to lead a group in a study of the Bible using the Kerygma resources and approach.

Before proceeding further you should read the Introduction (3 parts) and Theme 1, GOD SAVES A PEOPLE (4 parts). Read the appropriate portions of the *Resource Book* as well as this *Leader's Guide*. The materials in the Introduction and Theme 1 are representative of what is included for the other nine themes. By reading this material, you will understand the information, skills, resources, and guidelines outlined in this section more clearly. After planning and leading one or two themes, you will probably find it helpful to return to this article.

What Is Kerygma: The Bible in Depth?

"Kerygma," a Greek word, means "proclamation by a *herald*." In New Testament translations this is rendered as "message" or "teaching" or "gospel." We use the word here in its original sense. But we also use the word in a more inclusive sense as referring to the "message" of the whole Bible. It is that message persons will be introduced to in order to become more knowledgeable about the Bible as a whole and about the interrelatedness of the Old and New Testaments.

There are several distinguishing characteristics of this approach to the study of the Bible:

1. *Kerygma: The Bible in Depth* is *thematic*. It is not a book-by-book study, nor is it a literary, critical, or doctrinal study. It is unique in the way it explores the great experiential themes of the biblical story throughout the whole Scripture. Each of the ten themes involves participants with both the Old and New Testaments. The themes are not imposed on the Bible nor on its study; rather, they arise from Scripture and confront us as we read and explore the text. *Kerygma: The Bible in Depth* is not just a study about the Bible; it is a participation in and with the message of the Bible. Many portions of the Scripture are studied from different perspectives in more than one theme.

2. *Kerygma:The Bible in Depth* is *comprehensive* in scope, seeking to uncover as much of the biblical story as possible. Those who participate in this study should gain a sense of the Bible, including the Apocrypha, as one book and not just a collection of unrelated works of literature. The Apocrypha is included because it provides an important continuity, linking the Testaments together. Although each element of the Bible has its own integrity, there is a oneness and wholeness to which both Testaments and all of the books together bear witness. To see the Bible in this way helps to overcome any tendency to view it in a disjointed, incomplete way.

3. *Kerygma: The Bible in Depth* is both *historical* and *contemporary*, providing a means for enabling us to hear and participate in the biblical story. In this approach, the biblical story is first read from the vantage point of the people of God who lived it. The study is completed with the exploration of the meaning and significance of the biblical story for the lives of individual Christians and the community of the People of God today. *Kerygma: The Bible in Depth* is grounded in the conviction that Christians have a profoundly important religious heritage that finds its origin, its continuation, and its fulfillment in The Story of the faith and life of God's people as presented in the Bible. To mature in one's faith and life as a Christian requires knowledge of The Story, as well as the ability to translate that Story in the living of one's life.

4. *Kerygma: The Bible in Depth* is *incomplete*. The process is completed only when, and to the degree that, it becomes manifest in the faith and life of the people who participate in the study. This approach involves the people with a story, but that story comes alive only when people of faith begin to see their own story as a part of The Story. Thus the objective of *Kerygma: The Bible in Depth* is not simply to increase biblical literacy but to infuse biblical faith into the life experience of individuals and the collective life of the local church.

5. Finally, *Kerygma: The Bible in Depth* is primarily a *resource* and only one component to be integrated into the larger worshiping and working community of the church. It provides a guide to the reading and study of the Bible in the experience of the life of a local congregation. It is a process and it is a program that can be used within the life and ministry of Christian churches to assist their people in learning about, growing with, and walking in the light of the marvelous story of God's people as they live with God, with each other, and with others in the world.

Those Who Lead *Kerygma: The Bible in Depth*

You are most likely reading this *Leader's Guide* because you are considering the possibility of, or have already committed yourself to, leading a group of participants in a creative approach to studying the Bible. Whether you are a clergy person, a church educator, or a lay person, it is less important how much you remember about your previous study of the Bible than that you are now willing to engage in an intensive process of reading, studying, planning, and leading. There are no short cuts to a successful study of the Bible using the Kerygma approach. It will require a significant commitment of time and energy in order to accomplish the ambitious goals of *Kerygma: The Bible in Depth*.

In some churches there will be one study group with one leader. In other churches there may be several groups meeting separately at different times, each with its own leader. In still other churches it is possible that two or more persons may form a leadership team to share the responsibility for one or more groups. Whichever arrangement you find yourself in, you will discover your own study and preparation are enhanced when you are able to share your plans, questions, dreams, and satisfactions with others who have the same interests.

As a leader of a study group, you will function in a variety of roles at different times. You are first of all a *learner*. Being a Kerygma leader may be the best opportunity for learning more of the Bible you will ever be privileged to experience. You are not expected to be an expert teacher of the biblical material on which the course is based. However, you are expected to be prepared for each session so that you are able to guide the members of the group in a productive study.

As a result of all the reading in preparation for leading each session, you will also become a *resource person*. You will become familiar with tools for studying the Bible, audiovisual materials, resource books, and resource persons. Knowing which resource to use or recommend for a particular purpose or time is a helpful role. You are not expected to know all the answers to every question that is raised, but you should be able to direct group members to resources that will assist them to find answers for themselves.

Furthermore, you will be a *planner* who works intentionally to consider session plan suggestions, the time available, the needs, interests, and abilities of the participants, and the resources available in order to develop an appropriate plan for each session. The session plans provided in this *Leader's Guide* are very complete and offer more than you will be able to accomplish in the time you have. However, the best session plan is the one you construct, using the suggestions here as well as your own personal resources and experiences in order to meet the needs and interests of your unique group.

Being a *facilitator* of group process is also a very important role for you to perform. The thirty-four session plans include many activities that involve participants in processes of investigation, discussion, reflection, creativity, and application. The more comfortable you become in guiding group process, the more effective the study will be for others. At first, some participants may prefer having you tell them what they should know about a theme or passage. And, there are times you may be tempted to tell them all that you know. However, you will be most effective as a leader and the group will gain most from the course when they are guided by you in many different participatory activities as you explore the Bible together.

It is important for you to be a *listener*. You will not only listen to what is communicated in God's Word, but you will also listen to what the people in the group are saying. To be a listener is to care about persons, to be accepting of what they are sharing, and to be responsive to their needs and interests.

Throughout the course of study, you will be called upon to exercise several important qualities. With the constraint of time and the great body of material to study, you must be *flexible*. Unplanned questions will arise, activities will take longer than expected, and participants may want to go slower than you feel is necessary. This will require considerable flexibility on your part.

You will need to be *patient* with the authors when the written materials are confusing or unclear. Unprepared participants will test your patience. And unpredictable occurrences in the life of the group and the church will require patience.

Thirty-four or more weeks of reading, planning, and leading will require *endurance*. You may begin to feel more like a long distance runner than a sprinter. It requires pacing one's self, getting a second wind, and having a kick at the finish in order to endure such an intensive, extensive study.

Those Who Participate in Kerygma: The Bible in Depth

The people who choose to associate with a group that is studying the Bible using *Kerygma: The Bible in Depth*, do so for a wide variety of motives and bring with them many levels of readiness and ability.

When individuals are invited to attend a Kerygma group, they should be made aware from the beginning that this is not a study of the Bible where the leader does all the work of preparation and presentation. Every participant is expected to have read the appropriate material in the *Resource Book* prior to each session. Familiarity with this material is assumed by the session plans that are developed in the *Leader's Guide*. In addition to reading from the *Resource Book*, participants are expected to read at least the basic Bible texts that appear in boldface type and as many other recommended texts as possible.

Given the busy schedules most people have, there will be some times when persons come to a session with minimum preparation. You should not compromise the expectation of adequate preparation, because the experience for the whole group will suffer if the reading is not taken seriously. There are several ways you can handle the lack of preparation by the participants.

1. Encourage persons who have not read the assignments not to participate in the discussion until others have had a chance.

2. Provide some time, as a part of the session plan, to review the key texts that serve as the foundation for the session.

3. When working in pairs or small groups, be sure that those who are not prepared are distributed among the groups rather than grouped together.

Some participants will have had a lot of experience with studying the Bible, but for others this will be their first experience as adults to be involved in an in-depth study. It is important for each person to feel that he or she belongs to the group. You need to encourage both the experienced and inexperienced participants to be mindful and appreciative of each other.

Reviewing the Printed Resources

There are a number of printed resources that are included as part of *Kerygma: The Bible in Depth*. Each resource makes a significant contribution to the whole program.

The Bible

The major curricular resource for *Kerygma: The Bible in Depth* is the Bible. The *New Revised Standard Version* is the translation on which this course is based. However, participants will be able to engage in the study effectively with another translation. In fact, the study is enhanced by the presence of several translations. The approach is to study representative texts; thus one is not required to read the entire

Bible. Instead, participants are offered relevant passages for each theme that provide sufficient background and focus for the study of that theme. A study Bible with notes for each section of the text and other study aids is recommended for the leader as well as the participants. A number of good study Bibles are available. Among those containing good study notes are the *New Oxford Annotated Bible with Apocrypha (NRSV)*, *The Oxford Study Bible with Apocrypha*, and the *New Jerusalem Bible* (*with complete notes*).

The *Resource Book*

The *Resource Book* is a guide to reading the Bible thematically. This is the text that both leaders and participants will use to guide their study. There are four to six pages of text for each part of each theme, with all the related Bible passages identified clearly. The purpose of the text in the *Resource Book* is to identify relevant Scripture readings with sufficient information to explain the relationship of the various readings with one another and with the theme. This volume contains all the necessary information for the entire study to enable persons to participate responsibly in the group sessions. It is essential that the leader read the *Resource Book* in order to be adequately prepared to lead each session.

As you review the *Resource Book*, you will note that each part begins with a Summary and includes a listing of Basic Bible References and a Word List. In the main body of the text, the Basic Bible References are in boldface type. At the end of each part is a section entitled "For Further Study and Reflection." You will want to review this section with the option of directing the group members' attention to it generally or on a week-by-week basis. This section will from time to time encourage participants to use additional study resources. For this purpose the group should have available from the church library basic Bible reference books. These will include as a minimum a Bible dictionary, atlas, commentary, and concordance.

As a leader, you should read the *Resource Book* from beginning to end before undertaking leadership of a study group and before you start planning any particular sessions. This effort will provide you with an overview of the total study. As you then plan for each session, you will need to reread the appropriate material for this session.

The *Leader's Guide*

This is the book you have in your hands at this moment. It will be the indispensable resource you will use for planning each session. You will notice that the *Leader's Guide* contains:

1. The Table of Contents and this article, a session planning form and a description of other study resources.

2. The Introduction (three parts), Ten Themes (thirty parts), and a concluding session. The word *part* is used to designate a study session. Ordinarily there should be a minimum of one and a half hours of meeting time for each session. For best results, two or more hours are preferable. (See the section below on number of sessions and amount of time.)

Each of the thirty-four parts includes:

1. "Notes from the Author." Dr. James A. Walther provides background information on the content of the biblical texts referred to in the *Resource Book*. Included are helpful comments on ways of dealing with various issues that may arise in group discussion.

2. "Session Plans." Extensive suggestions for session planning are provided for each part. *Kerygma: The Bible in Depth* is a highly flexible resource, and its flexibility is evidenced in session methodology as well as in other areas. Kerygma groups have been successfully led with the lecture and discussion format as well as with an emphasis on participatory activities. Most clergy have derived much of their education from a lecture format and may be most familiar and most comfortable with this approach. There is, however, overwhelming evidence that adult learning is increased and enhanced when group members participate directly in the learning process. It is strongly recommended that all leaders review the session plans and incorporate as many suggestions as appropriate into each session. Further suggestions on the specifics of session planning will be found in the following sections entitled "Planning a Study Session" and "Additional Guidelines for Leading a Study Group".

Number of Sessions and Amount of Time

In the early stages of thinking about *Kerygma: The Bible in Depth*, a number of questions usually arise, such as:

How will this study fit into our adult education schedule?

How many weeks or sessions does it take?

How much time should be planned for each session?

Perhaps those questions have already been answered in your church and arrangements have been made for scheduling. If the questions have been answered, you and your group will have to adjust to what is already planned. However, if the questions have not been answered, you may want to consider a variety of options. A comprehensive and detailed review of the various issues noted above is contained in *The Adult Education Idea Book*, available from The Kerygma Program office.

Kerygma: The Bible in Depth is flexible enough to fit into a variety of church settings. Each of the thirty-four parts is presented as one session, with enough suggested in the session plans for a meeting lasting two to two and a half hours. This presumes a midweek or Sunday evening format where enough time is available. However, it is quite possible to divide the session plans for each part into two or three segments, so that each segment fits into the usual one-hour Sunday morning study format.

It is possible for a group to complete *Kerygma: The Bible in Depth* in thirty-four weeks. Many churches have done this, and it is quite an accomplishment. Another strategy is to schedule two or three themes for an autumn term, another two or three themes for a spring term, and continue over the period of two or more years to complete the program.

It is important for all who become involved in the study to begin with the Introduction and the first theme. Thereafter, it is possible to enter any combination of the other themes whenever they are presented. Once a study group has begun, it is advised that persons not begin the study in "midstream." If this is not practical, individuals should be given a review of the Introduction before joining the group. Another option is to add new persons at specified times, e.g., at the conclusions of Theme 3 and Theme 6.

Planning a Study Session

By reading the Bible texts, the *Resource Book*, the *Leader's Guide*, and any other supplementary resources, you have already accomplished a major task of planning for leading a study session. However, there is one more important task: preparing a workable session plan to use with the group. Even though there is a detailed outline of a plan for each session (part), it is important to prepare your own session plan appropriate for your group. Only you know the unique situation of your group; the number of participants, the amount of time for each session, the interests, abilities, and needs of each participant, and circumstances of the ministry of your church. Thus, you are the only one who can prepare a session plan that is truly appropriate for your particular group.

In preparing your session plan you will want to give special attention to the following elements that appear at the beginning of each part in the *Resource Book*.

1. *Summary*. This is the focus of the session. All that you and the participants will do during the session will be done to uncover the meaning of the summary statement in terms of its biblical and its contemporary significance.

2. *Basic Bible References*. These are the essential references that you and the participants must read. These Bible texts provide the basis for the study in the session. They will ordinarily be used in one or another of the suggested activities.

3. *Word List*. These words are used in the content of the study. They are usually unfamiliar words for many people. Yet they are words for which you, as the leader, should have a working definition. Check a Bible dictionary for assistance with meanings of these words. The comments by Dr. Walther will also be helpful.

The Session Plans in the Leader's Guide include:

1. *Learning Objectives*. The three to six statements presenting the learning objectives indicate what the leader will help the participants to accomplish as a result of their study. When leading adults, it is appropriate to share these objectives with the members of the group at the beginning of each session. The selection of activities is then guided by the objectives considered most important. The statements of learning objectives can also be used as a basis for evaluating whether or not the participants have accomplished what was intended. A word of caution: accomplishing the learning objectives is not all there is to leading a study group. Some of the most important things that happen among the participants in a group cannot be evaluated by learning objectives; forming of Christian community, growing in faith, developing the ability to speak comfortably about one's faith, nurturing the spiritual life, as well as other important matters regarding the Christian faith and life.

2. *Resources*. In addition to the Bible, *Resource Book*, and supplementary readings, a list of those resources that are needed for the various activities is provided.

3. *Leadership Strategy*. This is the heart of the session plan. The leadership strategy is organized in three sections:

a. "Setting the Stage" is a time for inviting persons to become involved with the subject of the session. Ordinarily it will take ten to twenty minutes for this segment of the session plan.

b. "Exploring the Scripture" is what the study is all about. Most of the time of the session will be spent with activities that enable exploration of several biblical texts which are integral to the theme. Usually three or more activities will be planned for this portion of the session.

c. "Closing" is a time to bring closure to the session, to summarize what has been explored, and to make applications of what has been learned to one's own faith and life experiences.

4. *Looking Ahead.* In order to work effectively at the next session, some special tasks may need preparation by some or all of the participants. For example, occasionally a brief report requiring advance preparation is called for. Participants are invited to volunteer for these assignments. Of course, the basic assignment for each week is reading the *Resource Book* and the recommended Bible texts.

As you prepare for each session, it may be helpful to use the Session Planning Form that is included at the conclusion of this section. You may make copies of these pages or develop your own form.

Using Leadership Strategies

As you read the suggestions in each Leadership Strategy, you will notice that several activities are usually offered for each part of the session. These activities are clearly separated by **or, and,** or **and/or** in the center of the page. Ordinarily no group would be expected to complete all the activities that are recommended for each session. And there will be times when you, as the leader, will decide to do something different from what is suggested. You should feel free to utilize your own creativity, but be sure that what you do relates directly to the subject of the theme and enables fulfillment of the learning objectives.

When choosing from among the options that are suggested, there are several things to keep in mind.

1. The *amount of time* available is a critical factor which influences your decision. When faced with the choice of trying to do two activities quickly (perhaps superficially) or doing one activity thoroughly, it is usually best to do the one activity.

2. *Activities that involve participants* interacting with one another, preparing a presentation to share with others, or working cooperatively on a task, will always take more time than it does for the leader to present the same information. However, when persons are significantly involved in the process of their own learning, they will be much more motivated and will accomplish more in the end.

3. Some activities are designed to probe in *depth*, and others are intended to provide an *overview*. On the other hand, there are activities for individuals or pairs or small groups or the whole group. The important thing is to develop a session plan that has balance, so that there are some in-depth and some overview activities. There also needs to be a balance between individual, small group, and whole group activities.

4. The *interests, abilities*, and *previous experience* of the members of the group will influence your choices regarding which of the suggested activities to implement. It is important for you to become acquainted with the members of the group in order to make such judgements. It may be self-defeating to plan an activity that you feel will be resisted by many in the group.

5. Your own *interests, skills*, and *concerns* must also be considered when deciding which activity to choose. You should be reasonably comfortable with the activity and confident that it can be used effectively to guide the group's study. However, as the course develops and you become comfortable with the group and the subject matter you should be willing to try some of the activities that are new to you. All of the activities have been tested and proven by other leaders so that you should have confidence that whatever activity you select from the session strategy will work for you as well.

6. Some activities rely more on *presentation* of information by the leader and/or some of the participants, and other activities require more *involvement* by the participants. Again, it is important to make selections of activities that will provide an appropriate balance of leader input and group participation.

Planning for leading a group's study is an art. There is no right session plan for every topic or every situation or every leader. Neither is there just one right way to go about planning. You need to be willing to practice the art of planning until you find a process that works effectively. It is important to be willing to try new strategies, new resources, and new approaches to working with the group. Through practicing the art of planning and leading a group in the study of the Bible, you, as well as the group members, will discover the ways that work best.

Guidelines for Adult Education

The following guidelines provide a summary of the most recent findings about adult education.

• **Adults are responsible for their own learning.**

  Therefore, it is important not to develop dependent relationships whereby the learners look to the leader as the authority and primary source of information.

• **Adults learn best when they can participate directly in the process of their own learning.**

  Therefore, opportunities should be provided in each session for participants to make decisions about what and how they will learn and to interact with the subject matter and other learners.

• **Adults represent a variety of learning styles as well as different stages of physical, emotional, and spiritual development.**

  Therefore, learners will be related to individually without assuming that all adults are the same. Learners will be encouraged to work at their own pace and to make applications that are appropriate to themselves.

• **Learning is reinforced best when adults have the opportunity to practice skills and to express ideas in their own words.**

  Therefore, in each session there will be opportunities to practice particular skills and to express personal insights and interpretation.

• **Learning occurs within an environment of trusting relationships.**

  Therefore, it is important to develop a process whereby persons will be encouraged to share feelings, needs, and concerns as well as information and ideas. In such a setting persons will be helped to become caring about and supportive of one another.

- **With adults it is not necessary to use competitive activities to motivate them to want to participate and learn.**

    Therefore, the activities and resources will represent a cooperative, collaborative style of learning.

- **Adults who have positive self-concepts are less threatened by new information and experiences.**

    Therefore, leaders will be encouraged to use strategies that enhance a person's sense of self-worth.

- **Adults will increase their knowledge and skill to a greater extent when they gain a sense of satisfaction and experience success in those activities that are planned for them.**

    Therefore, the session plans of the Kerygma Program study resources will present a variety of activities that are designed to enable participants to achieve satisfaction and success.

Additional Guidelines for Leading a Study Group

There are many factors that contribute to the effective, productive working of a group. What follows is an attempt to summarize some of the most important considerations about effective group leadership.

What kind of leader do you want to be?

An *autocratic* leader is one who takes charge, who assumes all the responsibility for the group, and who is primarily concerned about getting the task accomplished. There are times when it is necessary for a leader to present information to the group or to make a decision on behalf of the group. However, the Kerygma approach to the study of the Bible will be most successful when the leader does not do all the work for the group.

The *laissez-faire* leader is one who sits back, enjoys what is happening, and lets the group go its own way. It is important from time to time to relax and not be too agenda-conscious. But the approach suggested by the Kerygma Program assumes that the leader is actively engaged in guiding the group's process.

The *democratic* leader functions in a partnership style. The leader of this type shares responsibility with the group's members for the content and the process of the study. *Kerygma: The Bible in Depth* will be studied more effectively when led by persons who seek to involve others in sharing their questions, insights, and affirmations.

How will you keep the group focused on the theme or the task?

Because participants will have questions, opinions, and insights about many aspects of the study of the Bible, it will be very easy for the group to stray from the focus of the session. The leader needs to tread the narrow line between letting the discussion proceed with its own momentum and directing the discussion back to the planned task. Sometimes the leader can note the group's interest in a topic and schedule further discussion as part of another session. There are also times when it will be possible to use what the group is talking about by relating it directly to the next topic, question, or activity. On occasion the group may just need to be reminded that it has gotten sidetracked.

What will you do when someone offers a contradictory point of view?

If you encourage members of the group to think and speak for themselves so that there is a lot of interaction, then it should not be surprising that persons will feel free to offer contradictory ideas and will, on occasion, disagree with you, with Dr. Walther, or even with the Apostle Paul. When disagreements occur be thankful that the individuals feel free to express themselves. You can accept what persons say even if you disagree with them. You can encourage them to clarify what they mean or to give the evidence that leads them to their position. It is not necessary for you to defend Dr. Walther or the Apostle Paul; they can defend themselves by what they have written. However, it is important to be sure that you and the others have read carefully and worked hard to understand what was written.

How will you respond when you don't know the answer to a question?

There is nothing more frustrating to a group than a leader who tries to bluff his or her way through a topic or a question. A basic premise of this study is that the leader is a learner among learners. It is not necessary for the leader to be authoritative in all subjects of the study. It is much more important to know where to turn for the needed information, to encourage the group to work toward its understanding, and/or to be willing to admit that you do not know something when you don't.

How will you establish a climate that is relaxed as well as stimulating?

In order for effective group process to develop, there are several very simple, yet significant, things you as the leader can do:

1. Speak to persons by name and encourage everyone to share enough of himself or herself so that all members of the group feel that they know one another.

2. Arrange the room so that persons are in a circle or square, so that everyone can see all other members of the group. This arrangement suggests a cooperative style of participation.

3. It is preferable for participants to be seated at tables so that they do not have to juggle their Bibles, books, and coffee cups on their laps.

4. Have a pot of hot water handy and the makings for coffee, tea and hot chocolate.

5. If the group meets for more than ninety minutes in a session, take a short break about half way through the session.

6. Be sure the meeting space is comfortable with regard to heat, lighting, chairs, etc.

The Art of Asking Questions*

If we desire to involve persons in serious interaction with one another and with the subject of the session, we will enable that process by asking effective questions. Questions may be one of the most valuable resources available to the leader as well as to the participants. The leader with even minimal experience can learn to ask good questions. And the church with the smallest budget can still afford to invest in valuable questions.

Questions may be used in at least a dozen different ways to:

1. introduce a new subject

2. discuss a familiar subject

---

*Based on a chapter from *Teaching Teachers to Teach* by Donald L. Griggs, published by Abingdon Press, 1980.

3. review a subject studied earlier

4. invite interpretation of a biblical passage

5. connect a biblical concept to personal experience

6. evaluate a recording, film, or other resource

7. motivate further research on a subject

8. brainstorm solutions to a problem

9. interview a guest resource person

10. consider alternative actions

11. clarify personal values

12. guide expression of beliefs

There are many ways to categorize questions. In all the categories there seem to be generally three different types or levels of questions.

Type One: Information Questions

Questions of this type assume that there are right answers. As a result of remembering the information or the facts related to a subject, persons are able to give correct answers when called upon. Information questions tend to be limited in their ability to provoke exploration or discussion by the group. When leaders ask too many information questions, the participants may feel as if they are taking a test. People often sense that leaders have all the answers to the questions they ask, so it is important to have the right answer to please the leader. Information is very important for setting the context for studying a subject; however, there are many ways to present information other than asking questions. Some examples of information questions:

In what city were followers of Jesus first called Christian?

Where in a town did apostles often go first to present the gospel message?

Type Two: Interpretation Questions

Interpretation questions require participants to think about, analyze, explore, and evaluate a subject. Based upon previous experience, available information, or a given situation, group members are guided to reflect upon the experience or information in an interpretive or analytical way. Interpretation questions are open-ended. Several people can be asked the same interpretation question, each can offer a different answer and each answer can be acceptable. Interpretation questions assume that there is a variety of points of view, that the leader has no correct answer in mind, and that together the leaders and participants will find the question worthy of their time and thoughtfulness. Questions of this type motivate people to think and express themselves, to become more involved in the session. Interpretation questions can be introduced with phrases such as:

What are some reasons. . .?

Why do you suppose. . .?

Let's think a minute about why. . .?

What are some examples of . . .?

What is the possibility of. . .?

Who do you think will. . .?

What are the alternatives for . . .?

What are your thoughts about. . .?

Some examples of interpretation questions:

What are some reactions Jesus' followers in Antioch might have had to being called Christians?

Why do you suppose Peter, Paul, and others often went first to the synagogue to preach when they entered a new town?

Type Three: Personalized Questions

With personalized or identification questions, leaders encourage participants to apply the subject to themselves in a personal way that helps them express their own identity. Information and interpretation questions can be impersonal—unrelated to the participants' interests or values. Personalized questions are designed to help people express their own values, commitments, choices, or affirmations regarding a particular subject or issue. Personalized questions guide the members of the group to invest something of themselves as they identify with persons, events, or situations of a past, present, or future time frame. A discussion of value questions moves out of the hypothetical and abstract arena into a very real and personal space. Questions at this level are essential if persons are going to grow in their faith and life commitments. In using questions of this type we must be careful to avoid embarrassing the group members by getting too personal or putting them "on the spot."

Some examples of personalized questions:

> When someone identifies you as a Christian, what are some feelings or reactions you have?

> If you had been members of the synagogue in Ephesus when Paul came to preach, how do you think you would have responded to his message?

When preparing to lead a discussion that utilizes a variety of questions, there are ten guidelines that will be helpful to keep in mind.

1. *Ask questions that are more open than closed.*

   Questions with only one right answer or implying a "yes" or "no" response are more closed. These questions are more a test of memory than they are inquiry into subject matter. When tempted to ask a closed question, make a statement instead. Then ask open, analytical, probing questions.

2. *Ask only one question at a time.*

   More than one question is confusing to the participants. Leaders who ask several questions at once usually have not thought carefully or prepared adequately and are "fishing" for the right question.

3. *Present questions to the whole group.*

   Instead of putting one person "on the spot" by directing a question to one, offer the question to the whole group. By being aware of a person's readiness it is possible to recognize who wants to answer. A participant can be called upon to respond without the leader speaking a word—through eye contact, gesture with the hand, or a nod of the head.

4. *Provide feedback after a person responds.*

The leader can reinforce participants and facilitate further discussion by providing verbal and nonverbal feedback so that they will know the leader has heard and received the response.

5. *After an initial question and response, follow up with probing questions.*

Probing questions follow first questions. Probing questions lead to further inquiry and exploration in depth of the subject. Probing questions can also provide a degree of reinforcement and feedback.

6. *After asking a question, be silent.*

The best "next step" after asking a question is to be silent. If the question is clearly stated, and if the members of the group have sufficient data to answer, they need some time to think. Ten seconds is not too much time. However, ten seconds of silence can feel like an eternity to a leader who is a little anxious. Leave the burden of the silence on the group. Bite your tongue and relax; usually someone will respond.

7. *Use an inquiry style rather than an interrogation style.*

Inquiry is a style or approach that says to the group members, "I'm interested in what you think and say." Interrogation puts persons on the defensive and inhibits their ability to think and express themselves creatively.

8. *Encourage people to ask their own questions.*

Questions are not just the property of the leader but can also be used effectively by the participants.

9. *Avoid echoing participants' responses.*

There are two valid reasons for repeating participants' responses: to reinforce the answer or to state it loudly enough so that others can hear who might have missed it the first time.

10. *Accept responses as if they were gifts.*

When people venture an answer to a question, they are risking something of themselves. Every person hopes his or her answer will be accepted. They will feel more confident to respond to open questions than to closed questions. Also, leaders will be more able to accept responses to open questions. We are not always perfectly pleased with every gift we receive, but we are usually gracious in receiving even the ones that don't please us.

Closing Words

All that we have been talking about in this chapter should help you to feel ready to begin preparing to lead your first sessions of *Kerygma: The Bible in Depth.* You are engaged in an outstanding program that will not only enrich the lives of many persons in your church but will also enrich your life and faith. As a result of your own study, you will discover many new and exciting truths in the Scriptures and you will be pleased to have an eager group of learners with whom to share what has been discovered. As a result of leading others in their study of the Bible, you will be rewarded again and again by the satisfaction of seeing persons become newly empowered by the authority and relevance of God's Word for their life and faith experience. You, and those with whom you share this adventure of studying the Bible, will find that the time spent together, the discussions of different interpretations, the challenge of difficult passages, and the commitment to one another will all contribute to a bonding of Christian fellowship where God's Spirit is present and working in your midst. Your study of the Bible should lead from study to service—service through leading others, through responding to the needs of hurting people, and through representing the Christ who calls us all to be disciples. May you and your people be abundantly blessed by God as you seek to grow in faithfulness to God's Word!

Kerygma Leader's Session Planning Form

Course Name _____ Leader _____

Session _____ Date _____ Time _____

Learning Objectives:

Real Time (i.e. 7:30 - 7:40)	Strategies/Activities	Resources Needed

Real Time (i.e. 7:30 - 7:40)	Strategies/Activities	Resources Needed

Supplementary Books

for the Kerygma Leader

In earlier editions of Kerygma Program study resources the *Leader's Guide* recommended the purchase of several reference books and listed specific readings by page in preparation for each session. The concept was that leaders should be prepared to respond to questions related to issues raised in the session. While reference books were recommended, leaders were also alerted to the danger of relying too heavily on secondary references lest the group study become a study *about* the Bible rather than a study *of* the biblical texts themselves.

In subsequent years two issues have arisen that make identifying references by page problematical. The first is that many of the references originally selected have either gone out of print or have been published in new editions, making the identification of pages inaccurate. Secondly, the pricing of books has made some texts unreasonably expensive.

With this edition of *Kerygma: The Bible in Depth*, we continue to recommend that leaders have access to standard reference texts. By using the Table of Contents and the Index in the various volumes, relevant material is easily accessible. In the *Leader's Guide* there will also be suggestions from time to time about research on ideas and concepts found in such familiar resources as a Bible dictionary, commentary, etc. In addition, leaders should feel free to use whatever reliable texts they have available, most of which should be in a good church library. The Kerygma Program has in stock a short list of standard reference books which are identified in the following section titled "How to Study the Bible."

for the Participants

A primary goal of The Kerygma Program is to promote a responsible study of the Bible by adults. To facilitate and enrich such study we recommend that participants in Kerygma study groups use a good study Bible and have access to selected reference books. Several of these volumes are listed in "How to Study the Bible," which is also included in all *Resource Books*. Leaders should review this section for recommendations on standard reference texts and be prepared to discuss the material with members of the study group as they begin their work.

KERYGMA

the BIBLE in DEPTH

Revised Edition

LEADER'S GUIDE

NOTES FROM THE AUTHOR

About the Introduction

These three introductory parts emphasize the concept of the Bible as a whole, and it will be helpful to use the phrase "Bible whole" repeatedly. This insistence on a difference between "the whole Bible" and "the Bible whole" is intended to stress the point that we shall not study the Bible piecemeal. This does not mean that we are going to ignore the diversity of the Scriptures; it means rather that we want to overcome fragmentary knowledge. On the other hand, it does not mean that we propose to read or discuss everything in the Bible.

Our purpose is to emphasize texts and ideas that bind the Bible together in spite of its diversity. We do not aim to make the Bible fit some doctrine but rather to let the Bible speak for itself and demonstrate its own authority. I have reached personal conclusions, of course, from my own years of Bible study and teaching, but I have tried to let the Bible produce its own evidence and to help those who follow this program find out the message of the Scriptures for themselves.

The three introductory sessions also aim to convey an idea of the scope, design, and purpose of this Kerygma program. We shall think together about the Bible whole, recognize our need to know more about it, and realize how this study program can meet this need. Thus we are less likely to have false expectations. Such a wide-ranging survey as this cannot dwell at length on all the detailed theological questions that will surely arise. Neither shall we always be able to explore the relationship between biblical faith and our own life situations as extensively as we might like. These things are eminently worth doing, however. The foundation of biblical knowledge that this Kerygma study provides will facilitate such pursuits more effectively in the future.

About This Session

Be sure you have absorbed Donald Griggs' article on "Preparing to Lead *Kerygma: The Bible in Depth*." Since this will be the first group experience, encourage a free flow of ideas focused on perceptions of the nature of the Bible. Probably it will be the first time some have faced this question outside of a dogmatic framework. It is important for all to clarify their perceptions at this beginning point.

Someone may raise the issue of inspiration. This is really a theological doctrine, and its definition should take into account the formation of the canon, a subject that will be considered in Part 2. For now it should be enough to recognize that the churches have never spoken with a unanimous voice on this matter and to promise to consider the issue further at appropriate points. The name "Kerygma" (see *Resource Book*, page viii) indicates that our aim is to trace the message of the Bible whole. We must therefore sidestep many fascinating lines of inquiry that should be deferred to other courses or to private study.

In connection with this issue, it is important to distinguish between authority and inspiration. It is quite possible to agree about the Bible's authority and to disagree about just how the Bible is inspired. It should be clear at the outset that we have a very high view of the authority of the Bible. Otherwise we should probably not undertake a program such as this. This authority implies that in some way the Bible is uniquely inspired. I believe that we should find that inspiration in the proclamation (*kerygma*) of the Bible rather than approach the Scriptures with a preconceived idea or dogmatic view of how that inspiration has taken place.

Dr. Griggs urges you to be sensitive to the needs of the group. If the question of inspiration persists, it may be useful to note New Testament evidence about the views of the Old Testament Scriptures held by first-century Christians. For example, New Testament references to the Old Testament show a clear preference for certain books. Nearly half of the quotations and allusions come from five books: Psalms, Isaiah, Genesis, Exodus, and Deuteronomy. There are many allusions to the deuterocanonical books of Sirach and Wisdom of Solomon and to the pseudepigraphical book of Enoch. (The point may be made without pursuing the character of these books.) Quotations from the very early Greek translation of the Old Testament ("Septuagint") often show variation from the Hebrew. For two examples see Psalm 8:4, 5, quoted in Hebrews 2:6-8, and Isaiah 40:13 in 1 Corinthians 2:16.

About Learning the Books of the Bible

You should stress that learning the names of the books of the Bible in order is not pedantic drill-work. Assure the group that much time will be saved in later study if the organization of the basic textbook is mastered at the outset.

The Jewish classification of the Hebrew Scriptures merits examination. This represents the earliest organization of the books and helps to explain some difficulties that may arise from our usual classification. This is particularly important with regard to the "Writings."

Supplementary Reading

The Supplementary Books mentioned in "How to Study the Bible" will provide additional resources for your study. Not all the details in these books are equally applicable to the theme or part under consideration. The books are obviously organized on different plans, and they may be used in several ways. (1) You may read some of the books through and then review for each topic as appropriate. (2) You may check the indexes to find references appropriate to each subject as it occurs. (3) You may develop your own style of using references, one that suits you best.

Be sure to read the notes in the study Bible used by the majority of the group. Occasionally an article in the *New Oxford Annotated Bible* (NOAB) will be brought to your attention. Group members who use this study Bible may also be reading these articles. Sometimes articles in *Harper's Bible Dictionary* will be suggested as particularly helpful in the part being studied. You will readily find similar references in other Bible dictionaries.

For this part you will find helpful sections on the composition and formation of the canon in the *Lion Encyclopedia of the Bible, Introducing the Old Testament, Understanding the Old Testament, Introducing the New Testament, Understanding the New Testament,* and *Harper's Bible Dictionary.*

SESSION PLANS

Learning Objectives

This session is intended to enable participants to:

1. Recognize the members in the study group by sight.

2. Name the major categories used to group the books of the Bible and begin to recognize which books belong in each category.

3. Formulate brief working definitions of the terms in the Word List.

4. Define the word canon and explain briefly how the canon was formed.

Resources You May Need

Resource Books
Chalk and chalkboard
Newsprint, markers, and masking tape
Name tags and small markers
Copies of the supplementary books and other resources available to the participants
Church creeds or confessions about the Bible
Copy of the Apocrypha or a Bible containing the Apocrypha
Copies of the list of definitions for the Word List
Bible Bookshelf post cards or bookmarks
66 color-coded index cards with the names of the books
   of the Bible
Filmstrip of "A History of the Bible in English," (available from The Kerygma
   Program) and copies of the review sheet, "The English Bible: An Overview".
Filmstrip projector, screen, and cassette player

Leadership Strategy

SETTING THE STAGE

1. Provide nametags for the participants. Many groups have permanent nametags that can be used every week. If your group is large, this is particularly important. Don't forget to make a nametag for yourself!

2. After all the members of the group have gathered, begin the session with an opening prayer. This is an appropriate way to start each session.

Donald Griggs has developed a useful resource for this purpose entitled *Meeting God in the Bible: 60 Devotions for Groups*. Each activity comes with Participants Resource Sheets which may be duplicated for members of your group. Indexes listing the Bible passages used in the activities and suggesting particular activities for every theme and part in *Kerygma: The Bible in Depth* are included.

If you prefer to lead the group in a prayer of your own, focus on inviting God to join the group in their study and to open their hearts and minds to hear, understand, and obey God's word. You may want to make specific references to the theme for a particular session. Sometimes you may decide to use a written prayer, which the group can pray in unison. After a few weeks, ask particular members of the group to lead the opening prayer activities in future sessions.

3. Since this is the first time members of your Kerygma study group will meet together, it is important to spend some time getting acquainted. Don't rush this part. The time you spend helps the group begin to become a community. One of the biggest hurdles some people face is speaking in front of a group. By giving them an opportunity to share their names and some information, you are providing a chance for them to hear their own voices. This helps break down the barriers to participation.

If you have a small group, go around the room and have persons introduce themselves and respond to some of the questions below. Write them on newsprint or the chalkboard. If your group is large, divide into smaller groups for this get acquainted exercise. It is also a good idea to spend a few moments describing your own involvement in study groups and your reasons for being a Kerygma leader.

 a. What is a childhood memory you have related to the Bible?

 b. What are some previous experiences you have had studying the Bible?

 c. Why did you decide to participate in this study of the Bible?

 d. What are some of your expectations as you begin this study?

4. In "Preparing to Lead *Kerygma: The Bible in Depth,*" Donald Griggs describes some important characteristics of The Kerygma Program study materials. One part of his article you might review with the group is "Those Who Participate in *Kerygma: The Bible in Depth.*" See also the section entitled "Guidelines for Adult Education." These will help to clarify what you expect of the members of the group by way of preparation and participation, as well as the role you play as leader.

and

If the participants did not receive their *Resource Books* before this session, distribute them now. Invite them to do the following:

 a. Locate the Table of Contents and note the theme and part names.

 b. Look at Theme 1, Part 1, and identify the basic components found in each part of this study. These include the Summary, Basic Bible References, Word List, general text, and the section titled "For Further Study and Reflection." Explain that the material in this final section is optional, but that you will be asking them to complete some of the suggestions from time to time.

c. Note the amount of Scripture reading that is included in the text and call attention to the various categories by which the references are designated. (See page ix in the Preface of the *Resource Book*.)

If copies of the supplementary books and other resources will be available to the group, display them now and explain that there will be an opportunity to practice using them in Part 3 of the Introduction.

EXPLORING THE SCRIPTURE

1. On page 1 in the *Resource Book* the participants are asked to state in their own words a response to the question, "What is the Bible?" Ask them to brainstorm responses to this question. If you distributed the *Resource Books* before this session, members of the group can use the material they have prepared. List their ideas on newsprint or a chalkboard. Then lead the group in noting similarities among the ideas. Attempt to formulate a comprehensive answer to the question, incorporating the major ideas that were collected. Save your notes from this discussion for review in the final session of the program entitled "Last Things."

or

If your group is large, divide it into three or four smaller groups. Ask each small group to develop an answer to the question "What is the Bible?" A scribe from each small group can write the answer on newsprint and then share it with the total group. As the answers are presented, note their similarities and work to formulate a comprehensive answer to the question.

or

Distribute paper to the participants. Working individually the members of the group are to write two or three sentences that will complete the statement, "To me the Bible is …" Invite those who are willing to share their statements. Use them to create a composite list on one or two sheets of newsprint. Reflect on the list together. Note the similarities and differences among the responses.

and/or

Many denominations have developed credal statements about the Bible. Collect and copy several of these. Divide the participants into small groups and give each group one of the statements. Ask them to respond to these or similar questions:

a. How does the statement you are studying respond to the question, "What is the Bible?"

b. What parts of the statement were included in the list we prepared as a group?

c. What parts of the statement were not included in our list?

d. What parts of the statement do you question? What parts do you affirm? Why?

Ask the small groups to share what they have discovered as they complete the exercise.

2. Familiarity with the names of the books of the Bible and the groupings in which they are placed is an important part of this session. If the participants have not had an opportunity to read the Introduction, Part 1 in their *Resource Books*, give them a few minutes to scan pages 2-4.

and/or

Have the members of the group locate the chart titled "The Books of the Bible" on pages 249-250 in the Appendix of their *Resource Books*. Point out the different order in which the books of the Old Testament appear on the three lists. Note the names of the books of the Apocrypha. Display a copy of the Apocrypha or a Bible which includes these books. Discuss the major categories which are used to group the books in the Old Testament and the New Testament.

Explain that each part of the *Resource Book* begins with a Word List. They will find it helpful to write brief definitions for the words that are presented. Provide copies of the list of brief definitions of the terms in the Word List for this part, which you will find on page 10 of this book.

or

If you prefer, assign each of the terms in the list to a different person or pair. Ask the participants to scan the *Resource Book* to develop a definition to present to the total group. Discuss the definitions.

and/or

Supply each person with a copy of a "Bible Bookshelf." These can often be purchased in a bookmark or postcard size from local religious bookstores. If they are not available in your area you can make up your own. Compare the "bookshelf" with the list of books in the Appendix and note the categories in which the various books are listed.

or

Write the names of the books of the Bible on sixty-six index cards, color coding the book names to indicate the category to which each belongs, i.e., law book names could be written in orange, names of history books in blue, etc. Shuffle the cards, deal them to the members of the group, and ask them to exchange cards so that any person with more than one card will have only one color. Then have all of the participants move about the room to form small groups based on the colors on the cards.

Each small group then places the cards in canonical order. The small group members select a reporter who, when his or her group is called, will stand before the participants and read the names of the books they have in canonical order. Keep the various reporters before the group until a line is formed running from Genesis to Revelation.

and

Invite the members of the group who have memorized the names of the books of the Bible to share the methods they used to accomplish the task.

3. To reinforce the material that has been covered in this session, show the first part of the video cassette or the first thirty-three frames of the filmstrip "A History of the Bible in English," available from The Kerygma Program. (The remainder of the material will be used during the next session.) This portion of the filmstrip or video briefly covers the history of the Bible prior to its translation into English. The running time is under ten minutes.

Accompanying the filmstrip or video cassette is a review sheet entitled "The English Bible: An Overview." Provide copies of this sheet for the participants. Ask them to review the items related to the first part of the strip or tape so they will be familiar with the facts for which they should be listening in the presentation. Provide dim light during the viewing so persons can record their answers to the questions on the sheet.

Following the filmstrip or video review the answers participants have recorded to the questions. (An answer sheet is provided).

or

Give a mini-lecture about the formation of the Old Testament canon, using information found in the supplementary readings as well as other resources you may have.

and

Assign each of the seven basic Bible references (Matthew 5:17; Matthew 7:12; Luke 16:29, 31; Luke 24:44; John 1:45; Acts 28:23; Romans 3:21) to seven different people. Ask them to read the verses aloud to the group. Invite the participants to identify which particular books of the Old Testament they believe are meant by each of the various references to parts of Scripture.

CLOSING

1. If the members of the group have developed an answer to the question "What is the Bible?" re-read it. (Remember to save your notes from this activity for the final session of the program.)

and/or

Adapt one of the activities in Don Grigg's book, *Meeting God in the Bible*, for your closing.

and/or

Read in unison Psalm 78:1-4.

2. Many groups have found that a closing prayer which allows the participants to share their joys and concerns is extremely meaningful. If this is not done customarily with groups at your church, give serious consideration to beginning the tradition. You will soon see members of the group ministering to one another. Some leaders ask the group members to join hands in a circle while others choose to have the participants remain at their tables during this time of prayer. Do what seems to be most comfortable. Whatever you choose to do, do not rush this important time.

Looking Ahead

Invite the participants to bring their oldest, most unusual, and/or favorite Bibles to the next group session.

Item #3 under Exploring the Scripture in the next session suggests that five to eight members of the group report information about different translations of the Bible, using the worksheet "Eight Questions about the Bible." Ten versions are listed on the worksheet and you may think of others. Allow the volunteers some choice in deciding which versions to review. Supply copies of the Bibles the participants do not have.

Brief Definitions for the Word List

a. Torah: Law; Pentateuch; Books of Moses; first five books of the Old Testament.

b. Former Prophets: The Books of Joshua, Judges, Samuel, and Kings.

c. Latter Prophets: The Books of Isaiah, Jeremiah, Ezekiel, and The Twelve (Hosea, Joel, Amos, Obadiah, Jonah, Micah, Nahum, Habakkuk, Zephaniah, Haggai, Zechariah, and Malachi). Since these last twelve "books" all fit onto one scroll, the scroll was called The Twelve.

d. Writings: All of the books that are not classified as Law or Prophets. Note that Qoheleth is called Ecclesiastes in the Protestant Old Testament, and that Ezra-Nehemiah is one "book" or scroll (On the other hand, 1 and 2 Chronicles in the Writings, and 1 and 2 Samuel and 1 and 2 Kings in the Former Prophets required two scrolls for each "book.").

e. Catholic or general Epistles: Letters written to a general audience or an unidentified individual (James; 1 and 2 Peter; 1, 2, 3 John; Jude and sometimes Hebrews).

f. Apocalypse: The Book of Revelation.

g. Canon: List of books officially accepted as sacred Scripture.

h. Septuagint: The Bible of the Greek speaking Jews of Alexandria. Paul often quoted from the Septuagint.

i. Apocrypha: Means "hidden things." Fifteen books not included in the Hebrew Scriptures, but included (except for II Esdras) in the Septuagint and some early Christian versions of the Old Testament.

j. Deuterocanonicals: Deutero = second, canonicals = canon. Term used by Roman Catholics for twelve of the books in the Apocrypha (all except I and II Esdras and the Prayer of Manasseh).

How Did We Get the Bible?

NOTES FROM THE AUTHOR

About Different Versions of the Bible

You may wonder why we should take time at the start of this course to consider how we got the Bible. One important reason is that some people have strong preferences for one particular version. If they understand how the versions came to be, they will likely be more respectful of the choices of others. It may also lead them to compare translations, which adds to the interest and accuracy of their study.

I decidedly prefer the *New Revised Standard Version* (NRSV) and ordinarily quote from it. The facts seem to indicate that the NRSV is the most useful, for it is a kind of common denominator among the versions. Its lineage from the *King James Version* (KJV) is notable and should commend it to those who respect tradition. It takes account of advances in knowledge of ancient texts. It accepts changes in the English language in modern times. The *Revised Standard Version* (RSV), from which it is directly derived, has won wide acceptance among Protestant, Roman Catholic, and Orthodox Christians.

For those who prefer a translation into contemporary idiom free from conscious dependence upon older versions, the *Revised English Bible* (REB), *New Jerusalem Bible* (NJB) and *New American Bible* (NAB) are excellent. *The Good News Bible, Today's English Version* (TEV), is intentionally less literary and more in the popular speech, consciously limiting the range of its vocabulary. Among versions with a conscious conservative slant, *The New International Version* (NIV) has won wide acceptance.

Experience with pilot groups in this program verifies that a knowledge of how we got our Bible broadens and intensifies interest in the book. Its message becomes contemporary in a new sense. It becomes a living Bible from a new perspective. There is also an appreciation of the importance of the original languages of Scripture, so a leader who is familiar with those languages may refer to them without raising an unnecessary barrier.

Because of the ease of publication today more translations and versions will certainly appear, as the new *Contemporary English Version* shows. Studious Christians need to have a basis for discriminating in order to choose the best for effective Bible study.

The History of the English Bible

There is an abundance of study material on the history of the English Bible, and the supplementary readings provide plenty of resources. If you are a good story teller, you may be tempted to shine. Be careful, however, to honor discussion questions and to make sure the group members see the significance of the history.

Circumstances affect the translation process. The history of the NRSV goes back to the work of individuals, but group responsibility was recognized and established very early. The KJV, for example, was the work of forty-seven experts, many of them leading biblical scholars, carefully organized and operating under accepted rules. Events in the life of the church have influenced translations. For example, the *Genevan Version* was produced by exiles from persecution in Britain.

If your local situation warrants, it may be valuable to include a report on the history of Roman Catholic versions. Catholic interest in Bible study has expanded remarkably in the second half of this century, and it bodes well for interfaith dialog.

The suggestion to bring old or unusual Bibles to the group meeting is sure to arouse interest. It does not matter if many of these are of no particular significance to the history of translations. They will promote personal identity with this part of the study. (A broader-based, Bible-display event involving the local church or community can develop from this beginning.)

Supplementary Reading

The New Oxford Annotated Bible has an article entitled "English Versions of the Bible." Also check *Harper's Bible Dictionary* or other dictionaries and encyclopedias under "English Bible" or "Translations."

If this part arouses continuing interest, additional resources are available from the American Bible Society. Write for the latest catalog with material on the history of the Bible: ABS, 1865 Broadway, New York, NY 10023.

SESSION PLANS

Learning Objectives

This session is intended to enable participants to:

1. Name at least five major versions of the Bible in use today.

2. Distinguish between a translation and a paraphrase and describe the advantages of each.

3. Indicate which version of the Bible they prefer and give reasons for their choice.

Resources You May Need

Copies of at least eight major versions of the Bible (such as the *King James Version, Revised Standard Version, New Revised Standard Version, New English Bible* or *Revised English Bible, New Jerusalem Bible, Today's English Version, Living Bible, New International Version, New American Bible, The New Testament in Modern English*)

Copies of the chart "A History of the English Bible" from this *Leader's Guide*

A Hebrew Old Testament and a Greek New Testament

Filmstrip of "A History of the Bible in English," and copies of the review sheet, "The English Bible: An Overview"

Filmstrip projector, screen, and cassette player

Copies of the worksheet "Exercises in Translation"

Copies of the worksheet "Eight Questions About Bibles"

Copies of sample verses as they appear in several different Bibles

Leadership Strategy

SETTING THE STAGE

1. Welcome and introduce any new members of the group. Then start the session with a prayer thanking God for the Scriptures and those who have preserved and translated them across the years, or lead a prayer activity from Don Grigg's *Meeting God in the Bible*.

2. Invite those who brought special Bibles to show them to the group, explaining briefly why they selected them. As they do, record on the chalkboard or newsprint the versions that are represented. (Place the Bibles on a browsing table so the members can

examine them before and after the session. Locate copies of the Hebrew Old Testament and the Greek New Testament to include in the display.) You may also want to share a Bible that has special meaning to you.

EXPLORING THE SCRIPTURE

1. Distribute copies of the chart "A History of the English Bible" found in this part of the *Leader's Guide*. Using information from the "Notes from the Author," and supplementary resources you have read, review the chart with the group, clarifying its structure and highlighting some of the history. Pay particular attention to the material that begins at the *Tyndale New Testament*.

and/or

If you began showing the filmstrip or video "A History of the Bible in English," last week, begin this session where you left off. This second segment of the material traces the exciting history of the Bible as it was translated into English. Ask participants to read all of the remaining items on the review sheet, "The English Bible: An Overview," so they will be familiar with the information they should be gathering. Provide dim light during the viewing so members of the group can record their answers.

Then, invite the group to share what they discovered about the Bible. Go over their answers to the questions on the review sheet. Lead a discussion using the questions suggested in the "Presentation Guide" which comes with the filmstrip or video cassette.

and

Using information from the *Resource Book* under the headings "A Unique History," "An English Tradition," and "Which Versions Today?," make a brief presentation that will demonstrate the differences between:

- A new translation (such as the NEB, NIV, TEV and NJB) which endeavors to produce a dynamic cultural equivalent of the biblical texts for modern readers, and is not dependent upon earlier versions.

- A translation that is a revision of an earlier translation (such as the KJV, RSV, and NRSV). These versions attempt to preserve the earlier translation except where revisions are required by significant changes in contemporary English usage and new knowledge of the earliest Hebrew and Greek texts.

• A paraphrase (such as J. B. Phillips' *New Testament in Modern English* or *The Living Bible*) which may or may not be based on ancient texts and may allow commentary language to creep in.

Ask the members of the group to determine to which categories the Bibles they brought for display belong.

2. The process of translation is very complicated and requires great skill. One way you can help the group appreciate some of the difficulties faced by translators is to select one or more of the following options.

Option I

Distribute copies of a page from a Hebrew Bible. Invite the members of the group to notice the following things about the material:

a. The text is printed from right to left.

b. There are boldface letters. These are the consonants.

c. There are other markings such as dots, dashes, etc. These are the vowel points. Originally there were only consonants, no punctuation marks, and no spaces between words.

Option II

Give each participant a copy of the worksheet titled "Exercises in Translation" at the end of this part. It contains examples of texts without vowels, punctuation, or word division and a fragmentary text. In each case, spend a few minutes as a group trying to figure out the text which lies behind the copies. The first text is Psalm 23:1, 2 (NRSV). The second text is Psalm 73:1, 2 (NRSV). The fragmentary text is Jeremiah 34:1, 2 (NRSV).

Option III

Use the part of the worksheet "Exercises in Translation" which contains the Greek text and word list for Mark 8:35. Have the participants work individually or in small groups to provide a translation and compare versions in the total group.

or

In order to save time use the section of the worksheet containing Mark 8:35 from an interlinear Greek New Testament. The matching of the words has already been done.

The task is to try to use the words to form an English sentence that makes sense. Invite the members of the group to work in pairs to try to form a good sentence that carries the meaning of the verse. After approximately five minutes, share the sentences that have been written.

3. Selecting a study Bible is a complicated task. This exercise can help the members of your group understand some of the information that can be used to make that decision. If you assigned participants to do research on various translations and paraphrases at the end of the previous session, invite them to give their reports to the group at this time. The reports should take no more than two to four minutes each. They should present answers to as many of the items on the worksheet "Eight Questions about Bibles" as they could find in the material they had available. Provide all of the participants with a copy of the worksheet so they can follow the reports as they are presented.

or

Select five to eight versions of the Bible you want to review and form a small group for each version. Distribute copies of the worksheet "Eight Questions about Bibles" to each group. Also provide copies of the edition of the Bible the group is to study. Try to have several copies of each edition available.

After approximately twenty minutes ask the small groups to report their conclusions. Each report should take not more than two to four minutes.

and/or

Take a poll of the group to see which versions of the Bible they read most often. Discuss the reasons for their choices. Then describe the criteria for choosing a study Bible that Dr. Walther mentions in the *Resource Book* in the section "Which Version Today?" Compare his evaluation with those of the group.

and/or

In the Research section in the *Resource Book* Dr. Walther suggests comparing several texts in different translations. Ask the group to share the differences they note that are particularly striking. Discuss the value of using more than one translation.

or

Provide copies of one or two of the following passages (Genesis 1:1-8; Psalm 23; Matthew 5:1-12; 1 Corinthians 13) using a new translation (NJB, TEV, or NEB), a revision (RSV or NRSV), and a paraphrase (J. B. Phillips). Ask the participants to read the various versions and make note of some differences that are particularly striking. Discuss them with the group.

CLOSING

1. Divide into groups of three and invite people to share their earliest memories about the Bible. They might tell about when they received their first Bible or some of their early thoughts about the Bible.

2. Sing the hymn "Book of Books, Our People's Strength" (*Songs of Praise*, Oxford University Press), or another hymn that celebrates the written Word.

and

Ask the members of the group to share their joys and concerns. Include them in a prayer that also gives thanks for those who faithfully translate the Bible for our use today.

Looking Ahead

If you are going to use the learning center idea suggested in the session plan for the Introduction, Part 3, there are a number of preparations you need to make. Recruit one or two members of the group to design the necessary signs and help you gather the resources and supplies.

Ask someone to lead the group in an opening prayer or prayer activity at the next session.

A HISTORY OF THE ENGLISH BIBLE

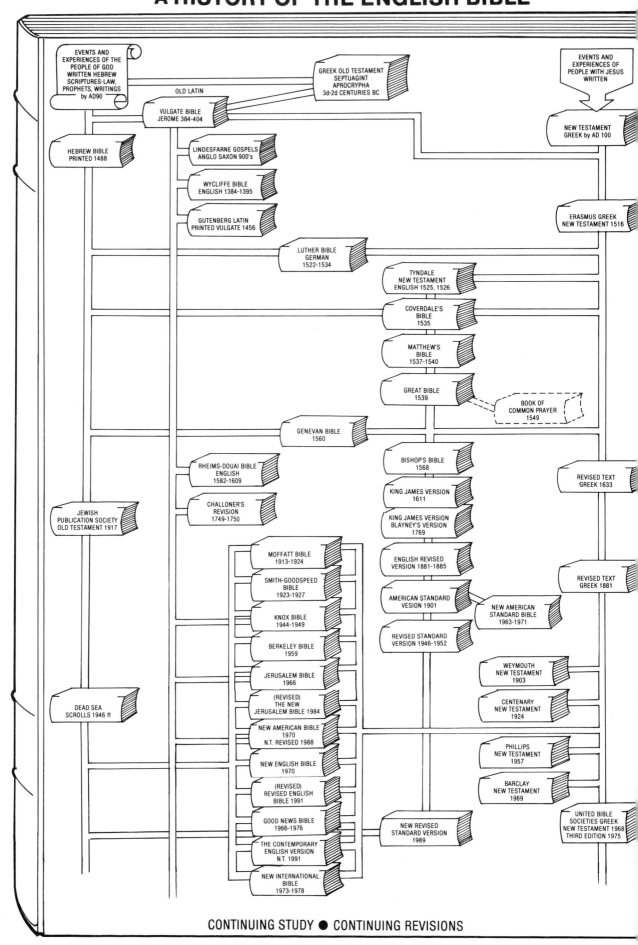

CONTINUING STUDY ● CONTINUING REVISIONS

Exercises in Translation

Examples of a text without vowels, punctuation, and word division:

a. thlrdsmshphrdshllntwnthmksmldwnngrnpstrshldsmbsdstllwtrs

b. trlgdsgdtthprghttthswhrprnhrtbtsfrmmfthdlmststmbldmstpshgnrlslppd

Example of a fragmentary text:

                e word that came to Jeremiah from the LORD wh
                Nebuchadrezzar of Babylon and all his army an
                kingdoms of the earth and all the peoples und
                on were fighting against Jerusalem and a
                ays the LORD, the God of Israel: Go an
                Zedekiah of Judah and say to him: Thus sa
                RD: I am going to give this city into the hand of the
                bylon, and he shall burn it with fire. . .

Greek Text of Mark 8:35

$$\overset{\text{hos}}{\overset{\grave{o}\varsigma}{}} \overset{\text{gar}}{\gamma \grave{\alpha} \rho} \overset{\text{ean}}{\mathring{\alpha} \nu} \overset{\text{thele}}{\theta \acute{\epsilon} \lambda \eta} \overset{\text{ten}}{\tau \grave{\eta} \nu} \quad 35$$

ψυχὴν αὐτοῦ σῶσαι, ἀπολέσει αὐτήν·
psuchen   autou   sosai   apolesei   auten.

ὃς δ' ἂν ἀπολέσῃ τὴν ψυχὴν αὐτοῦ
hos d' an   apolesei   ten   psuchen   autou

ἕνεκεν ἐμοῦ καὶ τοῦ εὐαγγελίου,
heneken   emou   kai   tou   euaggeliou

οὗτος σώσει αὐτήν.
autos   sosei   auten.

MAPKON.
Mark 8:35

Meanings of Words for Use in Translating Mark 8:35

an: Under the circumstances, in that case, anyhow, would, if; make a statement contingent

apolesei: Will lose, will destroy; other manuscripts use the subjunctive – would or might lose, etc.

auten: Him, it

autos: He, self, the same

autou: His, its

d' (or de): But, and, on the other hand

ean: If; when linked with hos (see below) it is usually translated whoever

emou: Mine, of me

euaggeliou:The good news, the gospel

gar: For; a conjunction relating a phrase to the previous idea

hene'ken: For the sake of, on account of, on behalf of

hos: Who, which, sometimes whosoever or whoever

kai: And, even

psuchen: Appetite, desire, soul, self, life, breath of life, person, identity, individual

sosai: To save, to rescue, to preserve from danger or death (physical or spiritual death)

ten or *tou*: The

thele: Would or might will, stick resolutely to, wish, or desire

Interlinear text of Mark 8:35

ὃς γὰρ ἂν θέλῃ τὴν   35
For   whoever   wishes   the

ψυχὴν αὐτοῦ σῶσαι, ἀπολέσει αὐτήν·
life   of him   to save   will lose   it;

ὃς δ' ἂν ἀπολέσῃ τὴν ψυχὴν αὐτοῦ
but whoever   will lose   the   life   of him

ἕνεκεν ἐμοῦ καὶ τοῦ εὐαγγελίου,
for the sake of   me   and   the   gospel

οὗτος σώσει αὐτήν.
(*)   will save   it.

*in the Interlinear New Testament this word is omitted.

MAPKON.
Mark 8:35

Eight Questions about Bibles

In order to answer the questions below about the Bible you have chosen to explore you will need to read its Preface and other introductory material. Skim its other pages and review any other information you can find related to it's publication.

Bibles to explore:

King James Version
Revised Standard Version
New Revised Standard Version
Good News Bible, Today's English Version
New Jerusalem Bible
Living Bible
Revised English Version
New International Version
The New Testament in Modern English
New American Bible

Questions to answer:

1. Who is the publisher? sponsor?

2. Who are the translators, the editors, the authors?

3. What is the purpose or the intent of the translation?

4. Who are the intended readers or audience?

5. What type of translation is it? literal? a revision of a previous translation? a cultural equivalent? a paraphrase?

6. What study helps are included in the edition you are using?

7. What is the style or format of the Bible?

8. What do you like or dislike about this Bible? Why?

THE BIBLE AS
A WHOLE

INTRO

How Shall We
Study the Bible?

PART
3

NOTES FROM THE AUTHOR

About the Kerygma Way of Bible Study

We cannot overstress the importance of studying the Bible *whole*. The merits of this emphasis of *Kerygma: The Bible in Depth* must be clearly seen by the group. Our further Bible study will gain much, however it may be organized, when it can rest on the foundation of knowledge of the Bible whole. Each part of Scripture finds its most authentic meaning when it can be related to all other parts.

The built-in difficulties of moving from one part of the Bible to another illustrate the need for this program. The great variety among the books of the Bible makes it hard to establish connections. For example, how does one relate Law (Leviticus), Prophets (Hosea), and Writings (Ecclesiastes)? Or how does Paul's thought relate to the teaching of Jesus? At this point it is necessary only to pose the problem clearly. The unity of the biblical books is not a simple matter, but it is certainly an important issue for study.

This is where the themes come in. They do not gloss over the real differences among books, but they clarify lines of continuity that run through the Bible. The fact that there are additional themes that could be introduced is irrelevant at this point. We are presenting a special way of looking at biblical material, and the success of the task will become evident only as we move along.

The recurrence of "God" and "people" in the theme titles is also very important. There are certainly other things that are common in the Bible, but these two word concepts are absolutely basic. The validity of the ten themes and their relationship to God and people will become apparent when they are studied and understood.

Study Tools

The Session Plans suggest ways of demonstrating the study aids presented in the *Resource Book*. At this stage it is probably unwise to recommend that each group member possess all of these resources. Different members of the group are coming from different backgrounds, and every effort should be made to keep from overwhelming any of them. Some are probably already awed by the prospect of a thirty-four part study.

Patient example will be the most effective way to promote the use of basic reference tools. Some members, of course, will plunge into the program and will be ready to purchase a small library of resources. Be careful not to let these persons monopolize the group sessions. For many of the participants diligent study of the *Resource Book* and the Basic Bible References given there will be a formidable task.

You are now at the brink of the study of the Bible texts. Experience has shown that the leader is likely to learn more than anyone else in the group, so you are embarking on an exciting enterprise. Members of the group will probably not shift into high gear for several sessions yet. I encourage you, and you must encourage them.

Supplementary Reading

Become thoroughly familiar with the ten themes, their titles and the overview of them in the *Resource Book*.

Review the use of the tools discussed in the *Resource Book*. If you are unfamiliar with the particular ones suggested, try to see them and note any differences from the ones you have previously used.

SESSION PLANS

Learning Objectives

This session is intended to enable participants to:

1. Explain the differences between the thematic approach to the study of the Bible and other methods.

2. Name the themes of *Kerygma: The Bible in Depth.*

3. Demonstrate the use of the following: Cross reference notes, a concordance, a Bible dictionary, and several of the suggested supplementary resources.

Resources You May Need

Chalk and a chalkboard

Newsprint, markers and masking tape

Concordance(s), *Lion Encyclopedia of the Bible, Understanding the Old Testament, Introducing the Old Testament, Understanding the New Testament, Introducing the New Testament, Harper's Bible Dictionary* or other Bible dictionaries

Several translations of the Bible, *Gospel Parallels* or a harmony of the Gospels

Signs and direction cards for each of four learning centers, scratch paper, pencils

An overhead projector, prepared transparencies and acetate markers

Leadership Strategy

SETTING THE STAGE

1. Lead the group in an opening prayer or introduce the person you have asked to lead the prayer or prayer activity.

2. The *Resource Book* asked the participants to review their own Bible study experiences. Invite them to name Bible classes and courses in which they have previously participated. Make a composite list on a chalkboard or newsprint. Discuss the similarities and differences in content and approach among the items on the list.

or

Make a list of the books or areas of the Bible about which members of the group feel least informed. Provide an opportunity for them to share their feelings about the Bible study experiences they have had.

EXPLORING THE SCRIPTURE

1. Some of the difficulties the group has experienced in their various Bible studies may be attributed to the diversity of the Bible and a piecemeal approach to its study. The concern in *Kerygma: The Bible in Depth* is to study the Bible whole rather than piecemeal. Following a thematic design is one way in which a holistic study can be carried out.

To help the members of the group appreciate the diversity and unity of the Scriptures, have them turn to the Table of Contents in their Bibles. Using the categories from the chart listing the books of the Bible in the Appendix, ask persons to name those that belong to the various groupings (e.g.,Law, Minor Prophets, Gospels, Apocalypse, etc.). Then discuss some of these questions.

a. What are some factors that make the Bible a diverse volume?

b. In what ways might some study approaches accentuate the diversity of Scripture?

c. How may a thematic approach help uncover the unity of Scripture?

d. The New Testament is packed with references to and quotations from the Old Testament. How may a thematic approach help us become comfortable with this use?

Suggest that the thematic approach used in *Kerygma: The Bible in Depth* is a method that focuses on the unity of the Scripture but also takes the diverse contextual factors into account.

and

Review the presuppositions mentioned on page 19 of the *Resource Book* in the section titled "A Thematic Approach," and invite questions and comments. With the *Resource Book* still open, guide the group through a review of the ten themes. Note how the themes focus on the relationship between "God" and "People." Invite the participants to suggest other possible themes that could be included in a study of the Bible.

or

Divide the participants into ten small groups. Provide each group with a sheet of newsprint and markers. Assign one of the themes to each group. The groups are to write their theme title on the newsprint. Then, using the information in the summaries for each theme in the *Resource Book*, they are to create a poster that lists topics that will be covered in the theme. They can also include the parts of the Bible they think might best be considered under their theme. After approximately ten minutes gather the groups and ask them to share their posters.

2. One of the educational principles affirmed by The Kerygma Program is that adults are responsible for their own learning. Because there will be a significant increase in the amount of preparation needed for the remaining sessions, spend a few minutes discussing these questions:

a. What does the statement "adults are responsible for their own learning" mean to you?

b. Preparation and participation are cornerstones of this study. Thousands of churches have used this format successfully. It requires, however, commitment on the part of both the leaders and the participants. How have you managed to schedule your preparation time to this point?

c. As we actually get into the study of the Scripture in the remaining sessions, you will find that the preparation time increases. What adjustments will you have to make to find the necessary time?

and

Encourage members of the group to try the following method of preparation. You may want to illustrate the procedure by using Theme 1, Part 1.

a. Begin with the summary statement at the top of each part.

b. Note the Basic Bible References and the Word List.

c. Read the material straight through rather quickly to get an overview of the content.

d. Go back and re-read the material, looking up the basic references and as many of the other references as time allows.

and

Suggest that everyone read "Some Suggestions about the Resource Book Material" found on pages viii-x in the Preface of that book before they begin preparing for the next session. It clarifies the terms and symbols used with different categories of Scripture references.

and/or

Theological diversity is a reality in all groups. Many successful groups find the formulation of "ground rules" for discussion very useful. They insure that everyone will feel free to express ideas, questions, and doubts without feeling "put down" by others. Here are three that work.

a. Everyone's viewpoint will be respected. (That does not mean you must agree with it.)

b. No one person's viewpoint will be allowed to dominate. (This includes the leader's.)

c. The sharings within the group are confidential. (Not the learnings, just the personal sharings that occur naturally as the group becomes a real community. Trust is an essential element of successful groups.)

Begin with this list and encourage others to suggest "rules" that seem important to them. If the group concurs, add them. Copy the final list on newsprint and keep it on display.

3. As Dr. Walther pointed out in the *Resource Book*, learning to use the "tools" of good biblical study should be a high priority. Acquiring the skills necessary to use concordances, Bible dictionaries, and cross reference notes is essential if the participants are to engage in serious study. During this course, suggestions that invite participants to prepare reports using information found in the supplementary books are sometimes included in the session plans. It is possible that some members of your group have never had the opportunity to use books like *Understanding the Old Testament, Introducing the Old Testament, Understanding the New Testament, Introducing the New Testament*, and the *Lion Encyclopedia of the Bible*. The following learning centers have been designed to provide hands-on experience in the use of these resources. Use only those that are appropriate for your group.

Each center will require a sign naming and defining the resource to be used as well as a copy of directions. Divide the participants into groups and have each group visit each center. If there are a number of copies of the resources at each center, the group members can perform the tasks individually. Otherwise, ask one participant in each small group to read the directions and demonstrate the work for his or her group at each center.

CENTER #1 - Cross Reference Notes/Study Bible

<u>Supplies at the center:</u>

Copies of the *New Revised Standard Version, Today's English Version*, and one other translation of the Bible; a copy of *Gospel Parallels* or a harmony of the Gospels; Center directions; scratch paper; and pencils.

<u>Sign at the center:</u>

Cross reference notes help us locate parallel passages that refer to the same events or persons or use the same language. The various editions of the Bible have different ways of indicating cross references. Some Bibles locate cross reference information at the bottom of the page. Others have columns that run from the top to the bottom of the page. *Today's English Version* locates cross references immediately under the text heading.

Center Directions:

1. Locate Jeremiah 31:31-34 in each of the Bibles. Compare the cross reference notes in each Bible. Locate the parallel passages. Read each passage in one of the Bibles.

2. Locate 2 Samuel 22:1-51 in each of the Bibles. Find the parallel passages. Which type of cross reference notes seems easier to use?

3. When do you think cross reference notes would be useful? What style of cross reference notes does your own Bible contain?

4. Look at the copy of *Gospel Parallels* or the harmony of the Gospels. Locate Mark 6:30-44. Read these verses and the parallels in Matthew, Luke, and John.

CENTER #2 - Concordance

Supplies at the center:

A complete concordance, such as *Strong's Exhaustive Concordance of the Bible*, and a concise concordance, such as *The Oxford Concise Concordance to the Revised Standard Version*, or a study Bible that contains a concise concordance; Bibles (the version needed will be indicated by the choice of concordances); center directions; scratch paper; and pencils.

Sign at the center:

There are four ways to find a Bible passage:

1. You remember where to find it.

2. You flip through the pages in search of it.

3. Someone who knows where it is tells you where to locate it.

4. You use a concordance.

A concordance is an alphabetical listing of words in a book with references to passages in which the words appear. There are two types of concordances:

a. Complete, analytical concordances, which include every word found in the book.

b. Concise, abridged concordances, which include only the key words found in the book.

In this exercise you will be looking at both types of concordances.

Center Directions:

1. Open the complete concordance to the word *covenant*. Note the number of listings. Is the word *covenant* spelled out or abbreviated in the listing of the verses?

2. Open the concise concordance to the word *covenant*. How do you think the editor of this concordance decided which verses to include? How does this concordance indicate the word covenant within the verses?

3. Using either concordance, locate the verse "He is mindful of his covenant forever..."

4. For additional practice locate the Ten Commandments and the LORD's Prayer. What key words will you use to locate these passages?

5. In what circumstances do you think a concordance might be useful?

CENTER #3 - Bible Dictionary

Supplies at the center:

Harper's Bible Dictionary and other Bible dictionaries, center directions, scratch paper and pencils.

Sign at the center:

Bible dictionaries are different from other dictionaries. Most dictionaries just provide definitions. A Bible dictionary gives definitions and much more. Brief essays are presented to provide background information. Biblical references are included and key words are often illustrated. Some Bible dictionaries are one volume. Others contain several volumes.

1. Look up at least two of the following words: Heaven, Jericho, manna, Matthew, name.

2. Write one interesting fact you discovered for each entry you explored.

3. Why do you think a Bible dictionary would be a good reference book for you to have available as you prepare for a session?

CENTER #4 - Supplementary Resource Books

Supplies at the center:

Copies of *Understanding the Old Testament*; *Introducing the Old Testament*; *Understanding the New Testament*; *Introducing the New Testament*; the *Lion Encyclopedia of the Bible* and other resources you have selected; center directions; scratch paper; and pencils.

Sign at the center:

These books provide supplementary background material for the study. They will be very useful when you are asked to do research on a particular topic.

Center Directions:

1. Select a book and open it to the Table of Contents. Skim the major divisions, titles and subtitles. Note the ones that seem especially interesting to you.

2. Turn to the subject index in the back of the book. Write down the page numbers where you will find information about a topic and review these pages.

3. Note any special features about the books, such as photographs, charts and maps.

or

If your group is very large (over thirty people), demonstrate the use of these tools by means of transparencies and an overhead projector. Try to provide some opportunity, however, for the participants to see the books first hand.

CLOSING

1. The participants have covered a lot of material during these first three sessions. Help them recognize their accomplishments by reviewing the learning objectives for the introductory sessions. Invite the members of the group to share their insights about the task they have undertaken.

or

Ask the group to brainstorm a list of things they have learned during the introductory sessions. Record them on newsprint as they are mentioned.

2. Read Jeremiah 31:31-34 in unison. Conclude with a prayer that asks God to write a covenant on the hearts of those in the group. Include any concerns and joys the participants have mentioned.

Looking Ahead

Item #5 of Setting the Stage in the next session suggests that a member of the group make a brief presentation about the significance of names in the Old Testament, with special emphasis on the name of God as given to Moses. Several of the supplementary resources and a Bible dictionary like *Harper's Bible Dictionary* (Names) will provide useful information.

The Exodus: Pattern of God's Saving Acts

NOTES FROM THE AUTHOR

About the Kerygma Way of Bible Study

The idea for the our thematic approach to Bible study came out of an experience at Pittsburgh Theological Seminary. Prof. Jared Judd Jackson and I were to team-teach the theological content of the Bible, and we were hunting for a way that would offer the fewest presuppositions and thus be most open to the message of the biblical texts. The typically Hebrew way of describing religious experiences was by narrative or in concrete statements rather than by theoretical discussion or in abstract terms. This second way was characteristic of Greek thought, but since the New Testament was for the most part shaped by the Hebrew way, we agreed that both Testaments could be studied best by following Hebrew patterns.

Professor Jackson and I described a number of themes, all expressed as concrete statements. We found that both Testaments may profitably be studied with such an organizing format and that the result is a fine understanding of the Bible whole. The ten themes chosen for this program are modifications of the decisions we first made at Pittsburgh. To supplement my own training and experience in New Testament studies, I have sought the professional advice and assistance of Professor Jackson and Professor Donald E. Gowan, both reliable scholars in Old Testament studies. They have saved me from avoidable mistakes and have made numerous helpful suggestions.

I recount this background to help you get a sense of the *Kerygma* way of studying the Bible. This way means several things. *First*, the *Resource Book* stresses taking the Bible on its own terms. This means that the themes we study are drawn and developed from the Bible itself. As far as possible we shall not let our thought be controlled by later theological reflection upon the Bible.

Second, this approach cannot avoid decisions about meaning—indeed, it should not. One such decision is that there are certain themes in the Bible that contribute to making it one book. A related decision is that simply reading the Bible from beginning to end is not a productive way to study it. It is also hazardous to study parts of the Bible, however closely, without seeking to understand how the parts are related to the whole.

Third, as we move through the themes, we shall be going through the Bible again and again, at least ten times. In the early themes, therefore, we shall have to make some general assumptions about the historical and literary frameworks of the Bible. Detailed development and dimensions will come as we move along. This is like taking several different tracks as one moves repeatedly through the same territory. Another way of putting it is that from time to time we shall drive pegs that we shall pass again and again, and each time we shall hang more material on them.

Each move through the Bible will bring increased detail. The success of the course will be proportional to the thoroughness with which each individual studies each part. It is appropriate to emphasize this and to urge that no one settle for minimum achievement.

About This Theme

In a sense this theme is a paradigm for the whole course. Its four parts provide a study with a certain completeness. More than a quantitative emphasis, however, is involved. I hope you will see that this theme is very close to the heart of the biblical message insofar as the Bible can be said to have one message. We shall quickly discover that the exodus deliverance is a key topic throughout the Old Testament, and the deliverance effected by Jesus Christ is certainly what the New Testament is all about. In a way the four parts are in an a-b, a'-b' pattern.

Part 1 zeros in on the Passover and exodus and traces references to them throughout the Old Testament. Part 2 looks at other examples of deliverance of God's people from the journey through the wilderness to the end of the Babylonian exile. A significant story from the intertestamental period is added from a deuterocanonical book.[1] Part 3 covers the deliverance by Jesus Christ and how it is stressed throughout the New Testament. Part 4 deals with how members of the first-century church were delivered, and it culminates in a first look at the book of Revelation.

---

1   This is evidence of the importance of the material on the deuterocanonical books mentioned in Introduction, Part 1.

Three Presuppositions

We take for granted three matters when we state this theme. *First* there is *God*. The Bible throughout assumes the existence of God. Theme 3 considers ways in which PEOPLE REFLECT ABOUT GOD, but even there God's being is hardly questioned. The Bible does not offer much help for philosophical speculation about the being of God. If we accept the biblical presupposition, however, we may indeed learn much about God.

The *second* presupposition is *people*. In the theme statements, *God* and *people* are always present. This program assumes that one thread of continuity in the Bible is in the people who have been conscious of a relationship with God, hence, *God . . . a people*. The thread continues because God continues. Thus the relationships of the people with each other are regulated for good or ill by their relationship with God.

Third, we presuppose that we can discuss God and people in a meaningful way. Philosophy of religion may consider alternatives to this assumption, but study of the Bible depends on our accepting that what the Bible says about God and people has meaning in itself and for us. This is another way of saying that we take the Bible seriously.

God and *people*, then, are prominent in every theme of this program. Our approach to the Bible begins with what it says about various aspects of the relationship between God and people. Reflection upon this material comes later.

Why Begin with Exodus?

Bernhard Anderson calls the exodus "the great watershed of Israel's history."[2] The people of Israel, whose particular relationship with God pervades the Old Testament, first began to be conscious of their national being at the exodus. Genesis contains stories and explanations of their origins and background—indeed, these include prehistorical narratives about human origins. This material furnished a story of how the Hebrew ancestors came to Egypt and it made them aware of their ancestral God, to whom they could address their complaining.

It is not easy to explain the exodus starting point to persons who have not reflected about it previously, but it is important that they understand it. Theme 2 moves back into Genesis to study the ancestor Abraham, and then Theme 3 addresses Genesis 1-11. Thus we move backward through the stories and ancestral recollections that caused Genesis to be recorded. You will find that this method provides a particularly sound basis for understanding the roles of Genesis and Exodus in the Bible whole.

---

2 *Understanding the Old Testament*, p. 9.

Enter Moses

Take care to establish Moses' character and his place in biblical history. In Theme 5 we shall look again at his leadership role, so here we concentrate on his relationship to the development of the religion of Israel. His part in the rise of Jewish monotheism is of great importance.

You cannot escape considering the name of the God of Israel, difficult as it is. The session plans direct you to this. Establish a habit of speaking of *Yahweh* in this context. Lifelong exposure to monotheism makes it difficult for us to understand the story of the burning bush and its sequel. Moses' experience had a twofold impact upon the Hebrew people: They learned that (1) they were under the guardianship of a God who was uniquely theirs, and (2) this God was the only true God and the supreme deity of creation. By comparison, other so-called gods were not real deities at all.

There is much interesting material on the Passover. Its function as a memorial gave it a vital role throughout the history of Judaism, for a memorial brings the past to encounter the present. Part 3 relates the Passover to the career and passion of Jesus, and Theme 9 reviews its role as worship, so you need not push discussion at this point.

About Theological Dilemmas

Some ticklish questions may surface in connection with the exodus events. How could God allow the death of the Egyptian children? Several times Yahweh promises to *harden Pharaoh's heart*, so how can Pharaoh be held responsible for his actions? Yahweh also takes credit for the destruction of the Egyptian army.

It may be disquieting to some of the group to be forced to consider the theological dilemmas posed by these and other events in the Bible. Be sensitive to the threats people may feel. Make it clear that we are not manufacturing these problems: They are already there. It is hard to reconcile the views of God in the exodus context and in the light of Jesus Christ. Christian faith declares that the New Testament revelation is definitive, but it also recognizes that it can be understood fully only in the light of the Old Testament.

You cannot resolve all difficulties in one magical moment. Be patient with the Bible and with the persons in your group. Try gently to move them along as steadily as possible. Have confidence in God's Spirit to bring a new kind of inspiration in this study: Familiarity with the Scripture that will carry you all to new, deeper, more comprehensive levels of understanding and appreciation.

When the question arises about how God could act in what appear to be ruthless ways, there are several ways to approach an answer. The first is deceptively easy: In an age when life was cheap, it posed no ethical issue to say that God killed children, made rulers do heartless things, and slaughtered armies. This really only relocates the problems: It implies that the observers and writers were mistaken in their perceptions, that the connection of such events with the welfare of God's people must be coincidence or due to the vivid imagination of early interpreters. In an age when God's people were not offended by such acts, there was no real difficulty in attributing the acts to Yahweh. But, says this explanation, the connections were only in the minds of those who preserved the memories.

Another approach is to recognize the crudity of the times, but to insist that it is unreasonable to expect God to act in such times in a manner to satisfy a future, Christian, ethical sensibility. That would force God to be anachronistic. It helps a little to perceive that the moral stature of Yahweh portrayed in these old documents is infinitely superior to that of other deities we know from prechristian times.

If you push this matter, ultimately you will be dealing with the problem of evil, especially how it relates to a good God. Quite evidently that issue did not occupy the thinking of God's people in the exodus years. The Hebrews were not at home in abstract, philosophical thought. Theme 3 will consider aspects of this problem. Difficult problems seldom have simple solutions, and every question cannot be answered in one session.

Could these accounts be explained as just literary inventions, written to illustrate the religious development of a people? It is true that history is almost always something more than simply factual records; it is practically impossible to avoid some admixture of interpretation. But we do not on that account dismiss history as untrue. The narratives in Exodus surely contain elements of interpretation, but that does not render them literary inventions. Israel's national memories sprang from real events, which from earliest times were associated with the interpretative perception that in those events God and a people were inextricably connected.

The exodus narratives also pose the problem of miracles. Our idea of miracle is usually ill-defined and far removed from the grand view of extraordinary events as presented in Exodus. What happened to Israel was understood to be wonderful acts of God. Since God was the creator and in direct control of all creation, natural processes could be controlled by the divine will. There is no suggestion of magic. A miracle was what the derivation of our word implies: Something to be wondered at.

It will also become evident in subsequent stories that these great acts did not produce exuberant trust that God would provide for all future emergencies. We may observe from this that divine miracles do not necessarily lead human observers into a lasting faith relationship.

Someone may want to press this discussion. Your sense of timing, your skill as a discussion leader, and the inexorable turn of the clock will tell you how far you should go now. The questions will return, so it is not unreasonable to limit discussion here.

The introduction of material from Deuteronomy may raise a question about the development of the Pentateuch and Moses' relation to it. Again, there will be time ahead for this matter. You will be well advised to stick to fairly elementary discussion. (Advanced students may be helped outside of group time.) Deuteronomy is plain evidence that there are complex strands of tradition in the Pentateuch, but it will almost certainly be unprofitable to bring up documentary hypotheses at this point.[3] It is not evasive to repeat that we shall return to these problems again and again.

Supplementary Reading

A Bible dictionary will be very helpful in preparing for this session. See especially articles on names of God, Yahweh, Exodus and the Red Sea or Sea of Reeds.

SESSION PLANS

Learning Objectives

This session is intended to enable participants to:

1. Explain the significance of names in the Old Testament, especially the importance of Moses receiving God's name.

2. Retell in their own words the major events of God's deliverance of the Hebrews from Egypt as recorded in Exodus 1-15.

3. Describe how this deliverance was a central focus in Israel's understanding of God.

4. Locate several references to the Passover and exodus in other parts of the Old Testament.

---

3 A Kerygma elective, *Interpretation*, deals with this matter in some detail.

5. Reflect on the relationship of these events to their own pilgrimage of faith and contemporary experiences of deliverance or liberation.

Resources You May Need

Materials for making a time line
Chalk and a chalkboard
Newsprint, markers and masking tape
Directions for six groups working on the exodus
Sets of cards listing the events in Exodus 1-15
A large map of the exodus route
Directions for composing newspaper headlines
Words and music for "Go Down Moses"
Copies of the paragraph from the Seder service
Copies of the litany from Psalm 136

Leadership Strategy

SETTING THE STAGE

1. Experienced leaders of this course have noted that while the thematic approach is an excellent way to study the Bible whole, it does present one serious problem for many learners. Because you will be "going through the Bible again and again," the members of the group may become somewhat disoriented. A large time line that can be referred to by the group at all times helps address this situation. One leader started her time line on shelf paper at a corner of the room near the ceiling. Another leader who was using a large multi-purpose room designed a time line that could be contained on two large window shades that were pulled down during group time. Beginning with this theme, dates, events, and people covered in the various sessions may be added to the time line as you go. The general dates to use will be found on the chart in the Appendix of the *Resource Book* titled "Chronology of the Bible." Allow space on your time line for the period called prehistory and follow the date column along the left side of the chart.

2. In the plans for this and future sessions we will not include suggestions for opening prayers and prayer activities, but assume you will select or design your own.

3. When people struggle with Scripture, questions arise. All questions are important, if only to the persons who raise them. One way to deal with them is to ask the group for unanswered questions from their reading for this session. List them on a sheet of

newsprint you have labeled "Loose Ends." Indicate that some of these questions will be discussed in the course of the session. Others may be held over for later sessions where they are more appropriate. Finally, some questions, particularly theological ones, may never be answered to the satisfaction of everyone in the group. Assure them that this is appropriate. No one study can answer all questions!

Do not fall into the trap of thinking that as the leader you should be able to answer, or even need to answer, all the questions that are raised. With your help the group can take responsibility for doing research on some of the questions. Unless they are easily answered, add new questions to your list as they arise during the session.

At the beginning of each session continue to ask for unanswered questions, either from the previous session or from the reading that was done. Some groups schedule in a "loose ends" session after every two or three themes, when all of the unanswered questions are discussed.

4. Some of the participants may be wondering why this study begins with the book of Exodus, rather than with Genesis. In the "Notes from the Author" Dr. Walther answers this question in the section titled "Why Begin with Exodus?" on page 35 of the *Leader's Guide*. Share these comments with the group.

or

Events have shaped each person's faith journey. In order to help the members of the group focus on their individual journeys, ask them to think about their pilgrimages of faith. Then ask this question: "If you were to identify an event, a series of events, a period of time, or a significant relationship as being the pivotal place of your faith story, where would you begin?"

Invite the members of the group, if they are willing, to tell the beginning of their personal faith stories briefly. Reflect on the similarities and differences. Note that the beginning of the story is not necessarily the chronological beginning. Other experiences, before and after, are often understood in light of particular key events. Such is the case with God's people understanding their story of faith.

5. Ask participants to reflect on the meaning of their own names or an experience they have had in naming a child or changing a name. If the group is small (8-12 persons) provide time for those who wish to share a brief story related to their name or the

experience of naming. If the group is larger, you can do the same exercise in sub-groups of six to eight.

and/or

You or a participant who has prepared ahead of time can then make a brief presentation about the importance of names in the Old Testament, with special emphasis on the name of God as given to Moses. *Understanding the Old Testament, Introducing the Old Testament*, and Bible dictionaries such as *Harper's Bible Dictionary*, will provide the necessary information. Look in the index under "names" or "Yahweh."

EXPLORING THE SCRIPTURE

1. As the title of this part suggests, the exodus presents the pattern of God's saving acts. In Dr. Walther's words, "In that experience a particular people became aware that they were a special people with a special relationship to God." There are a number of ways to review the story of Exodus 1-15. The amount of time and the resources available will determine your choice of activities.

Divide the participants into six groups. Each group needs sufficient space to work. Provide sets of markers and sheets of newsprint. Assign each group one of the Scripture references below and provide them with a copy of the directions.

Group 1 - Exodus 1:8-2:25
Group 2 - Exodus 3:1-20; 4:1-23
Group 3 - Exodus 5:1-6:13
Group 4 - Exodus 6:26 through chapter 11 (a quick overview is
all that is required)
Group 5 - Exodus 12:1-51
Group 6 - Exodus 13:17-14:31; 15:21

Directions:

Your assignment is to read a part of the exodus story and to create a poster that summarizes the major events of the story. You will share the poster and the story with the whole group. You have twenty-five minutes to prepare and a maximum of five minutes to share your part of the story.

a. Read the story individually.

b. Discuss your part of the story as a group. What is happening? Why? Who is involved? What are the dramatic highlights?

c. Discuss what symbols, illustrations, words, or drawings might be used to help others understand the drama of the events.

d. Together, create a poster that can be used as a visual aid in telling the story to the whole group.

e. Decide how you will share the story using your poster. One or more persons may tell the story. Others may provide sound effects if appropriate.

After twenty-five to thirty minutes, gather the groups and have them retell the story of the exodus. As the groups finish, hang the posters on the wall. Be prepared to add any significant points the presenters overlook.

or

Divide the group into clusters of five persons. Give each cluster a set of cards on which you have typed the fifteen events listed below. Do not include the order number or the Scripture reference on the cards. Shuffle the cards before you distribute them. Ask the clusters to place the cards in chronological order and find the chapter and verses in Exodus that confirm the order. They are to write these references on the cards. After approximately twenty minutes, have the participants in their small groups retell the story of the exodus using the cards. They can include details that were not part of the fifteen events.

a. Moses is born and placed in the bullrushes. (Exodus 2:1-4)

b. Moses is adopted by Pharaoh's daughter and raised in the palace. (Exodus 2:5-10)

c. Moses sees a fellow Hebrew mistreated and kills the taskmaster. (Exodus 2:11, 12)

d. Moses flees to Midian. (Exodus 2:13-15)

e. Moses encounters the burning bush. (Exodus 3:1-17)

f. Moses and Aaron approach Pharaoh and ask him to permit the Hebrews to worship God in the desert, but God hardens Pharaoh's heart. (Exodus 5:1-5)

g. Pharaoh commands the taskmasters to make the Hebrew slaves find their own straw to make the bricks. (Exodus 5:6-19)

h. God sends the plagues on Egypt. (Exodus 7-11)

i. God smites the firstborn of Egypt, but the Israelites are spared. (Exodus 12:1-14, 29-30)

j. Pharaoh sends the Israelites out of Egypt. (Exodus 12:31-42)

k. The Egyptians pursue the Israelites. (Exodus 14:5-9)

l. The people complain to Moses and announce they were better off as slaves in Egypt. (Exodus 14:10-12)

m. The Sea of Reeds is parted and the Israelites pass through on dry ground. (Exodus 14:21, 22)

n. The Egyptian horses and riders are thrown into the sea. (Exodus 14:23-29)

o. Miriam leads the Israelites in a song and dance of celebration. (Exodus 15:20, 21)

and

Use a large wall map or the smaller map in the Appendix of the *Resource Book* to trace the probable route of the exodus. Several of the supplementary books provide details about the journey you may want to relate to the group.

2. To encourage reflection on God's saving act as seen in Exodus 1-15 discuss some of the following questions:

   a. In what ways is God acting as deliverer in this story?

   b. How are individuals or groups responding to God's actions?

   c. What for you is the most remarkable aspect of the story?

   d. What experiences have you had or witnessed that have something in common with the story?

or

Divide the group into five subgroups. Assign each subgroup one of the following references and ask them to write a newspaper headline on newsprint for the story from the perspectives indicated beside the reference.

Exodus 2:1-10   From Moses' mother's point of view
                         From Pharaoh's daughter's point of view

Exodus 5:1-5	From Moses' point of view
	From Pharaoh's point of view
Exodus 5:6-21	From the slave's point of view
	From the taskmaster's point of view
Exodus 12:29-36	From the Israelite point of view
	From the Egyptian point of view
Exodus 14:26-29	From the Israelite point of view
	From the Egyptian point of view

Have the subgroups share their headlines with the whole group. Then ask questions such as these:

a. How did the different viewpoints influence the headlines that were written?

b. How would you describe the Israelite view of the exodus?

c. Describe a contemporary event that might be viewed differently by people with varying perspectives. How do you see this event?

d. What are some experiences you have had of interpreting an event in your life from the perspective of faith in God?

3. The numerous references to the exodus and the Passover in the Old Testament emphasize their importance in the life of the people of God. As Dr. Walther says in the *Resource Book*, "God's people came to understand that it was characteristic for God who had delivered them from Egypt to save them again and again."

Ask three volunteers to present a dramatic reading of the family Passover scene in Deuteronomy 6:20-23. They will assume the roles of a narrator, a young son, and a father. Give other members of the group cards with one of the following references printed in large letters: Exodus 20:2; Deuteronomy 5:15; Deuteronomy 6:12; Joshua 24:16, 17; Judges 6:8, 9; 1 Samuel 10:18; 1 Samuel 12:6; Psalms 78:12-16; Hosea 13:4-6. After the players have presented their brief drama have the others in the group hold up their cards and read their verses in rapid succession.

or

Several supplementary passages in the *Resource Book* are related to the Passover, e.g., Numbers 9:1-5; Deuteronomy 16:1-8; 2 Kings 23:21-23; Ezra 6:19-22a. Invite four participants to read these passages to the group. Then ask those who have been to a Seder to share their impressions of that memorial celebration.

4. Review the questions on the "Loose Ends" list. Mark off those that have been answered. Discuss any that seem appropriate at this time. Ask the group members where they think answers may be found to those that are left. Invite volunteers to do research on the remaining questions.

<u>CLOSING</u>

1. Divide into clusters of three or four. Discuss one or more of these questions:

   a. Who are some people today who might be identified with Pharaoh and the Egyptians or Moses and the Hebrews?

   b. What are some examples of oppression and/or deliverance in the 20th century?

   c. What are your personal experiences of oppression and deliverance?

or

As a group, brainstorm a list of things from which individuals or groups need to be delivered today. Discuss the question, "In what ways do you sense God acting to bring about deliverance?"

2. Sing, read, or listen to the spiritual, "Go Down Moses."

or

Have the group read in unison this section from the Seder service:

"Praised are you, O LORD our God, King of the Universe, who has redeemed us and our ancestors from Egypt and has enabled us to observe this Passover, the feast of the unleavened bread. May we rejoice in your salvation and be gladdened by your righteousness. May your will be done, so that Your Name shall be sanctified in the midst of all the earth, that all people be moved to worship you."

or

Use the litany based on Psalm 136:1-3, 10-16 that is printed on the following page.

Looking Ahead

Item #1 under Exploring the Scripture in the next session suggests that a member of the group make a presentation on the period between the Testaments. Suggestions for resources are listed with the activity. Tell the presenter that the time for the report will be five to seven minutes.

A Litany from Psalm 136

Leader: O give thanks to the LORD, for he is good,

Group: *for God's steadfast love endures forever;*

Leader: O give thanks to the God of gods,

Group: *for God's steadfast love endures forever;*

Leader: O give thanks to the LORD of lords,

Group: *for God's steadfast love endures forever;*

Leader: who struck Egypt through their firstborn,

Group: *for God's steadfast love endures forever;*

Leader: and brought Israel out from among them,

Group: *for God's steadfast love endures forever;*

Leader: with a strong hand and an outstretched arm,

Group: *for God's steadfast love endures forever;*

Leader: who divided the Red Sea in two,

Group: *for God's steadfast love endures forever;*

Leader: and made Israel pass through the midst of it,

Group: *for God's steadfast love endures forever;*

Leader: but overthrew Pharaoh and his army in the Red Sea,

Group: *for God's steadfast love endures forever;*

Leader: who led his people through the wilderness,

Group: *for God's steadfast love endures forever.*

GOD SAVES
A PEOPLE

THEME

1

Deliverance after
the Exodus

PART

2

NOTES FROM THE AUTHOR

Facing Your Task

If the first session on our first biblical theme went well and if you covered what you thought you ought to cover, then you may approach this second session with satisfaction and confidence. If your achievement was less than you hoped for, however, do not be discouraged. This is a difficult undertaking, and you may need several sessions to get it all together.

You cannot cover all the material suggested in the *Resource Book* in a two-hour session. Each member of the group should have studied the material in the *Resource Book* carefully. Let us hope they spend at least as much time in outside preparation as they spend in the group sessions. This creates a burden and a blessing for you as leader. It gives you a solid base from which to follow the session plans, but it challenges you to substantial preparation. Resist the temptation to rehash *Resource Book* material and embroider it a bit with some other stories and a few additional Bible references. Nothing is deadlier to the prospect of success in this project.

The members should quickly become accustomed to bringing their questions to the group. The session plans allow for this. When you do not know the answer to a question, it is far better for you to admit this than to have persons feel they cannot ask freely. Do not expect to be an authority on all questions raised. You are an enabler. Together with the questioner and others in the group you will find an answer that will help you all grow in your knowledge of the Bible.

Some questions can be followed up at once. I suggest that you always have a concordance at hand so that you can quickly find passages that may help in answering some questions. Some questions are ill-timed. Sometimes answers should be deferred, not because you do not know how to treat the question, but because the answer will be more clearly understood with more background or in a more appropriate context. Some group members may grow impatient with what they perceive as stalling, but as your credibility as leader grows, their patience will stretch.

One regular aim is to become familiar with details in the continuing story of God's people that are important in later biblical reflection. In this part, notice item #4, under Research in the *Resource Book*. Here references to New Testament usage are to be located. Part 3 will refer to several of these items. To help you see how this aim works out in practice, let us look at some of the material from this part.

The Exodus

Part 1 makes the point that the exodus experience became a persistent memory and a recurring reference in Israel's later life. This is the springboard for this part, and the material begins by jumping onto it.

The Manna Story

This curious detail in a series of wonders that befell Israel in the wilderness is referred to in several books of both Testaments, and "manna" finds its way into English dictionaries. It is a crucial reference when one is exploring Jesus' meaning in the *bread of life* discourse, John 6.

Deuteronomy

This is not the time to introduce Deuteronomy in detail, but the setting of the book at the threshold of the Promised Land offers an opportunity to locate the book in relation to the rest of the Old Testament. Note the words *beyond the Jordan*, which indicate an editorial perspective of a time much later than the time of Moses. (If discussion will bear it, you may note that the same phrase occurs in Genesis 50:10, 11.) This is not intended to show a skeptical approach to these records, but rather to help participants to accept before all else the theological nature of these documents. Our intention is to take the Bible seriously. Let it say what it says; don't make it say what you think it should say!

Joshua

The *Resource Book* passes over Joshua quickly. You may mention that some scholars use the term "hexateuch" as a way of indicating the continuity of the stories in the first six books of the Hebrew Bible. Introduction 1, however, shows that Jews take Joshua as the beginning of a different part of the canon.

Judges

The period of the Judges presents a new situation. One important value is the pattern of experience that is presented. The people fall away from their right relation with God—they sin. They undergo oppression. They call to Yahweh for help. Yahweh saves them through a human deliverer. Gideon is the best illustration for this theme. Other judges appear in Theme 5.

Kings

These stories present a special temptation to digress. The point in this theme is that God delivered the people through the agency of kings or by direct divine action in the time of a king. Themes 5 and 6 deal with kings extensively.

Elijah and Elisha

The role of these prophets is important. Elijah became the prototype of the Old Testament prophet; see, for example, Malachi 4:5 and Mark 9:4. The contest with Jezebel and the priests of Baal demonstrates that God's deliverance was not always from foreign political enemies. The story is a great one. (Note that Jezebel's name became a synonym for wicked woman; see, for example, Revelation 2:20.) The personal deliverance of Elijah is bound up with the national destiny.

Another aspect of God's saving power relates to those outside the Israelite nation. Jesus mentions Elijah's stay in Zarephath and the healing of Naaman under Elisha's direction (Luke 4:25-27; note Research 4). The implication of God's concern for outsiders was not a welcome message among Jesus' hearers in Nazareth. This incident will show up several times in later sessions.

About Miracles

Several of the stories in this part will likely raise a question about miracles. It is important to understand that a study of miracles would quickly land us in dogmatic theology or philosophy of religion. The Bible accepts but does not discuss miracles. Try to keep three things separate: (1) What the text says; (2) what the text intends its readers to learn; and (3) wherein lies the authority of the text. Now (3) is primarily a matter for theological study. Does the authority of the text depend upon its conformity to twentieth-century understanding of natural laws and processes? I do not think so. When Moses left Egypt, the world contained all the raw material necessary to make a diesel truck, and I suppose we may say that God knew how to make one. How handy it would have been to haul the tabernacle and other baggage!

But God does not deal in anachronisms. That is a foible of God's people in modern times. So it will be relatively profitless to debate about whether the donkey actually talked with Balaam. The meaning of the story is clear in its own setting. It is somewhat like the story of a messenger of God who was running his own way when a large fish stopped him! Balaam must deliver precisely the message God directs and do it on God's terms.

Similar analysis applies to the miraculous details in the Gideon story. It is clear throughout that the wonders take place to establish beyond question that it is Yahweh who is delivering the people. Gideon does not save the people, God does! So it is beside the point to explain away the military action. Then one must explain away the fleece and dew. And so on. Again, the intent of the story is plain. To insist that the value of the story depends upon whether the events seem possible to us is to miss the point.

This is not a rejection of the possibility of miraculous events. God remains LORD of creation, and we must never be closed to the limitless possibilities of divine power. The authority and inspiration of Scripture, however, do not depend upon making it conform to our ideas of what is possible nor upon accepting perceptions of ages whose understanding of nature was radically different from ours. Do not use your time in debates that are likely to be fruitless.

This goes, too, for the Elijah-Elisha cycles of stories. Do not spoil the grandeur of Yahweh's displays of power by trying to explain how ravens fed Elijah or how bathing in the Jordan healed Naaman—nor by insisting that questions about either story imply disbelief in the Bible.

The Prophets and the Exile

Details about the relationship of the latter prophets to the monarchies and the exile are covered in other themes. The focus here is upon deliverance. Jeremiah is mentioned only to give scope to the period leading into the exile.

It is probably safe to assume that Ezekiel is relatively unfamiliar. Note that his preexilic threats and pleas are aimed at persuading the people to let Yahweh deliver them from the road to ruin that they were pursuing. Once the exile becomes a reality, Ezekiel offers comfort and hope for deliverance. The vision of the valley of dry bones is one of the most dramatic passages on the deliverance theme in the Old Testament. This vision should be rescued from its place in popular folk religion and restored to its proper setting in God's deliverance of a distressed people. Ezekiel 37:11 is a key: *These bones are the whole house of Israel.* Yahweh delivers from death to life.

Events and Prophets of the New Exodus

There is only one mention of the second part of Isaiah (45:1). These chapters (40-55) provide extensive resources for this topic, but literary problems prompt us not to use them here. Likewise, details about Ezra, Nehemiah, Haggai, and Zechariah are more appropriate in Theme 5.

Study of Daniel is confined to the story elements in chapters 1-6. If a question comes up about the visions and Daniel's interpretation of them, you may point out that the details of the future are known only to God, and God helped Daniel to interpret what God rather mysteriously revealed. Further pursuit of this would lead far afield. The rest of the book of Daniel is off limits here but will be considered in an appropriate place. The manifest point of the Daniel stories is the faithfulness of Daniel and his friends and God's response of deliverance.

A little about the person Daniel may help at this point. There was in the Hebrew traditions a pious man named Daniel. We know little about him except general references in Ezekiel 14:14, 20 and, of course, the stories in the book that bears his name. Other Near Eastern traditions knew of a legendary person named Daniel—see the footnotes to the Ezekiel passages in NRSV. It helps to remember that the Hebrew canonical process did not place Daniel in the "prophets" collection but in the "Writings," which were received last into the official Jewish scriptures.

The Maccabean Period

In the several centuries leading up to Jesus' time, what do we really know about the views of the so-called "person in the street"—the Hebrew term is "the people of the land" (*'am ha-ares*)? We gather these views largely by implication, but the Gospels indicate that they were the backbone of Jesus' following. Jesus interacts with official opponents and with the crowds. The views of the opponents we can recover fairly well, but the common people leave no literature. These people live by a combination of day-to-day experiences and folk traditions. Our evidence implies that in Jesus' day the common people felt at least three strong pressures. One was the impact of official and traditional Jewish religion. Another was the Roman occupation, a day-to-day reality. It had brought to an end the period of relative national independence won by the Maccabean revolution. Finally, memories of this independence must have engendered a strong hope for a repetition of that moment in history, just two hundred years before Jesus appeared on the public scene.

This is therefore an important part of biblical history to recover. Alexander the Great does not appear in the Protestant canon, but 1 Maccabees begins with him in 1:1. If our

Introduction has been well absorbed, use of the Apocrypha should not raise a problem now. Its relevance here should reinforce what we studied earlier.

Supplementary Reading

Once again your Bible dictionary will be a key supplementary resource. The *Lion Encyclopedia of the Bible* also has helpful information on the people and events which are central in this part.

SESSION PLANS

Learning Objectives

This session is intended to enable the participants to:

1. Identify at least six experiences of deliverance in the Old Testament between the exodus and the birth of Jesus.

2. Describe at least three of these experiences and explain how God acted to save those involved.

3. Compare similarities and differences among these events and discuss possible parallels in contemporary life.

4. Use a concordance, Bible dictionary, and/or cross references to locate several Old Testament events and describe how the writers use these references in the New Testament.

Resources You May Need

Chalk, chalkboard
Newsprint, markers, masking tape
Copies of the worksheet "God as Deliverer in the Old Testament"
Bibles with cross references, concordances, Bible dictionaries
Overhead projector and transparencies
Copies of the closing litany or the antiphonal reading of Ezekiel 37:1-14

Leadership Strategy

SETTING THE STAGE

1. If you have begun a time line, add items to it from the wilderness period up through the Maccabean Revolt. See the chart in the Appendix for details.

2. Ask the group for unanswered questions from their reading for this session. Add those you cannot answer briefly to the Loose Ends list you started during the last session. Invite those who located answers to previous questions to share them with the group.

3. While the exodus is the most important experience of deliverance in the Old Testament, the pattern set by this event is repeated over and over again. The passages suggested in the *Resource Book* include at least a dozen other deliverance events, although not all of them were indicated as Basic Bible References.

   With the total group brainstorm a list of saving events and record them on newsprint or the chalkboard. If necessary, participants can prompt their memories by skimming the *Resource Book* text. After the list is completed to the satisfaction of the group, ask them to suggest categories of deliverance that are present in the events, e.g., from physical danger, from military threat, from false religious practices. Have them indicate the proper category for each item in the list of deliverances they compiled.

   or

   The deliverance events that were introduced in the *Resource Book* have contemporary parallels. Divide into five groups. Assign these portions of this part of the *Resource Book* to the groups as follows:

   > Group 1 - From Sinai to the Promised Land
   > Group 2 - Invasion and Settlement in Canaan *and* Deliverance in
   >   Samuel's Time
   > Group 3 - Elijah and Elisha
   > Group 4 - Into Another Slavery *and* The New Exodus from Exile
   > Group 5 - Two Later Resources

   Tell the groups to review the material they have been assigned and list the deliverances that are discussed. For each experience they list they are to think of a contemporary situation that requires deliverance and complete a sentence similar to this:

Long ago God delivered _____ from _____; today _____ need(s) deliverance from _____.

After ten minutes call the groups together for them to share their sentences.

EXPLORING THE SCRIPTURE

1. Now that the group has had an opportunity to recall some of God's saving acts, they are prepared to take a closer look at several of the events.

   Divide into six groups. Assign these passages:

   > Group 1 - Judges 6:1-16 and 7:19-22
   > Group 2 - 1 Kings 18:17-39
   > Group 3 - 2 Kings 5:1-16
   > Group 4 - Ezekiel 37:1-14
   > Group 5 - Daniel 6:1-24
   > Group 6 - 1 Maccabees 1:1-2:48 (skim)

   Give each group a copy of these directions:

   a. Individually, read the passage(s) assigned to your group.

   b. Together, decide what the people were in bondage to and how deliverance was accomplished.

   c. Plan some way to share your story of deliverance with the other groups. Be sure to include a description of the situation indicated in the passage, the need for deliverance, and how the deliverance was accomplished. Some possible ways include a cartoon strip, a dramatic reading, an eyewitness news report, a reunion of those who were present retelling the story, a newspaper editorial. You have twenty minutes to prepare.

   After twenty minutes gather the groups for them to present the examples of deliverance they have prepared. Set the scene for each group's presentation with a brief comment on the historical situation surrounding the event.

   or

   Provide each person with a copy of the worksheet at the end of this part titled, "God as Deliverer in the Old Testament." Assign the passages to individuals or groups so that all ten are read and the questions related to them answered. After the participants have completed their assignments, review each of the events using the information they have gathered. When the sharing is complete discuss some of these questions:

a. Which of these instances of deliverance do you think is the most significant? Why?

b. What do you learn from these passages about God as deliverer?

c. In what ways do we describe or believe in God as deliverer today?

d. What can we hope for today in terms of God's acting as deliverer?

and

The period between the Old and New Testaments is one most people know little about. At this point you or a member of the group selected ahead of time can present a brief report lasting five to seven minutes about the intertestamental period. Focus primarily on the situation of the Israelites during the reign of Antiochus IV and how the books of the Apocrypha help us understand the background of the New Testament. Information can be found in the *Lion Encyclopedia of the Bible, Understanding the Old Testament*, and *Introducing the Old Testament*.

2. According to Dr. Walther, "One valuable focus, especially for this part, is on those details that are important in later biblical reflection." The events or persons listed below are some of the ones that New Testament writers refer to again. Cross reference notes, a Bible dictionary, and a concordance should become a regular part of preparation for the group members. These resources will help them locate key events and persons in the Old Testament and find references to them in the New Testament.

Divide into pairs. Assign one of the items to each pair.

a. The serpent on the pole

b. Manna in the desert

c. Balaam

d. Elijah and the widow

e. Elisha and Naaman

f. Joel's prophecy about the coming of the Spirit of God

Using concordances, Bible dictionaries, and cross reference notes the pairs are to find the basic reference to the item in the Old Testament and then locate other references to it in the Old Testament and in the New Testament. When they have located the New Testament passage(s), they are to answer this question: What use of the Old Testament passage seems to be made by the New Testament writer?

After ten minutes gather the groups and have them share their findings.

or

If your group is large and/or the number of supplementary reading books is limited, lead the group in this exercise using an overhead projector and transparencies of appropriate pages in the concordance.

3. Go back to the Loose Ends list and mark off any questions that have been addressed during the session. Ask volunteers to research any unanswered questions.

CLOSING

1. Ask the group to brainstorm a list of things from which individuals need to be delivered. After the list is compiled use it to lead the members in a litany. Their response will be "Deliver us, O LORD." (For example, "From our bondage to *schedules*, Deliver us, O LORD." "From slavery to our *addictions*, Deliver us, O LORD.")

or

Provide copies of this responsive reading for the members of the group.

Deliverance

Leader: From slavery to telephones, calendars, and clocks, the "shoulds," the "ought to's," and the "musts," from all the things that hinder our spontaneity and keep us from being truly ourselves,

People: Deliver us and help us to be more aware of possibilities in our lives.

Leader: From submission to our addictions: Alcohol, cigarettes, soap operas, drugs, food, compulsive behaviors; from our desire for power and control and one-up-manship,

People: Save us and show us how we can replace these needs with others that build us up rather than tear us down.

Leader:	From bondage to old habits and ways of doing things; from the fear of risking and growing and vulnerability,

People:	Release us and awaken us to new beginnings.

Leader:	From the tyranny of anger, hate, resentment, greed, envy, and ambition; from the bonds of loneliness, despair, hopelessness, worry, the fear of dying and the fear of living,

People:	Liberate us and empower us to be all that you would have us be. Good LORD, make us whole so that we will be free to move out into your world, to love and care and support all who need us.　　　Amen.

or

Use this antiphonal reading based on Ezekiel 37:1-14 with the group. Group 1 will read the prophet's words, Group 2 will read God's words.

Group 1	The hand of the LORD came upon me, and he brought me out by the spirit of the LORD and set me down in the middle of a valley; it was full of bones. He led me all around them; there were very many lying in the valley, and they were very dry.

Group 2	Mortal, can these bones live?

Group 1	O, LORD, God, you know.

Group 2	Prophesy to these bones and say to them: O dry bones, hear the word of the LORD. Thus says the LORD God to these bones: I will cause breath to enter you, and you shall live. I will lay sinews on you, and will cause flesh to come upon you, and cover you with skin, and put breath in you, and you shall live; and you shall know that I am the LORD.

Group 1	So I prophesied as I had been commanded; and as I prophesied, suddenly there was a noise, a rattling, and the bones came together, bone to its bone. I looked, and there were sinews on them, and flesh had come upon them, and skin had covered them; but there was no breath in them.

1:2

Group 2	Prophesy to the breath, prophesy, mortal, and say to the breath: Thus says the LORD God: Come from the four winds, O breath, and breathe upon these slain, that they may live.
Group 1	I prophesied as he commanded me, and the breath came into them, and they lived, and stood on their feet, a vast multitude.
Group 2	Mortal, these bones are the whole house of Israel. They say, "Our bones are dried up, and our hope is lost; we are cut off completely." Therefore prophesy, and say to them, Thus says the LORD God; I am going to open your graves, and bring you up from your graves, O my people; and I will bring you back to the land of Israel. And you shall know that I am the LORD, when I open your graves, and bring you up from your graves, O my people. I will put my spirit within you and you shall live, and I will place you on your own soil; then you shall know that I, the LORD, have spoken and will act.

2. Invite the members of the group to share their joys and concerns. Incorporate these into your closing prayer.

Looking Ahead

Item #2 under Exploring the Scripture in the next session suggests that a member of the group prepare a report on Dr. Walther's remarks under the heading "About Fulfillment" on pp. 62-63 of the *Leader's Guide*.

God As Deliverer in the Old Testament

	What is the situation?	From what/whom is there need for deliverance?	How was the deliverance accomplished?	What were the results after the deliverance?
Numbers 20:1-13				
Numbers 21:4-9				
Joshua 4:1-14				
Judges 6:11-24				
1 Samuel 7:7-14				
1 Kings 18:17-39				
2 Kings 5:1-16				
2 Kings 19:20-37				
Daniel 6:1-24				
1 Maccabees 1:1-2:48 (skim)				

1:2

NOTES FROM THE AUTHOR

The Gospels and Our Kerygma Study

As we focus on the Gospels for the first time, let us remember that we aim to use the Bible as the sourcebook for Christian faith. Its contents, therefore, must become well-known, and so we constantly emphasize both details and interrelationships of the biblical books.

By studying the biblical material through themes drawn from the Bible itself, we gain maximum opportunity to learn the Bible on its own terms. A great value of this structure is that it enables us to learn responsibly what the Bible as a whole is about.

To relate biblical details to the themes requires another move. We have to give careful attention to the setting of the particular passages as we move along. Thus, when we are studying about Jesus, it will not do to pick indiscriminately among the materials in the four Gospels. Our group members need a growing awareness of the relationships among the Synoptic Gospels—the so-called "Synoptic problem"—and we cannot avoid the question of the relationship of the synoptics to the Gospel of John. We shall not explore problems in unnecessary detail, but when open study and inquiry are invited, serious questions will arise. They should be dealt with constructively, but we must avoid overkill.

About Technical Matters

Some of the material in this part requires basic familiarity with research in Gospel studies. If you the leader do not feel adequate in this area, a few ideas here should see you through. If you do have confidence in these matters, be careful not to parade your learning. Our goal is to understand the texts, not to see how technical we can become.

Perhaps the most important observation on the Gospels in relation to this theme is that a Gospel is not intended to be a biography of Jesus. John 20:31 expresses well the purpose of a Gospel: *These [signs] are written so that you may come to believe that Jesus is the Messiah, the Son of God, and that through believing you may have life in his name.* What we learn about the life of Jesus is to be viewed in light of the primary goal of the Gospels. Although we have information from only a few of the years of his life, we do have data upon which to form a fair view of his career. An important example is the sequence of events centering in Peter's confession at Caesarea Philippi. In all four Gospels this seems to constitute a turning point. (The confession in Matthew 16:13-20, Mark 8:27-30, Luke 9:18-21; John 6:67-71 is somewhat parallel.) From then on, Jesus turns inexorably toward Jerusalem and the dramatic conclusion of his ministry.

Another conclusion of Gospel research is that each of the Gospel writers was a theologian in his own right. This is one of the factors that accounts for the existence of four different Gospels. The star news reporters of each TV network file stories on the same events, but each report bears the distinctive character of the individual. So it is with the Gospel writers.

A challenging example is Matthew's story of the flight to Egypt (2:13-15). No other Gospel writer even hints at such an episode, and it is not, of course, an essential detail for studying Jesus' ministry. Matthew, however, makes a theological reflection that brings the story into direct bearing on this theme. *This was to fulfill what had been spoken by the LORD through the prophet, "Out of Egypt I have called my son."* This quotation from Hosea 11:1 refers to Exodus 4:22. Thus, a very brief detail in one Gospel becomes a part of the pervasive exodus theme. It also associates Jesus again with the figure of Moses. Among many other Moses examples, see John 3:14, 15.

About Fulfillment

Now just a few words about the idea of "fulfillment." When the occasion offers itself, help your group to understand that we deal with several kinds of fulfillment in Bible study. The most common is the sort we have just mentioned. The New Testament writer observes that something that has occurred reflects appropriately something recorded in the Old Testament. (Matthew particularly points out such connections.) The New Testament writers were probably convinced that there was a providential relationship between the Old Testament citation and what they were recording, but this is primarily the inspired insight of the writer. If we treat fulfillment as a mechanical ordering of history, it undermines the meaning of human existence.

Another meaning of fulfillment is related to this. Sometimes the relation between Old and New Testament events or texts shows a bringing to completion of what started in the past. Matthew's citation of Isaiah 7:14 is sometimes misused because of the inclusion of the

Greek word for "virgin,"[1] but here think about *Emmanuel . . . God is with us.* The presence of God in Isaiah's thought now finds its ultimate meaning in Jesus. This is also one meaning in Jesus' words about the presence of the Kingship of God. In Theme 6 we trace how the perception of God as ruler comes to a new and complete understanding in Jesus' mission and message.

A third kind of fulfillment concerns things Jesus said and did that are related to his Old Testament heritage. The relationship is intentional even when not explicit. Two items are very important: (1) The influence of the servant-figure from Isaiah 40-55 upon Jesus' evolving mission. Another way of putting this is to say that Jesus accepted the role of suffering servant-savior of God's people rather than that of political messiah. (2) Jesus' deliberate choice of Passover time for the climax of his ministry. Thus he died as the sacrificial paschal lamb for the new people of God (as Paul observes in 1 Corinthians 5:7).

One more kind of fulfillment is that which the modern reader professes to see between texts. It is valid when it relates God's law or saving power to a sequence of experiences. It is highly questionable when it associates events with passages perceived as predictions of the far future. This latter practice is subject to the interpretative whim of each person who comes to the texts. It applies particularly to claims of fulfillment in modern world events. In this course we make regular and intensive use of thematic relationships among texts from the two Testaments, but we scrupulously avoid identifying this as fulfillment unless the Bible itself introduces the association. Perilous mischief can be done through the indiscriminate connection of texts by the subjective ingenuity of someone who will not seriously study the Bible whole.

About Beginning at the End of the Gospels

It is important to the development of this theme to understand why we begin at the end of the Gospels. When the evangelists compiled their Gospels, they were living after the climax of God's saving act in Jesus Christ. The Gospels were written in the light of the church's knowledge that Jesus had risen and that he was relating to his followers in a new way. This is a presupposition of the New Testament understanding of God, and it explains why a new view of the people of God developed. There is a parallel to the exodus story, which gave new meaning to the events that had happened to God's people before that time.

The Emmaus road passage, Luke 24:13-35, provides a narrative view of the transformation that was taking place among Jesus' followers. Cleopas and his friend were in a dilemma: They were not ready to accept the reports about Jesus' resurrection, yet they could not give up their hope that he might bring a new day to God's oppressed people. Their discussion

---

1 We consider this in another context. Do not allow it to intrude here.

with the unrecognized traveler turns on continuity between the old revelation and the new time. They recognize Jesus during a meal, which directly connects them with experiences from his earlier ministry. This breakthrough disclosure of the resurrection immediately leads the two to join the community that is sharing support and witness. This kind of response and action becomes distinctive of the life and work of God's people in the New Testament.

Peter's quotation of Joel 2:28-32, recorded in Acts 2:17-21, begins with the addition of the words *In the last days*. The events following Jesus' resurrection were viewed as a decisive fulfillment of Old Testament expectations. The fact that the *portents in the heaven above and signs on the earth below* had not literally taken place is ignored in Peter's affirmation. Luke anticipated a fulfillment by his use of the word *exodus* when Moses the law-giver and Elijah the prophet were talking with Jesus at the transfiguration (Luke 9:31). Now, Peter says, what Joel wrote is taking place: *God declares. . . I will pour out my Spirit upon all flesh*. Because of what has happened in Jesus a new time in the life of God's people has begun.

The New Deliverance

This theme concentrates upon the importance of the resurrection as the initiation of a new deliverance for God's people. Part 4 looks at how this immediately affected the church, and other themes will consider other facets of what Jesus did. No one line of description exhausts the significance of Jesus' accomplishment. Through the centuries theologians have held what are called "theories of the atonement"—that is, explanations of what Jesus did for the relationship between God and people. Each focuses on one or more aspects of the truth, but the whole truth is greater than the sum of these expressions. The New Testament includes many ways of describing the new condition and how it took place: "entering the Kingdom of God," "receiving life," "being justified by faith," "being reconciled," "being redeemed," and so on. This theme emphasizes one descriptive view, which has the immediate value of using terms that we have just studied in Old Testament traditions.

This is how the earliest Christian community understood what Jesus did. We should also ask, "How did *Jesus* understand his mission and accomplishment?" The *Resource Book* touches this question. What did Jesus think he was doing? How do we discover this? Do the Gospels tell us enough that we can recover Jesus' own intention? Of course we cannot explore the ranges of Christology, nor can we pursue technical details of how the Gospels were formed. The objective is to set the records we have within a framework that will facilitate understanding this theme.

Mark's three predictions of the passion are significant. This must surely reflect an emphasis in Jesus' teaching. Note the setting of the first warning (Mark 8:31). The collection of incidents (whatever their sequence in each Gospel) marks a turning toward the climax of Jesus' ministry, so we may take it that Jesus foresaw how it would end.

Jesus' perception of the socio-political situation differed radically from that of most of his contemporaries. We have stressed the background of the Maccabean successes followed by the Roman occupation. Jewish nationalists in Jesus' time seem not to have understood two things. (1) The unsettled conditions under Antiochus' rule were different from the hard reality of Roman imperial power. (2) The Maccabean revolt was as much a spiritual achievement as it was a military victory. Thus Jesus' contemporaries who had high political ambitions did not recognize that the relationship between God and a people is primarily moral and spiritual, not physical and political.

Old Testament prophets tried to say this, and it was an essential emphasis in Jesus' teaching. It finally reached theological formulation in the letters of Paul. He declared that in the cross and resurrection God had delivered a people from the ultimate slavery, which Paul identifies as *sin and death* (Romans 8:2). The rest of the New Testament, especially the Gospel of John, supports this interpretation.

The Scope of Deliverance

If there is one New Testament theme that embraces the others it is this one about God's saving acts. The material in the *Resource Book* provides a framework for this theme. You have the responsibility of seeing that any diversion is turned back to the focal point.

The theme indicates that there is a new people of God, but we must not lose sight of the continuity with God's people before the New Testament. "New" implies an old. Once slavery to sin is seen as the universal problem of people, God's deliverance must be announced beyond national boundaries. Do not miss the importance of Jesus' Nazareth sermon in this respect. Note particularly his use of Isaiah 61:1, 2 as a program for his ministry. His choice of illustrations shows the broad scope of his vision. Think how this would speak to the second-generation church. This is expanded in Theme 4.

Supplementary Reading

A review of articles in a Bible dictionary on the items in the Word List will be helpful. You might also do some background reading on "Messiah," "Resurrection," and "Kingdom of God."

SESSION PLANS

Learning Objectives

This session is intended to enable participants to:

1. Describe the impact the crucifixion had upon the disciples.

2. Retell the story of Jesus' resurrection in their own words.

3. Explain three ways Jesus is seen as the fulfillment of the Old Testament.

4. Compare the similarities and differences between the deliverance in the exodus and the new deliverance accomplished by Jesus.

5. Describe the nature and purpose of the new community.

Resources You May Need

Chalkboard and chalk
Newsprint, markers, masking tape
A recording of "Were You There When They Crucified My Lord?"
A recording of *Jesus Christ, Superstar*
Record player or cassette player
Large sheets of construction paper
Hymnbooks or copies of a hymn about the resurrection

Leadership Strategy

SETTING THE STAGE

1. Add dates for Jesus' and Paul's ministries to your time line.

2. Ask the group for any questions from previous sessions or the present reading to add to the Loose Ends list.

3. The story of Jesus' crucifixion is so familiar to us that it is easy to overlook the impact it had on his followers. In order to experience the joy of the resurrection, we need to reflect upon the death of Jesus.

Tell the participants to close their eyes and pretend they are the followers of Jesus. Set the scene by saying, "It is Saturday morning. Yesterday you saw Jesus placed on the cross and crucified. His dead body was removed and placed in a tomb. All night you have met in small groups, talking over the events that have just taken place. There is no way to know what today will bring. Your grief and pain overshadow everything else."

Dim the lights and play a recording or have someone sing the spiritual, "Were You There When They Crucified My Lord?" After the final verse is sung, have the whole group hum the melody.

Divide into groups of four. Remind the participants that they have just experienced the loss of the person in whom they have invested their hopes and dreams. They have gathered to share their confusion, fear, grief, disappointment, and pain and to give support to one another. Ask them to share their feelings about the death of Jesus with one another.

or

The musical *Jesus Christ Superstar* has become a classic. The selection titled "Crucifixion" (running time 4:04) is very moving. Ask the members of the group to imagine that they are followers of Jesus and are witnesses to the event of the crucifixion. Play the music and then ask what impact the experience of the music had on them.

and

Many events, including the story of the crucifixion, are told with varying details in all four Gospels. Dr. Walther states, "Our group members need a growing awareness of the relationships among the Synoptic Gospels...and we cannot avoid the question of the relationship of the Synoptics to the Gospel of John." Give a mini-lecture about the purpose and composition of the Gospels using information found in resources such as *Understanding the New Testament, Introducing the New Testament*, and the material under "About Technical Matters" in "Notes from the Author."

EXPLORING THE SCRIPTURE

1. After the despair of Saturday came the amazement and hope of Sunday. Luke 24 presents three different encounters with the resurrected Messiah. Divide into three groups. Assign these passages of Scripture:

Group 1 - Luke 24:1-12
Group 2 - Luke 24:13-35
Group 3 - Luke 24:36-53

Give these directions to each group:

a. Select someone to read your passage aloud to the group. The remainder of your group will form a "listening team."

b. Listen for and record the "evidence" that caused the followers to believe that Jesus had indeed been raised from the dead.

c. Together, make a composite list of the information your group has gathered.

d. Choose someone to present your list to the other groups.

After ten minutes gather the groups so they can compare the evidence that is mentioned in each case.

Then divide into clusters of three and invite the participants to respond to this question: "What has convinced *you* that Jesus has been raised from the dead?"

or

Divide into three groups. Assign each group one of these portions of Scripture: Luke 24:1-12; Luke 24:13-35; Luke 24:36-53. After they read the assigned verses, the groups are to decide how to present the central message of their accounts of the resurrection to those who do not understand its importance. Some suggestions are a dramatic reading, a TV interview using eyewitness accounts, a pantomime, a mural, or a poster. After the presentations reflect on these questions:

a. What is similar or different in the attitudes and responses of the women, the two disciples, and the others?

b. What is it that makes the most difference in these responses?

c. Who or what has influenced your response to the resurrection?

2. The idea that Jesus is the "fulfillment" of the Old Testament hope is presented in many New Testament passages. In his notes Dr. Walther says that there are several senses in which fulfillment is used in Bible study. Engage the group in a discussion of these different meanings of fulfillment by asking questions such as:

a. What do you think Luke means in chapter 24:44, 45 when he says that Jesus "opened their minds to understand the scriptures"?

b. To what extent do you think Jesus' followers saw him as the fulfillment of Scripture before the resurrection?

c. What do we mean when we say that the Gospels were written backwards, beginning with the resurrection?

or

Introduce the person who prepared a report based on Dr. Walther's comments in his notes under the heading "About Fulfillment" on pages 62-63 of the *Leader's Guide*.

and/or

The early church understood Jesus consciously to have related his mission and message to the Old Testament. Assign the following passages to small groups and ask them to summarize the texts and share with the whole group how they see Jesus linking himself with the history of Israel in each passage.

Matthew 26:1, 2, 17-29   Luke 9:28-36

Luke 4:16-30   Mark 15:33-39

Conclude by asking the group to name titles for Jesus (the Good Shepherd, Vine, Lamb) and discuss how these also link him to the Old Testament.

3. Up to this point we have been concentrating on the continuity between Jesus and the Old Testament. In Romans 6:1-11 Paul indicates that our bondage and the deliverance secured by Jesus Christ are different from those involved in the exodus.

On the chalkboard or two sheets of newsprint create a chart that will help the group compare the first exodus with Jesus' death and resurrection. Head one column "Exodus 1" and the other "Exodus 2." Ask the members of the group to respond to these questions:

a. Who is in bondage?

b. What is the nature of the bondage? to what? to whom?

c. What is the means of deliverance?

d. What is the nature of that deliverance? by what? by whom?

e. What is the result of the deliverance?

or

Dr. Walther says, "The Gospels were written in the light of the church's knowledge that Jesus had risen and that he was relating to his followers in a new way. This is a presupposition of the New Testament understanding of God, and it explains why a new view of the people of God developed." While the church understood its relationship to what had come before, it also recognized that God's saving act in Jesus Christ ushered in a new type of deliverance from bondage.

Ask the group to skim the material in the *Resource Book* under "Discontinuity with the Old Testament," "Jesus' New Message," and "Paul and God's New Salvation" to locate ways in which the deliverance brought about by Jesus' death and resurrection differed from the exodus experience of the Hebrews. Write their suggestions on a chalkboard or newsprint. Conclude by discussing these questions:

a. In what ways can Jesus' death and resurrection be seen as the second exodus?

b. How are the first exodus and the second exodus similar? dissimilar?

c. The Israelites were God's special people of the first exodus. What people were/are a part of the second exodus?

4. The deliverance brought about by Jesus resulted in the formation of a new community. The resurrection was the trigger that set this new community in motion and mission. Review with the group the following texts, asking what each one discloses about the nature and purpose of this community.

Matthew 28:18-20	Acts 1:8
Luke 10:30-37	Acts 2:14-42

Discuss these question in the group:

a. According to these passages, what was the nature and purpose of this community?

b. In what ways do the life and work of your church reflect the meanings of these texts?

or

The church's ministry and mission reflect the life, death and resurrection of Jesus Christ. The unity and diversity of each community of faith depends upon its understanding of what Scripture discloses about the nature and purpose of the church. Divide into small groups. Provide large sheets of construction paper and markers. Assign each group one of the following passages:

> Luke 10:30-37
> Matthew 28:18-20
> Acts 1:8; 2:14-42

Tell the groups to imagine they are founding members of a new church community. They want to spread the news about their church's ministry through the local newspaper. Using the assigned passages for inspiration, each group has ten minutes to create an advertisement that discloses the nature and purpose of this new community and encourages others to become a part of the church.

Gather and share the advertisements.

and/or

Ask the participants to describe the path by which they came to be members of their present congregations. Were they members of the same denomination previously? What branches of the church and what nationalities do they represent? Discuss as a group how their diversity reflects the nature of the community described in the passages listed above.

CLOSING

1. Go over the Loose Ends list and respond to those questions that can be answered at this point.

2. The following verses to "Come, You Faithful, Raise the Strain" tie in the exodus theme with both the Old and the New Testaments. Sing or recite the words in unison. The hymn tunes St. Kevin or Ave Virgo Virginum can be used.

> Come, you faithful, raise the strain of triumphant gladness;
> God has brought forth Israel into joy from sadness;
> Loosed from Pharaoh's bitter yoke Jacob's sons and daughters;
> Led them with unmoistened foot through the Red Sea waters.

'Tis the spring of soul's today; Christ has burst his prison,
And from three days' sleep in death as a sun has risen;
All the winter of our sins, long and dark, is flying,
From his light, to whom we give laud and praise undying.

or

Select another resurrection hymn to sing.

3. Stand, join hands, and invite the members of the group to share their joys and concerns. Include these in your closing prayer.

Looking Ahead

Item #2 under Exploring the Scripture in the next session suggests that two individuals or two small teams prepare brief presentations reflecting opposing views of the church's relationship to civil authority. Scripture references and discussion questions are listed with that activity.

Item #3 suggests that a member of the group present a summary of the characteristics of apocalyptic literature. Sources of information for the presentation are included with the activity.

*GOD SAVES
A PEOPLE*

THEME
1

*Deliverance of
the Church*

PART
4

NOTES FROM THE AUTHOR

About This Session

What is the central message of the New Testament? As you begin this session, clarify your thinking by working out a definition of that message. It is not necessary to use the key words of this theme, but your statement will probably relate to its ideas. The following may help you get started:

> God's determination to save a people emerges in the New Testament as deliverance from the severed relationship between people and God (= "sin"), and this deliverance depends uniquely upon the death-and-resurrection victory of Jesus Christ, which brings renewal in every area of human life.

Part 4 deals extensively with stories about physical freeing of people, first in the Gospels and then among the early church leaders. The episode in Mark 2:1-12 is a prime example of the new focus of God's saving action in the New Testament. The onlookers were startled by how Jesus' word of forgiveness is related to bodily healing—and we should certainly give it a second thought. Some people in Jesus' day believed that physical deformity was a punishment for sin. This man, however, was still unable to walk after the declaration that his sins were forgiven. In John 9:1-12 Jesus restores sight to a blind man and denies a causal connection between sin and physical affliction. The point of the Mark story is surely that Jesus is able to deliver the whole person.

Jesus' status as a healer is prominent in the Gospels; see Martha's and Mary's comments in John 11:21, 22. In Mark 2 the healing is accepted, but a problem arises when Jesus speaks words of forgiveness. In view of widespread interest in faith healing today you should carefully examine Jesus' acts of healing and their relation to his total ministry.

The Book of Acts

This part includes considerable narrative material from Acts, and there are some details that may prompt discussion. Here (as always) you will have to be time-conscious so that you do not jeopardize your session plans. No Memory Bank verses are assigned in this part, but Acts 4:12 and 4:33 merit attention. The connection between salvation and the resurrection has been stressed. The cross is the very visible symbol of the whole saving history of Jesus Christ, which culminated in the resurrection.

The story of Ananias and Sapphira raises some difficulties. It is best understood in relation to the emerging life of the young church. The Christian community was saved from the selfish deceit of some of its members. Likewise, the stories about release from prison are related to the needs, activities, and witness of the Christian communities where they occurred. Consider carefully the *Resource Book* note that the narratives make no capital out of miraculous aspects of the deliverance experiences.

Paul

The conversion of Paul is introduced here because it is a prominent instance of the church being saved from its enemies. Paul was painfully aware of the enormity of what he had done before he became a Christian (1 Corinthians 15:9), but he was able to recognize that God's purpose was being worked out in his life (see Galatians 1:15, 16).

Paul develops the perception, already present in the Gospels, that God's people need to be delivered from the enemy within, identified as *sin*. He appears to be somewhat indifferent to external enemies and to social and political slavery except as these affect the success of Christian mission. The story of Philemon and Onesimus is classic on this subject. Slavery and freedom for Paul have to do primarily with the human relationship to sin and therefore to God. For further study, see Romans 6:17, 18; 1 Corinthians 7:21-24; 2 Corinthians 3:17; Galatians 4:1-11; 5:1.

The corporate aspect of Christian salvation is essential in Paul's theology. Salvation of course affects individual persons, but Paul always views these persons in community. In 1 Corinthians 12:12-27 Paul points out that the body is made up of parts, but the parts live in the body. We return to the life of Paul in Theme 5.

A Note About the Time of Salvation

At some point you may find it helpful to know that salvation (being saved) occurs in the New Testament in four different time structures. (1) In 1 Corinthians 1:18, 15:2, and 2 Corinthians 2:15 the verbs show salvation in a linear, present-time frame. (2) In Romans

8:24, 1 Corinthians 1:21, 1 Timothy 1:15, and Titus 3:5 the verbs point to a point of past time. (3) In Romans 5:9, 10; 10:9, and 1 Corinthians 3:15 they indicate a future event. (4) In Ephesians 2:8 the verb is in a completed or perfect aspect, i.e., salvation begun in the past and continuing into the present.

Political Enemies

Paul was not really indifferent to the social context outside the church, but he saw it always in connection with the church. So his attitude toward the Roman government is moderate. If we knew more about his last days, we might find that his attitude changed when it became clear that Rome would finally suppress his witness.

This leads to consideration of the salvation of the church from civil government. Mark 13 demonstrates that Jesus anticipated a radical confrontation between God's people and imperial power. Since this chapter has often been cited to support modern end-time expectations, the *Resource Book* directs the reader to note the setting that is clearly stated in the first four verses. The parallel in Matthew 24:1-3 implies that the disciples made a connection to end-time, but in the verses that follow, Jesus does not encourage this. See also Luke's report in 21:5-8.

Commentators note that the tone of 1 Peter changes rather abruptly at 4:12. There is no indication in the earlier verses that there is a *fiery ordeal* in the offing. The doxology and *Amen* at the end of verse 11 point to a suddenly worsened situation. This warning, then, is a step beyond Paul's situation, and nearer to the circumstances of Revelation.

The Book of Revelation

The immediate reason for introducing the Book of Revelation at this relatively early stage of our study is that it forms a fine conclusion to the theme. When it is properly interpreted, it also forms a fine conclusion to the biblical canon. This implies that the Spirit led the early church to make wise and right choices. We therefore return to the book at the end of Theme 10.

You and members of your group may have misgivings about getting into a book that has been so troublesome to interpreters. This leads to two other reasons for tackling it as early as we can.

(1) The hesitation of many people to study the book seriously and carefully has left a clear road for irresponsible and superficial expositors to present wild interpretations that mislead and upset undiscriminating persons. Such interpretations usually find in the book some blueprint for the end of the world, which, they insist, is imminent.

(2) I find the book to be timely. I find not a fantastic, apocalyptic scenario, but a carefully and impressively drawn message of assurance to God's people in the terribly threatening situation in which they lived, confronted by a government gone demonic. The Christian community longed for God to step in and bring them powerful deliverance. We have seen such situations more than once in the twentieth century. I consider it significant that when the German bishop Hanns Lilje was imprisoned by Nazi power in World War II, he spent time writing a commentary on the Book of Revelation.

So put aside fear and hesitation. If you do not already appreciate and use this book, it is time to do so. It is not necessary to undertake extensive, detailed study at this point. That can come with Theme 10. Revelation shows the characteristics of apocalyptic literature. One writer has summarized these: Pseudonymity, secrecy, division of history into periods, determinism, belief in the nearness of the end, an other-worldly or cosmic dimension, pessimism, and mythological symbolism. You should be able to identify these characteristics when they appear in the text.

The historical setting of Revelation is a primary element in its interpretation. The book is addressed to real, live, first-century churches. The details in each letter of Chapters 2 and 3 are appropriate to the particular church. For example, Pergamum had a prominent temple for the worship of the emperor; so *Satan's throne*, 2:13. Laodicea was a banking center; so *rich . . . poor*, 3:17. It is essential always to remember that the book meant something immediately appropriate to the people to whom it was first directed. Any attempt to center the meaning of the book in a time yet in *our* future is evidence of choosing the easy spectacular rather than serious wrestling with the book.

The explanation of the first vision, given in Revelation 1:20, is a key to sorting out the bewildering details of the later chapters. The Christ figure is among the *lampstands*, symbols of the churches, and he holds their *angels* (see Psalm 91:11) in his *right hand*. The ultimate security of the church is guaranteed no matter how terrible the future appears in Chapters 6-20.

The scene shifts from earth to heaven in Chapter 4, and a vision of the Creator God establishes a secure foundation that nothing can destroy. How can one describe heaven? Recall how cautious Scripture is in references to God. Milton and Bunyan have probably colored our thinking about heaven and the presence of God more than attentive reading of the Bible itself. Hymns appear in Revelation 4:8 and 4:11, the first of many in the book.

Chapter 5 provides a link to much that follows. The Lamb is the only one who can *open the scroll*, so the Lamb is the key to the future. Both the Lion of Judah and the Lamb are clearly figures of Christ. Christ *has conquered*, and the future of God's people depends upon his victory. The opening of the seals of the scroll will involve much of the rest of the book.

The seer will return again and again to the heavenly scene where the victory of Christ is celebrated.

It is helpful to approach Revelation as drama. Theaters were prominent in the cities of western Asia Minor, so such an association is not out of line. This drama is staged, as it were, in a kind of cosmic theater. Scenes shift back and forth between earth and heaven (first-century audiences were familiar with a two-level stage). The visions in Revelation fit the stage better than the framework of literary narrative. Simultaneous episodes, flashbacks, and symbolic actions are easily portrayed in the theater. Try this idea as you study the book.

Supplementary Readings

A very usable, up-to-date commentary on Revelation is the volume by M. Eugene Boring in the *Interpretation* series published by John Knox/Westminster Press.

SESSION PLANS

Learning Objectives

This session is intended to enable participants to:

1. Describe at least four experiences of the deliverance of persons or the Christian community in the New Testament.

2. Compare two attitudes toward the civil government that are reflected in the New Testament.

3. Define the term "apocalyptic" and list three or four characteristics of this category of literature.

4. Identify examples of God's promise of deliverance in Revelation.

Resources You May Need

Chalk, chalkboard
Newsprint, markers, masking tape
Copies of Dr. Walther's summary of the central message of the New Testament
Map of Asia Minor
Cards with directions for small groups
Recording of the "Hallelujah Chorus" or copies of Revelation 11:15-19

SETTING THE STAGE

1. Add any new items to the Loose Ends list. Decide when you or others in the group will respond to them.

2. In the "Notes from the Author," Dr. Walther suggests that you begin the session by clarifying the group's thinking about the question, "What is the central message of the New Testament?" Divide into small groups of three and ask each group to write a one to three sentence statement responding to the question.

   After five to seven minutes gather the small groups and ask each to share its answer. Discuss the similarities and differences among these responses.

   or

   Divide into small groups and give each group a copy of the sentence Dr. Walther provides about the central message of the New Testament on page 73 of the *Leader's Guide*. Ask the groups to revise or expand the sentence so that it reflects the members' understanding of this central message. When the groups are finished, have them share their responses.

   or

   Ask the total group to brainstorm a list of phrases that help answer the question, "What is the central message of the New Testament?" Record these phrases on a chalkboard or newsprint. Together, using the phrases the group feels are the most relevant, develop an answer to the question.

   and/or

   As a review, list on newsprint the title of this theme and the titles of its parts. Ask the group to summarize the kinds of deliverance by which God has saved.

EXPLORING THE SCRIPTURE

1. God saves individuals, but these individuals live in community. In this part we see how God delivered people from enemies within themselves and enemies who were external to the community.

The following passages are key examples of deliverance mentioned in the first half of the *Resource Book* text:

Mark 2:1-12   Acts 9:1-22
Acts 4:1-22   Acts 12:1-19
Acts 5:1-11   Acts 16:16-32
Acts 5:17-42   1 Corinthians 5:1-13

Assign one reference to each member of the group. They are to read the passage and then answer these four questions:

a. Who is saved?

b. From what?

c. By what means?

d. What are the results?

When all have had an opportunity to complete the assignment, invite them to share their answers beginning with Mark 2:1-12.

or

Divide into seven groups of at least two people. If you do not have enough persons to do this, eliminate a passage or two to accommodate the number of participants you have. Give each group one of these references and a copy of the directions.

Mark 2:1-12   Acts 9:1-22
Acts 4:1-22   Acts 12:1-19
Acts 5:1-11   Acts 16:16-32
Acts 5:17-42

Directions:

a. Read the passage individually.

b. Together discuss what is happening. Who is being saved? What are they being saved from? What is the means of deliverance? What are the results?

c. Decide how in sixty seconds you can pantomime your story so that the other groups will be able to identify it and retell it.

After fifteen minutes gather the small groups and have them present their pantomimes in random order. The other participants must wait until an entire skit is presented before they identify the experience of deliverance being demonstrated. After it is identified, the whole group can join in retelling the story.

and/or

The situation described in 1 Corinthians 5:1-13 offers an excellent opportunity for discussion. Provide some background about the context, using information from *Understanding the New Testament, Introducing the New Testament*, or a Bible commentary. Then divide into several groups and designate a leader in each group to read this passage aloud. The members are to assume the role of the Corinthian Christians who are hearing Paul's words for the first time. They are to discuss his message and draft a reply for the leader to send back to Paul. After each group has completed this task have them read their responses.

2. Several passages in this part suggest ambiguity in the young church's relationship to civil authority. At first it appears that Paul supports the Roman government. However, in other situations it appears that the Christians may risk punishment by professing their faith.

Have an individual or a small team of people who have prepared in advance present the position that the Roman authorities were installed by God and are worthy of obedience. They can use texts such as Romans 13:1-7 and Acts 22:25-29. Have another individual or team counter this presentation with the position implied in Mark 13:1-13 and 1 Peter 4:12-19. Then discuss these questions as a total group:

   a. How may the different historical circumstances of the authors have influenced their outlooks?

   b. What sort of deliverance was promised to the generations of Christians who lived under Roman authority? To Christians in turbulent situations today?

   c. What are some recent historical examples of viewing civil authorities as God's servants, or the opposite?

   d. How is deliverance viewed from each of the two perspectives?

or

Present a mini-lecture summarizing the two positions toward civil authority represented by the passages mentioned above. Additional help can be found in a good one-volume commentary such as *Harper's Bible Commentary*. After the presentation lead the group in discussing the questions listed above.

3. As seen above, views about civil authorities were mixed in the early church. The author of Revelation, however, lived in a time when the civil authorities were persecuting the church. His message is one of warning about the trials that are to come and reassurance about the deliverance of the community.

   Revelation reflects the characteristics of a literary form known as apocalyptic. Because this type of literature is difficult to understand, a brief report about these characteristics might be given by you or a participant who was selected at the previous session. Dr. Walther has provided some information on page 76 of this *Leader's Guide*. More help can be found in the commentary on Revelation by M. Eugene Boring in the *Interpretation* series (John Knox/Westminster Press). Additional information is contained in an article on apocalyptic literature in the *New Oxford Annotated Bible*.

and/or

Set the scene for an introduction to Revelation by describing the occasion for its writing. Indicate that the book was a circular letter to be read in public gatherings of seven churches in Asia Minor. Point out on a map the location of the cities of these congregations listed in Revelation 1:11. Information found in the readings above will provide additional details.

and

Ask the participants to imagine they are members of the church at Ephesus. Read Revelation 1:1, 2; 2:1-7; 5:1-14 to the group. As they listen, they are to jot down any phrases that seem to offer hope of deliverance from the dangers they are facing from the state.

At the end of the reading ask persons to share the phrases they have identified. Then discuss these questions:

   a. If you had been a member of the church in Ephesus, how would John's words have given you hope of deliverance?

   b. How is God delivering the church today?

or

Divide participants into seven small groups. Each small group is to assume the role of one of the churches mentioned in Revelation 1:11 and study the appropriate passage in Revelation listed below:

Ephesus, 2:1-7	Thyatira, 2:18-29
Smyrna, 2:8-11	Sardis, 3:1-6
Pergamum, 2:12-17	Philadelphia, 3:7-13
Laodicea, 3:14-22	

Have the small groups prepare a summary in their own words of the message to their church and how they see this message as related to God's promise of deliverance. Reassemble in the total group and have each subgroup present its summary. Discuss questions such as the following:

a. Of the churches we studied, which is your favorite church? Why?

b. What do we learn about God's deliverance from these passages?

c. What connection do you see, if any, between some of the characteristics of these churches and your church?

CLOSING

1. In Revelation 11:15-19 we find the words that form the basis for the "Hallelujah Chorus" from Handel's *Messiah*. Read the words in unison or, better yet, play the music while the class mediates on God's saving love.

or

Since you have come to the end of the first theme, it would be appropriate to have the group stand and affirm its faith using the Apostles' Creed or another appropriate affirmation.

2. As in the past, God's deliverance is needed today. Ask the members of the group to identify circumstances from which individuals, groups, or nations need this deliverance. Make a composite list on the chalkboard or newsprint. Invite them to pray silently for one or more of those listed. Conclude with a prayer to God who has delivered, is delivering, and will deliver.

Looking Ahead

Item #3 under Setting the Stage in the next session suggests that a member of the group present a brief summary of material on covenants and ancient treaty forms.

Item #2 under Exploring the Scripture suggests that five members of the group give brief presentations on one of the prophets, using the Scripture references cited.

PEOPLE FIND GOD IS FAITHFUL

THEME **2**

Promise and Covenant in the Hebrew Scriptures

PART **1**

NOTES FROM THE AUTHOR

About This Theme

Theme 2 introduces a unique and valuable feature of *Kerygma: The Bible in Depth.* We go back to Genesis and start through the Bible again! Our emphasis this time will be different from that in Theme 1, but we shall not lose sight of what we studied there. When we have done this with ten themes, we should be familiar with most of the Bible. This will help us understand better the foundations of the Christian faith.

We move back to the setting of Theme 1, Part 1, by stressing that the people enslaved in Egypt appealed to the God of their ancestors for help. Their consciousness of God gave them a kind of unity. They considered themselves to be descended from a common ancestor, Abraham. Exodus 3:15, 16 assumes that they had a living memory of the ancestors whom we call the patriarchs. This memory was kept alive in traditions that must have been handed down orally through many generations. (Such oral tradition is still practiced among Middle Eastern tribes and villagers.)

The Noah Story

The story about the covenant with Noah illustrates this theme well. It is part of a section (Genesis 1-11) to be considered in the next theme, so do not allow the use of this story to sidetrack the covenant idea. Other distractions—amateur search for remains of Noah's ark, debate over the extent of the flood, accommodations for the animals in the ark—are really useless for understanding the significance of the story in the ancient tradition.

Let me challenge you again about your own thinking in this regard. Openness to learning what the Bible says, on its own terms, must not be confused with a doctrine of inspiration. These two things are not mutually exclusive, but they must be kept clearly separated. The Bible provides material from which theological doctrine develops, but if a dogma keeps

2:1

one from hearing the biblical message, then the cart has been put before the horse. So concentrate on what the story means for this theme. God saved a family. This is an earlier step toward what we have already studied, that GOD SAVES A PEOPLE. God makes promises and keeps them. God makes and keeps covenants. PEOPLE FIND GOD IS FAITHFUL.

Abraham and His Family

Abraham is the central character in Genesis. The stories about his life and the lives of his immediate descendants develop the relation of the clan to God and explain how later descendants happen to be in Egypt. Abraham and Joseph appear again in Theme 5, but here is the principal place to cover the stories of the patriarchs. The thread of the whole story is necessary to fix the relationships and relative importance of the various persons. The "little creed," Deuteronomy 26:5-9, is a capsule summary of the story from Abraham to the Promised Land.

Details may be judged important to this theme on two bases. (1) They demonstrate the covenant relationship between God and people, and (2) they figure significantly in later Scripture. Thus Genesis 15 is important though it is difficult. God takes on a covenant obligation. Its one-sidedness is fundamental. The human side is also important, but God's faithfulness puts it in proper perspective. Human failure does not change God, and human faithfulness ought to be a conscious response to God's covenant promises.

The matter of circumcision (Genesis 17:9-14) is likely to raise problems. Your Supplementary Reading should be helpful here. If you can discuss the matter with a Jewish rabbi, by all means do so. The culture of Abraham's day was absolutely male dominated. Modern Judaism has wrestled with this problem—ask the rabbi.

About Masculine-Oriented Language

The first mention of the problem of masculine language, particularly third-person pronouns, appears in *Resource Book* footnote 4, page 55. I bring it up for two reasons. First is the obvious fact that our versions of the Bible have not been able to eliminate the problem. This is understandable and unavoidable. Attempts to remove all gender-specific language from Old Testament references to God usually produce unacceptably awkward language. Faithfulness to the original setting compounds the problem.

Second, however, notice Dr. Metzger's reference in the footnote to "masculine-oriented language related to people." This can and should be changed. In most contexts—and certainly with reference to covenant faithfulness—there is no intention to exclude women. It is not always easy to make the language inclusive, and one may not always agree with how the translators have solved the problem. In your own dealing with language, I hope you will be very sensitive to this matter.

David and the Prophets

There are two major foci in this part: The patriarchal stories and the prophetic proclamation of the covenant. Other details are related to these emphases. For example, the narratives show a direct connection between the covenant with David and his descendants and the later history: Judah had one ruling family until the exile. (Details are treated in Theme 6.) This, of course, influenced popular expectation during the exile and after. Eventually it became part of what we know as messianic expectation—thus the New Testament occasionally associates the title "Son of David" with Jesus. The promise to David is the background of these developments.[1]

The prophets are the later preachers of the covenant. Be aware that the prophets faced a dilemma. God made certain promises to the people. The people from time to time acted completely contrary to the spirit of such promises. Someone had to call the people to account without questioning the integrity of God's promises. Here we introduce five prophets (not in canonical order).

Amos shows Yahweh's faithfulness in three ways: (1) Yahweh's demands are consistent in requiring Israel as well as foreign nations to be accountable for sin (2:4-16). (2) This requirement stems precisely from Yahweh's special relationship with Israel (3:1, 2). (3) There are notes of hope and assurance (9:8, 11-15). Some commentators think the hope in Chapter 9 is a later editorial addition, but the form of the book that became fixed in the tradition included these statements, and we may take them as part of the message.

The material in Micah 4:1-8 is important and well-known. The reference to Bethlehem in 5:2 is significant here only in connection with the promise to David. Connecting this to Jesus is not easy and should not be discussed here.

Hosea is a particularly effective commentary on this theme. Family ties are a common symbol for the relationship between Yahweh and Israel in the Old Testament, and the figure of the unfaithful wife is applied to God's people a number of times. The poignancy of Hosea's story adds a special dimension to the understanding of God's faithfulness.

Jeremiah lived through the dissolution of the Kingdom of Judah and was deeply involved in the events that took place then. This gives special meaning to his enunciation of the *new covenant* in 31:31-34. The exodus is mentioned, and so are both parts of the divided nation. Yahweh is the *husband* and takes the initiative in the covenant relationship.[2] Theme 5 takes up again the career of Jeremiah.

---

1 "Messiahship" is considered in later themes; it is not appropriate for discussion here.

2 Jeremiah often uses the figure of sexual unfaithfulness; e.g., 2:20-25; 3:1-14; 5:7-9.

Isaiah 55 is one of the great chapters of the Old Testament—if one is making such distinctions. The covenant theme here turns from God's love for David to the covenant responsibility of Israel. The house of Israel will now fulfill the role that was the earlier responsibility of David's house. The second part of Isaiah (chapters 40-55) is important for understanding Jesus, but special study of it comes in later themes.

Supplementary Reading

Preparation for the activities in the Session Plans will lead you to information in the supplementary books on covenant, promise, circumcision, and the five prophets studied in this part.

SESSION PLANS

Learning Objectives

This session is intended to enable participants to:

1. Trace the development of the covenant between God and the Hebrew people through the Patriarchs, Moses, and David.

2. Discuss what it means to say that God is faithful with regard to each of the covenants studied.

3. Describe how at least three of the prophets interpreted God's promises in relation to the covenant tradition.

Resources You May Need

Chalk and a chalkboard
Newsprint, markers, masking tape
Recording of a ceremony involving people taking vows
Index cards with Bible passages and directions
Copies of Bibles with background information on the various books
Copies of Deuteronomy 26:5-9 to use in closing

Leadership Strategy

SETTING THE STAGE

1. If you are using a time line, you may want to include important persons from this session, such as Abraham, Isaac, Jacob, Moses, David, Amos, Micah, Hosea, Jeremiah, Isaiah.

2. Ask the group for unanswered questions from their reading for this session or previous sessions. Add them to the Loose Ends list.

3. In *God is Faithful to People* you have your second chance to look at the Old and New Testaments in a thematic way. This time you will be focusing on promise and covenant. Covenant is a very important concept in the Bible. In this session you will examine the term and the impact God's covenants had on the people. Covenants are not found only in the Bible. With the total group, brainstorm and record on newsprint or the chalkboard a list of covenant type relationships that people enter today, i.e., a loan, marriage, baptism. Then divide the participants into triads. Ask each triad to select two of the contemporary "covenants" listed and answer the following questions you have written on the chalkboard or newsprint.

   a. What parties are involved?

   b. Who initiated the relationship?

   c. What are the terms of the agreement?

   d. What period of time is covered?

   e. What sign or symbol of the agreement is given, if any?

   After ten minutes ask the triads to share what they discovered about one of the covenants they explored.

   or

   Read or play a recording of a segment from a baptism, wedding, or other ceremony where people are heard taking vows. Discuss as many of the questions listed above as seem appropriate.

4. Introduce the person who agreed at the last session to give a mini-lecture about covenants and ancient treaty forms. The indexes in many of the supplementary books will lead you to the relevant information.

or

Divide the group into pairs. Provide each pair with a resource such as *Harper's Bible Dictionary, Understanding the Old Testament*, or *Introducing the Old Testament*, and ask them to explore the concept of *covenant* from the Old Testament perspective. These questions can guide their reading.

    a. What is the meaning of covenant?

    b. What are the mutual obligations of a covenant relationship?

After ten minutes invite the pairs to share their findings with the group.

EXPLORING THE SCRIPTURE

1. Covenants played a very important part in the lives of God's people. Through these covenants the people came to understand God's faithfulness. The covenants explored in the *Resource Book* during this session will help the group trace the development of God's covenant with Noah, Abraham, Isaac, Jacob, Moses, and David.

Write the following passages and directions on index cards. Divide the group into nine small groups and give each one a text, directions, newsprint and markers.

<u>Passages:</u>

Genesis 9:8-17	Genesis 28:10-22
Genesis 12:1-7	Exodus 6:2-8
Genesis 15:1-21	Exodus 24:3-8
Genesis 17:1-22	2 Samuel 7:1-17
Genesis 26:1-5	

<u>Directions:</u>

Read the passage and search for answers to four questions.

    a. Who are the main characters in the text?

    b. What promises or commitments are made by whom and to whom?

c. What are the conditions or restrictions involved in the relationship, if any?

d. What sign, if any, is given to "seal" the covenant?

Using symbols, create a poster that will retell the covenant event to the other groups. You have twenty minutes to prepare. Be sure to decide how the sharing will take place.

After twenty minutes gather and have the groups share their posters. Invite additional comments.

or

Construct a chart on a chalkboard or several sheets of newsprint using these headings:

Biblical References	Promise(s)	God's Responsibilities	Human Obligations	Sign
Gen.9:8-17				
Gen.12:1-7				
Gen.15:1-21				
Gen.17:1-22				
Gen.26:1-5				
Gen.28:10-22				
Ex.6:2-8				
Ex.24:3-8				
2 Sam.7:1-17				

Depending on the number of persons available, assign the passages to individuals or small groups. They are to read the passage and locate the appropriate information to add to the chart. (Not all references will contain material for all of the headings.) When the chart is complete, review the information and ask for additional comments or insights.

2. God's faithfulness to the covenant promises was demonstrated over and over again. Israel's failure to observe the requirements of the covenants, however, is a major theme in the prophets, the "preachers of the covenant." Amos, Micah, Hosea, Jeremiah, and Isaiah present different portraits of God's response to Israel's behavior.

Divide the participants into small groups of two or three. If possible, have them work with different people from those with whom they worked in the previous activity. Each group will study passages from one of the prophets.

Amos 2:4-16; 3:1-3; 9:11-15   Jeremiah 31:31-34; 33:14-16

Micah 4:1-8; 5:2-4; 7:18-20   Isaiah 55:1-5

Hosea 11

Provide copies of *Today's English Version* or study Bibles such as *The New Oxford Annotated Bible* and ask each group to read the Introduction or background material for the prophet they are studying. Then they are to read the suggested passages and reflect together on these questions:

a. What is the nature of the covenant about which the prophet writes?

b. What promises are made by God?

c. What is expected of the people?

d. How does God respond when the people are not faithful to the covenant?

In the total group share the insights that have been gained from reflecting on these questions.

or

Introduce the five persons selected the previous week who will use the passages from the above prophets to give brief presentations (two to five minutes) describing Israel's unfaithfulness and God's response. They can use the background resources and discussion questions listed above to shape their remarks. After each presentation allow a few moments for the group to question the "prophet." An alternative is to wait until all five speakers have finished and then compare their messages regarding God's loyalty to the covenant.

CLOSING

1. God is faithful. As God's people, we have experienced that faithfulness. Too often, like the people of Israel, we fail to keep our part of the covenant, our promises to God.

Invite the group to discuss these questions:

a. What is the relevance of the concept of covenant for our relationship with God today?

b. What causes covenants to be broken?

c. How can broken covenants be restored?

and/or

Invite two or three persons to tell of an experience of God's faithfulness in their own lives or in contemporary culture.

2. Answer or arrange for the group members to find answers to any unanswered questions on the Loose Ends list.

3. Recite in unison Israel's "Little Creed," Deuteronomy 26:5-9. If a variety of Bible translations are used by the members of the group, it may be necessary to print the words from one translation on a sheet of newsprint or a handout so all can read the same words.

and/or

Ask members of the group to share any joys or concerns they are experiencing. Then ask them to pray silently, giving thanks for God's faithfulness and asking forgiveness for their own unfaithfulness.

Looking Ahead

Ask for two volunteers to read the narrative of Luke 4:16-30, which is found in Item #1 under Exploring the Scripture in the next session.

The Closing section of the next session suggests that your group celebrate the Lord's Supper or an abbreviated "agape feast." If your denomination permits this practice, you will need to make the necessary arrangements for the worship setting and prepare the elements of the sacrament.

*Promise and Covenant
in the New Testament*

NOTES FROM THE AUTHOR

Prophecy and Fulfillment

God's faithfulness must deal with covenant promises, so we are involved throughout this part with considering how those promises have been kept. This leads quite directly into associating Old Testament covenant promises with events and ideas in the New Testament. This is not an easy subject, but it is important to what fulfillment does and does not mean.

Right up front is the problem of the understanding of prophecy as literal prediction. For some people this becomes a deadly serious game of finding precise, literal links between the Testaments, and these are interpreted as fulfillment. Such an approach must also find ways of explaining away those passages where prophets' anticipations do not fit subsequent events.

Old Testament prophets do regularly look to the future, and they make some predictions. Forecasting events, however, is usually incidental to their principal task of speaking for Yahweh. (Thus, "prophecy" is "forth-telling" rather than "foretelling.") This involves declaring Yahweh's promises, and if GOD IS FAITHFUL, those promises must find a fulfillment. Since the New Testament is a sequel to the Old Testament, it is natural to look there for fulfillment. How we do this is very important to our understanding of the Bible. Not only does it concern the internal relations of biblical passages, it also affects how we interpret the Bible for our day.

Prediction vs. Promise

Some biblical predictions may be shown to have been fulfilled in a literal way. It is crucial, however, not to expect this as an essential part of biblical revelation, and it is especially perilous to get wrapped up in hunting for such fulfillments. Consider the outcome of the promise to David about his dynasty. No reasoning, however tortuous, can find in the New

Testament a literal fulfillment of the assurance that there would forever be a Davidic ruler on the throne of Israel. The exile broke that succession abruptly, and the attempt at restoration after the exile failed. We noted in Part 1 that Isaiah 55:3-5 broadens the promise to David to lay responsibility upon Israel as a whole. Jesus' contemporaries wrestled with this problem and went so far as to consider him *the Son of David* (Matthew 12:23). But there was no national throne, nor has there ever been since then. Jesus himself argued that the matter had to be totally reconsidered (see Mark 12:35-37). Israel's future depended upon a new sense of responsibility to the God who makes promises.

The Old Testament prophets were remarkably accurate in their assessment of the future, but they were affirming the faithfulness of God rather than foretelling just how that faithfulness would work out. This same approach is valid in studying New Testament views of the past and the future. Consider this in a figure of contrasting viewpoints. One may stand in the New Testament and look at the Old and conclude that the Old has been fulfilled in the New. One must not stand in the Old Testament and look at the New and say that the New is precisely what the Old envisioned.

Interpreting Fulfillment (review the Notes in Theme 1, Part 3)

Think about the sequence of Themes 1 and 2. God's saving actions were interpreted as evidences of a covenant relationship. In the Old Testament this relationship kept breaking down from the human side. In the New Testament Jesus' followers believed that in him the relationship was consummated. That is, he revealed God's faithfulness by being one who completely kept covenant with God. Thus Jesus established the *new covenant*, and in this sense the New Testament is a remarkable fulfillment of the Old.

Crucial and unique as the mission of Jesus was, however, it must be understood in relation to what went before. The *New* Covenant implies an *Old* Covenant. In the second century the Christian church rejected as heresy an attempt to eliminate all Old Testament elements from the Christian Scriptures and faith. Neither Jesus nor Paul nor any other New Testament writer can be divorced from the Old Testament background.

It should be no surprise that God acts again, for God is faithful and keeps covenant promises. What is new is how God does it. Consider Peter's sermon on Pentecost. The text was recorded at least a generation after the event, and so the church accepted this rendering of what happened and what was said. Peter cites Joel 2:28-32, and declares that the words have been fulfilled. The details have certainly not all taken place literally—no *portents in the heaven*, etc.—but the intent of what the prophet expected has taken place in what has happened to and through Jesus. His resurrection is interpreted as fulfilling words of the psalmist David (Psalm 16:8-11). God's promise has been made good in a quite unexpected way. The *exalted* Jesus lives and has given his promised Holy Spirit to the people. If they respond, *the promise is for* them.

Hebrews

The letter to the Hebrews is particularly valuable in studying covenant in the New Testament. The book is not easy, and probably most in your group will not be well acquainted with it. If problems of authorship or addressees should come up, do not get sidetracked. The most we can say with confidence is that Paul did not write the book, a fact already acknowledged in the third century. Who the readers were is a very involved problem without any answer being agreed upon.

Hebrews 1:1, 2 sets out our present theme: Jesus has fulfilled what God affirmed through the prophets. The uniqueness and finality of this revelation are implied by the phrase *in these last days*. Chapters 1-10 may be summarized by the simple statement, "Jesus is better." (Chapters 11-13 are perhaps more familiar, but they are not our concern here.) The book is difficult to outline, for there are sermonic digressions, but even those are related to the idea of fulfillment.

Chapter 8 merits special attention. The word-for-word quotation of Jeremiah 31:31-34 gets right at the heart of this theme. Part 1 considered what Jeremiah was expecting and how he understood covenant. The point in this part is how Christ's new covenant met that expectation. Just how new is it? Verse 13 gives the radical answer.

The argument in Hebrews 9:15-22 is subtle, and the use of the word that means covenant, testament, and will is not easy to follow. We are familiar with the detail that a will takes effect only on the death of the person making the will. The rest of the passage introduces liturgical and sacramental ideas that are dated and difficult. The main point is how the death of Christ and his blood relate to the covenant.

Paul and Galatians

Paul's use of the double meaning of covenant/will in Galatians is somewhat like that in Hebrews. Both books also stress the importance of faith. Paul's line of thought, however, differs from that of Hebrews. He emphasizes the permanent validity of a covenant, not the way it is ratified. Both books introduce God's promise to Abraham, but Paul associates him with the new covenant while Hebrews does not. Hebrews points out how Christ fulfills the old covenant, while Paul identifies faith in the new covenant with Abraham's faith in God's promise.

The figure of Abraham is quite important in Paul's letters. The most curious reference is Galatians 4:21-31, which is introduced in Research 3. Paul's background as a Jewish rabbi often creeps into his explanations of Christian faith.

Circumcision is an important problem for Paul. His question is a practical one: What does the rite really mean? Paul assumes that for most of his readers it means that the one circumcised takes on all the obligations of traditional Judaism. This is diametrically opposed to Paul's understanding of the commitment and freedom of Christian faith. It is, if you will, a choice of the old covenant in the face of the new. Paul discusses this in Romans 2:25-29, where he concludes that circumcision should be an interior experience, *a matter of the heart—it is spiritual and not literal.*

Paul's Interpretation of Scripture

A note of caution may be sounded here about how Paul interpreted Scripture. It is not enough just to say that he had been a Jewish rabbi. He became *the* apostle for the church, and his writings were canonized. Some people, then, assume that we may follow his lead, particularly in regard to allegorical interpretation and proof-texting.

Several responses may be made. To begin, other writers in the New Testament do not follow his methods. This suggests that Paul's methods ought to be used with the same care and reserve that he shows. The allegory in Galatians 4, for example, falls into place without further elaborate explanation, and it does not cause problems with respect to other things Paul has written. His own beliefs were carefully reserved, so he may not be taken as a model for devising far-out ways of interpreting Scripture.

In Galatians 3:16 Paul uses the singular noun *offspring* to be a kind of prophecy of Christ (older translations used *seed/seeds*). The reference in Genesis 12:7 is most naturally taken as a collective expression, promising descendants. Paul fits his knowledge of Christ into this ancient text and uses it as an illustration. If we do not read this as a *necessary* prophecy-fulfillment sequence or as a piece of messianic expectation, probably no harm is done.

Let me also point out that Paul is not always precise in his Scriptural quotations, at least insofar as we can check the texts. Usually he quotes from the Septuagint (some form of which was the Bible in most of the churches he addressed). Sometimes this is modified by his knowledge of the Hebrew text. Sometimes we just cannot account for his reading. It is quite possible that in some instances he quotes from memory when his memory is not precise. After all, handy desk-sized copies of the Scriptures were simply not in existence in Paul's day, and he could not always visit the local synagogue to check his references.

A Neat Summary

The *saying* in **2 Timothy 2:11-13** is a remarkable statement about Jesus Christ. Observe how the fourth line breaks the pattern of the first three. This surprise affirmation is emphasized by an added clause (something God can't do: *Deny himself!*). Here is a concise declaration of what this theme is about.

Supplementary Reading

Additional information on the context and content of Hebrews and Galatians will be helpful in your preparation for this session. You may also want to consult a volume such as *Harper's Bible Commentary* on the Basic Bible References and other key passages.

SESSION PLANS

Learning Objectives

This session is intended to enable participants to:

1. Describe how the author of Acts 2 saw Jesus and Pentecost as a fulfillment of Old Testament promises.

2. Summarize how Jesus linked himself with the Old Testament in his inaugural sermon at Nazareth.

3. Cite at least two ways in which the new covenant is "better" according to the Book of Hebrews.

4. Explain how Paul relates faith in Christ to the covenants God made with Abraham and Moses.

Resources You May Need

Chalk and a chalkboard
Newsprint and markers
Photocopies of the first eight paragraphs in "Notes from the Author"
Scripts for reading Luke 4:16-30
Copies of the words used in the sacrament of the Lord's Supper in your congregation
Directions for the study of passages from Hebrews and Galatians
Materials for celebrating the Lord's Supper or an "agape feast"
Small slips of paper and a basket
Copies of Hebrews 1:1, 2 and 13:20, 21

SETTING THE STAGE

1. Add to the Loose Ends list any questions the participants have from their preparation for this session.

2. Distribute photocopies of the eight paragraphs under the headings "Prophecy and Fulfillment," "Prediction vs. Promise," and "Interpreting Fulfillment" in Dr. Walther's "Notes from the Author." Ask the members of the group to read the material, marking any statements they question or find confusing with a question mark in the margin and any statements they find interesting or insightful with an exclamation point. When all have had an opportunity to read and mark the paragraphs, lead a discussion using these or similar questions:

    a. Which statements did you find to be the most interesting or insightful? Why?

    b. Which statements raised questions in your mind?

    c. What surprised you most in this material?

    d. How did it help clarify your thinking about fulfillment?

Before moving on, you may want to respond to some of the issues raised under question "b" or add them to the Loose Ends list.

or

Give a mini-lecture on the relationship of the Old and New Testaments, using Dr. Walther's material and other information found in the supplementary books.

and

Ask the group to brainstorm a list of all the ways they believe the New Testament fulfills the Old Testament. Record these on newsprint or a chalkboard. Then divide the group into two sections. Each section will note the ways the writer of Acts indicates the events of the New Testament are the fulfillment of Old Testament promises from the perspective of a particular passage. Section 1 will read Acts 2:1-21. This passage records the Pentecost experience, which is interpreted by Peter to be a fulfillment of the prophecy in Joel 2:28-32. Section 2 will read Acts 2:22-39. Here Jesus is seen as the fulfillment of David's hope. Quotations in this passage come from Psalms 16:8-11; 132:11; and 110:1.

With the whole group list the results of this analysis and compare this list with the list they arrived at through brainstorming.

EXPLORING THE SCRIPTURE

1. Jesus viewed his mission in light of the Old Testament covenant. The message he presented at the synagogue in Nazareth, in which he read from Isaiah 61:1, 2 and reflected on stories from 1 Kings 17:1, 8-16; 18:1 and 2 Kings 5:1-14, underscores that identification.

Ask the group to imagine they are worshipping in the synagogue at Nazareth on the day of Jesus' appearance there. They have already heard tales of his activities in nearby Capernaum, but this is the first time they have had an opportunity to hear this "hometown boy" preach. Remind them of some of the challenges the people of Israel were facing in the first century A.D. They were under the political oppression of Rome, the memories of unfulfilled Old Testament prophecies were a source of frustration, and lately there had been appearances of several persons claiming to be the long awaited Messiah. Then select two people to present this material adapted from Luke 4:16-30 in the NRSV.

Jesus   The Spirit of the Lord is upon me, because he has anointed me to bring good news to the poor. He has sent me to proclaim release to the captives and recovery of sight to the blind, to let the oppressed go free, to proclaim the year of the Lord's favor.

Narrator   And he rolled up the scroll, gave it back to the attendant, and sat down. The eyes of all in the synagogue were fixed on him. Then he began to say to them,

Jesus   Today this scripture has been fulfilled in your hearing.

Narrator   All spoke well of him and were amazed at the gracious words that came from his mouth. They said, "Is not this Joseph's son?" He said to them,

Jesus   Doubtless you will quote to me this proverb, "Doctor, cure yourself." And you will say, "Do here also in your hometown the things that we have heard you did at Capernaum." Truly I tell you, no prophet is accepted in the prophet's hometown. But the truth is, there were many widows in Israel in the time of Elijah, when the heaven was shut up three years and six months, and there was a severe famine over all the land; yet Elijah was sent to none of them except to a widow in Zarephath in Sidon. There were also many lepers in Israel in the time of the prophet Elisha, and none of them was cleansed except Naaman the Syrian.

Narrator   When they heard this, all in the synagogue were filled with rage. They got up, drove him out of the town, and led him to the brow of the hill on which their town was built, so that they might hurl him off the cliff. But he passed through the midst of them and went on his way.

Following the reading discuss some of these questions:

a. How did you feel as Jesus read the prophecy from Isaiah?

b. In what way did Jesus say he would fulfill the promise in Isaiah?

c. What impressed you most about his message?

d. With what in his speech did you most agree?

e. What did he say that angered others in the congregation? In what ways did you identify with this anger?

or

In Luke 4:16-21 Jesus declares that his life and ministry are the fulfillment of five promises from the prophecy of Isaiah. Post five sheets of newsprint which each bear one of the following phrases:

a. bring good news to the poor

b. proclaim release to the captives

c. proclaim recovery of sight to the blind

d. let the oppressed go free

e. proclaim the year of the Lord's favor

Then read the passage from Luke to the group. Work together to find examples from Jesus' ministry that are the fulfillment of each of the promises, especially items *a* to *d*. Record the responses on the sheets of newsprint.

2. Jesus seems to consider his whole mission to be a fulfillment of God's covenant promise. His words at the Last Supper make the connection clear. Like Jeremiah he speaks about a "new covenant."

Provide members of the group with copies of the words used in their congregation's worship during the Lord's Supper (Communion, Eucharist). Ask them to compare the biblical account of the words of institution (Mark 14:24; 1 Corinthians 11:23-26) with those used in your congregation. How do the words remind them of connections with the Old Testament? In what way can it be said that the cross ratifies the covenant?

or

If your denomination permits the celebration of the Lord's Supper in the setting of group study you could do this as a closing for the session. If this is not possible, you may be able to locate materials for an abbreviated "agape feast" or celebration.

3. Paul and the author of Hebrews describe how the new covenant in Jesus is related to the previous covenants. Read the first paragraph of the introduction to Hebrews in *Today's English Version* or *The New Oxford Annotated Bible* (NRSV) to the group. As you read ask everyone to note the ways Jesus is a more complete revelation of God. Record these on a chalkboard or newsprint.

and

Hebrews 8:1-13; Hebrews 10:11-18; and Galatians 3:15-29 describe how the new covenant in Jesus fulfills the previous covenants. Divide into groups of no more than five participants. Assign each group one of these texts and provide them with sheets of newsprint, markers, and a copy of these directions:

a. Assign one person in your group to read the passage aloud.

b. As the passage is read, jot down reasons the author cites to explain how the new covenant is different.

c. Share your lists with each other.

d. Together create a poster using symbols and/or words to summarize your ideas.

e. Be prepared to interpret your poster to the other groups.

After approximately twenty minutes call the groups together and have them present their posters.

or

Write these questions on newsprint or the chalkboard:

a. What was Jeremiah expecting in the new covenant?

b. Why was the new covenant necessary?

c. In what ways is the new covenant "better" than the old?

Ask two persons to read aloud to the group Hebrews 8:1-13 and Hebrews 10:11-18, both of which refer to Jeremiah 31:31-34. Then discuss the questions. If you did the first activity described above after number 3, compare the answers to the last question with the list prepared from the introduction to Hebrews. Discuss any differences.

and

Briefly summarize Paul's background as a rabbi and the context in which Galatians was written. Information in the introduction to Galatians in *Today's English Version* and most study Bibles will provide the material you need. Next, review the terms of the covenants with Abraham and Moses studied in the previous session. Finally, ask the members of the group to read Galatians 3:15-29 and write a two-or-three sentence summary of Paul's argument that the new covenant in Christ is a fulfillment of the promise to Abraham. Ask several volunteers to share their summaries and then invite the group to speculate why Paul might have used the reasoning process he did and to share to what extent they agree with Paul's argument.

CLOSING

1. If you have decided to celebrate the sacrament of the Lord's Supper or an "agape feast" be sure to allow an appropriate amount of time. Either of those activities will take the place of the other "Closing" suggestions.

or

Check the items left unanswered on the Loose Ends list. Invite the group to help clarify any of these questions. Assign those that are still unanswered to members of the group for reports during the beginning of the next session.

2. Distribute small slips of paper to the group members. Invite them to write down joys and/or concerns they have. Pass a basket around the group to collect these. Then pass the basket a second time and ask the members to remove one of the slips. Begin a

prayer asking God to hear the joys and concerns that are being raised. One-by-one persons are to contribute the sentence(s) written on the slips they drew.

and/or

Read in unison Hebrews 1:1, 2 and Hebrews 13:20, 21.

Looking Ahead

Item #3 under Exploring the Scripture in the next session suggests that three people present brief reports on various names for God in the Old Testament. Each will need a Bible dictionary.

PEOPLE REFLECT
ABOUT GOD

THEME
3

*Thinking about
Who God Is*

PART
1

NOTES FROM THE AUTHOR

About This Theme

The first three themes form what may be called "a module." There is a kind of logical connection among them. The first theme begins with the exodus experience of deliverance. Although this became highly important in Israel's traditions, it implied knowledge of God prior to the exodus. This earlier connection and later events made it clear that God is faithful to covenant promises. Perhaps this involved an element of wonder: God does not respond as humans do in the face of disappointment. We assume that some such track led to reflection about the kind of God who manifests such character. This analysis is artificial, for the process was surely not so simple.

Another useful approach to these themes is to consider their starting points. Theme 1 begins at the exodus in the book of Exodus. Theme 2 goes back into Genesis and begins at Abraham (with a cameo look at Noah). Theme 3 finally starts at the beginning of the Old Testament with Genesis 1-11. In the New Testament, Theme 1 begins at the end of the Gospels with the resurrection. Theme 2 goes to the beginning of the Gospels, but there the parallel ends. New Testament texts in Theme 3 become prominent only in Part 3.

The delay in treating Genesis 1-11 is deliberate and, in my experience, constructive. The common practice of plunging into those chapters as a starting place for biblical study obscures their nature and makes it practically impossible to establish the term "prehistory." Backing into this material helps students understand and appreciate its nature and function in the Scriptures.

These chapters, however, loom large in the thinking of most Bible students. Your credibility may be at stake if you are maneuvered into a dogmatic confrontation. You should not get off track into a "history of religions" lecture. Theology is centrally concerned with learning about God, and these Genesis traditions have much to tell us if we interpret them carefully and sympathetically. Stick to the session plans.

The choice of passages to be emphasized in this theme may seem somewhat arbitrary, but reflecting about God is a very broad task. You must start with Genesis 1-11 in Part 1. The other texts are certainly not the only ones that might be appropriate, but they have proven to be effective for our purpose.

About Genesis 1-11

It is important to understand the sense in which these chapters may be referred to as "pre-history." This requires an appreciation of where this material came from and how it was preserved. Since we do not know precisely how the traditions developed, we may conjecture that Terah told the ancient stories to Abram and his brother in Haran. We can imagine Abram telling his nephew Lot, perhaps around campfires as they journeyed westward. Later Abraham tells Isaac, Isaac tells Jacob and Esau, Jacob tells his large family, and so on. Most ancient peoples felt the need to explain how the world and its creatures came to be. Primitive Near Eastern texts are available in a number of books.[1] Native American mythology also provides useful comparisons. But the Hebrew traditions about creation seem to us to be unique in their understanding of God and in the quality of the earliest ancestral memories.

Comparison with nonbiblical traditions readily shows that the Genesis narratives are remarkable for their beauty and reserve. There is a simplicity about the creation story, for example, that is not found in other Near Eastern literatures. God's relationship to primeval events and to the earliest life of God's human creatures is succinct yet grand. The focus on God as creator pervades these chapters of Genesis and recurs throughout the Psalms. This is due in large measure to the monotheism of the people who preserved and recorded the material.

There is a mountain of technical scholarship dealing with these matters, and it is a challenge to keep it from intruding needlessly into this study. It is beyond the scope of this course to deal with documentary hypotheses, but some of the evidence that led to these hypotheses cannot be overlooked. There surely are strands of tradition that have been combined and/or edited. One clear example is the two stories of creation. Remember that here we are not primarily concerned with literary theories; we are trying to understand the texts as they come to us. Careful consideration of the two creation stories offers a commentary on the transmission of the traditions. Since our focus here is on how and what the Israelites thought about God, the use of different names for God is a prime point to consider. It is observable in our English versions, and we shall return to it later in these notes.

---

1   See section on supplementary readings.

Anthropomorphism

This subject appears in earlier parts, but it is explicitly introduced here. The *Resource Book* directs attention to the first two commandments. It may seem strange that people who indulged in so much anthropomorphic language forbade any physical representation of God. The Hebrews felt a close identity with God (*created . . . in the image of God*) and at the same time sensed an inviolable distance (taboo at Sinai). Their traditions rejected nonhuman ideas about God (hence anthropomorphism), but there was a definite distinction between humans and God (God and Moses on the mount). Anthropomorphism was—and is—unavoidable if we are to speak meaningfully about the God of the Bible. At the same time, it raises the same basic questions about God that arise in the Bible.

The use of the first person plural pronoun in sayings attributed to God presents a problem. There are several ways to explain this. The one in the *Resource Book* is favored by the Old Testament scholar I consulted about this material. Another literary explanation is possible. The Hebrew word for God, *elohim*, is a plural formation and may have influenced the use of the plural pronoun. The "plural of majesty," which monarchs have used throughout history, may be illustrated from the lengthy introduction to the King James Version, where the king speaks of himself as "we." Note that in Genesis 11:5 and 11:8 Yahweh acts alone, and this may influence how we interpret verse 7.

One other explanation is to be rejected if it should come up in discussion. People sometimes propose that the plural pronoun is early evidence of the Trinity. There are at least two serious errors in this idea. First, texts showing a trinitarian understanding of God do not appear until the New Testament period, and even there the idea is not prominent. It had to be so. If we take seriously the divine incarnation in Jesus Christ, there could be no trinitarian belief until Jesus appeared as a human being. But even more importantly, trinitarian faith must never imply belief in three Gods. Belief in a "triune" God has never thereby superseded the ancient belief that God is one. In Mark 12:29 (and parallels) Jesus affirms the fundamental tenet of his Jewish heritage: *Hear, O Israel: the LORD our God, the LORD is one*. To propose that *us* in Genesis 11:7 (or 1:26) implies the Trinity is irresponsible theological error. Let us (you and I!) hope that it doesn't appear in your group.

About Changing God's Purpose

Genesis 1-11 is the principal concern in this part, but the *Resource Book* introduces several additional matters. One is the question whether God can be influenced. Put in more theological terms, is God immutable, unchangeable? The question was in the background in Theme 2, and it will appear again. An easy way to deal with the problem is to explain it as anthropomorphism, but that really dodges the issue.

We must go further and ask whether the Judeo-Christian faith does not at some point require us to use vocabulary of change in respect to God. It is hard to avoid a theological dilemma. We cannot enter into the consciousness of God as ultimate deity, but reason seems to demand that God to be ultimately God must be unchangeable. But our experience with life—the quality of being alive—demands change. Furthermore, the Bible takes seriously the creation of humankind as creatures with wills, responsible for their choices and answerable to God. But humans do not always do God's will—unless we make the nearly impossible inference that God wills people to stand against the divine purpose.

What happens when we pray? Is it all decided before we pray? Abraham and Moses both argued with God. Dare we? These are among the most difficult theological questions we can ask. Perhaps they will not come up from your group, but you should think about them just in case. A satisfactory response—one that will hold until the next time the question arises—may be found in distinguishing between drawing rational conclusions about God and receiving insight by experience. Our present task is to seek insight from the experiences of God's people as recorded in the Scriptures.

Other Matters

Three more details are addressed in the *Resource Book*.

(1) How does God communicate with people? Theologically, what is the nature of divine revelation? Our Old Testament texts show how the methods of God's communication are related to how the PEOPLE REFLECT ABOUT GOD. The diversity of such communication should warn us not to be dogmatic or hasty in our interpretation of the texts.

(2) The relationship of Yahweh to other gods is difficult for us to deal with because of our long exposure to monotheism. Be prepared with information about other Near Eastern gods of the Old Testament period; it will be valuable at some point. Information on Baal is easy to come by. Review Elijah's contest on Carmel and consider what that story tells about Elijah's understanding of God, about the people's understanding, and about Baal worship.

(3) The biblical names for God are not all of equal importance. Review the meaning of the name "Yahweh" and how it is translated in English versions. "LORD" is inescapably a masculine title. NRSV and some other versions stay with it because of the long tradition in earlier versions and because of the extreme difficulty of working around it. NJB eases the problem by using "Yahweh," but that is not likely to become popular. You may hear the Hebrew substitution of *adonai* if you attend a Jewish service today. "Yahweh Sabaoth" occurs in Protestant hymnology. "Sabaoth" must not be confused with "sabbath." *(LORD God of Sabaoth* means "Lord of hosts"—Lord of all the forces that operate at God's command throughout the whole creation. The term is always translated in NRSV.)

Part 2 studies Job. The name "Shaddai" occurs there without "El," translated by NRSV *the Almighty* (for example, in 5:17). The Greek name "Kyrios" will be familiar to those who sing liturgical music, for it occurs in the prayer Kyrie eleison, "Lord, have mercy."

Supplementary Reading

If you have access to a library that has *The Ancient Near East: An Anthology of Texts and Pictures*, Volume I, edited by James B. Pritchard (Princeton: Princeton University Press, 1958), you will find much background material for this part. You will also find useful information on Genesis 1-11 in *Understanding the Old Testament* and *Introducing the Old Testament*.

SESSION PLANS

Learning Objectives

This session is intended to enable participants to:

1. Imitate the art of "oral tradition" by retelling a story from Genesis 1-11.

2. List the major similarities and differences between the two stories of creation in Genesis 1 and 2 and describe in one or two sentences the main point of each of these stories.

3. Recall several places in Genesis 1-11 where God is described in human terms and discuss the advantages and limitations of using anthropomorphic language.

4. Recall and explain three names used for God in the Old Testament.

5. Recite the first two commandments and briefly describe their meaning.

6. Complete the phrase "Ancient Israel thought of God as one who..." with at least five different endings.

Resources You May Need

Chalk and a chalkboard
Newsprint and markers
Ancient Near Eastern Texts by J. B. Pritchard
Copies of the questions for analyzing the creation stories in Genesis
Bible dictionaries
Copies of Psalm 8 or Psalm 139:1-8 for a responsive reading

SETTING THE STAGE

1. Begin the session by describing the relationship of the first three themes. For this purpose review the first paragraphs under "Notes from the Author." This discussion will serve to provide a rationale for "backing into" Genesis 1-11 and lay a foundation for considering the early chapters of Genesis as "pre-history."

and/or

Divide the group into subgroups of six to eight persons and invite participants to recall stories they have been told about their birth or early childhood. Allow time for several stories to be shared. Then explore in the whole group how the stories were transmitted. Were they based on written accounts, pictorial records, oral reports? Who told them to whom? Have they shared them with anyone else?

This exercise will easily lead into a discussion of the way the stories in Genesis 1-11 were handed down from generation to generation by word of mouth, until the "oral tradition" became written. You may want to illustrate this discussion with examples of stories from other cultures found in *Ancient Near Eastern Texts*, by J. B. Pritchard.

and/or

Ask members of the group to recall stories recorded in Genesis 1-11 and make a list of their responses on the chalkboard or newsprint. Select two or three stories on the list (Creation, Fall, Cain and Abel, Noah and the Flood, the Tower of Babel, etc.) and retell them or have someone else do so, using a storyteller's style and speaking as if the tale were being told to people totally unfamiliar with it.

or

The stories in Genesis 1-11 are sometimes referred to as etiological tales. That is, they answer a question or explain why something is the way it is. Ask members of the group to think of questions the stories in Genesis 1-11 might answer, such as "Why do humans hate snakes?" or "Why are there so many different languages?" List these questions on a chalkboard or newsprint and ask the group to select one or two questions. Then retell the appropriate biblical stories that answer these questions.

EXPLORING THE SCRIPTURE

1. Divide the group in two sections and assign one half Genesis 1:1-2:3 and the other half Genesis 2:4-25. Ask each section to answer the following questions, which you have listed on the chalkboard or newsprint or given to each member on a worksheet. If the assigned Scripture doesn't provide an answer to a question the small group should note that.

Questions:

How long did creation take?

Where did creation take place?

When in the process was man created? From what substance?

When in the process was woman created? From what substance?

What is the relationship between male and female?

What is the relationship between humans and God?

What is the main point or idea of the story?

When the sections have completed their work, reconvene the total group and have both sections report their answers to the questions, one at a time. Record the responses on a large chart. Note the similarities and differences between the stories. Discuss what the two stories tell us about who God is.

(This exercise is reproduced by permission from *20 New Ways of Teaching the Bible*, by Donald L. Griggs. Nashville: Abingdon, 1982)

or

Divide the group into pairs. One person is to tell the creation story from memory, without using the Bible. The other person is to act as a scribe and write down the main points. Then together they are to find the Bible references to the facts which were listed and determine if the material has come from one or both of the Genesis accounts of creation.

Reconvene the group and compare the results of the activity. Discuss why the Bible includes two creation stories and what each story tells us about who God is and what God does.

2. The issue of using anthropomorphic language to describe God arises in all of the stories in Genesis 1-11. It is sharply focused in narratives which imply that God's intention can be altered. Three other passages that reflect this view are Genesis 18:16-33; 32:22-32, and Exodus 32:30-35.

Review these stories as a group or assign one to each of three sub-groups. Analyze each passage for:

   a. The details of the conflict between God and the individual.

   b. The implications of altering God's plan for the person or group concerned.

   c. What the story reveals about God.

Also discuss:

   a. What is the value of using anthropomorphic language to describe God?

   b. What are the limitations or problems caused by using such language?

   c. How do you interpret such language when you encounter it?

If you use sub-groups for this activity, pick up any loose ends from the discussions when the total group reconvenes.

or

Ask the group to list "off the top of their heads" specific instances where anthropomorphic language is used to describe God in texts they have read for this session. Record these on a chalkboard or newsprint. Discuss questions such as the three listed above.

3. Have three members of the group who have been selected beforehand give brief reports on each of the following names of God:

   El Shaddai (Exodus 6:2-3; Job 5:17)
   El Elyon (Genesis 14:18-24; Daniel 4:32, 34, etc.)
   Yahweh Sabaoth (Psalm 24:10; Psalm 46:7; Isaiah 6:3, etc.)

Ask the participants what each name contributes to our understanding of the God of the Bible.

or

List the above Bible references on the chalkboard or newsprint and ask a different person to look up each one. Compare translations among the group and examine any footnotes to discover how the term was used in the original language. Then summarize from a Bible dictionary the origin and meaning of the term.

4. The discussion of anthropomorphism and the different names for God may raise the question of whether the ancient Hebrews were really monotheists. Ask members of the group to recall the first two commandments from memory. Continue to take suggestions for the wording of these commandments until the group agrees on it. Record this wording on a chalkboard or newsprint. Then compare the group's versions of the commandments with Exodus 20:1-6 (Deuteronomy 5:6-10).

Carry on a mock debate by asking members of the group to recall evidence that indicates that the Hebrew understanding of God was similar to views in the surrounding culture. Among the items to consider are:

- God meets people in special places such as Sinai.

- God seems identified with particular patriarchs or leaders.

- The first commandment does not expressly exclude the existence of other gods.

Then have the group summarize the evidence that distinguishes the Hebrew concept of God from other contemporary views, such as:

- The second commandment expressly prohibits idolatry.

- Later prophets and writers denounce other deities. See, for example, Isaiah 40:18-26; Psalm 115:1-8.

Discuss what this evidence implies about the nature of God in early and later Hebrew faith.

or

Summarize material contrasting Israelite and Canaanite faith in a mini-lecture and relate this material to the first two commandments. Ask the group to cite additional instances of Israel's struggle with syncretism. Discuss the way in which this issue continues to be a problem for the church today. You will find basic information in the supplementary resources on the Old Testament and a Bible dictionary.

CLOSING

1. Ask the group to sum up the ways God communicated with people in the Scripture references for this part. List them on newsprint and save the list to review in Part 3 of this theme.

or

Write the following phrase on the chalkboard and have members of the group complete it in as many ways as they can think of.

In the Scripture for this session God's people think of God as
one who...

or

Ask persons to share any insights they have about who God is. Discuss how these have altered ideas they previously held. Read Psalm 8 or Psalm 139:1-18, perhaps responsively, in closing.

Looking Ahead

Item #3 under Exploring the Scripture in the next session suggests that nine members of the group be asked to prepare brief summaries of various aspects of the book of Job. See the activity for details.

PEOPLE REFLECT ABOUT GOD

THEME
3

Asking How God Can Be Both Just and Loving

NOTES FROM THE AUTHOR

The Central Question in This Part

We have been considering perhaps the oldest theological question: What is God like? This part really continues the question with some specific details. You will recall that the Hebrews answered fundamental questions about God and life by referring to experience rather than to speculative reasoning. They thought and wrote mostly in concrete terms.

Our Western religious heritage, influenced by Greek philosophy, leads us to reflect upon experience, to exercise reason, to tie up our answers in neatly logical outlines. Of course it is not always possible to arrive at satisfactory explanations of what has happened. Our Bible study begins by examining the experiences of God's people and asking what those experiences meant to them. Sometimes we can move smoothly to their meaning for us, but sometimes such a move is difficult and takes us into the realm of theology.

Biblical records tell us that God's people confront both love and justice in God's acts and revealed will. When it appears that love and justice are at variance, we face a difficulty. Since God is one, this must be resolved. Exodus 34:6, 7 is one of the clearest affirmations that God is both loving and just; hence it is placed in the Memory Bank. Yahweh's love is expressed in at least six terms. Then Yahweh's justice is announced. No attempt is made to reconcile the two parts of the declaration, and the text seems to see no contradiction. The tension is allowed to stand.

The Hebrews approached the problem from experience and so found the tension in their own human character. Accordingly they could frame their approach to God in several ways. They observed that they had surely sinned; then they could cry, "Have mercy!" When they felt that they were not sinful, they could cry, "Be fair!" Sometimes this second approach took the form, "We have not sinned as badly as the wicked people." When evildoers appeared to be prosperous, it called into question a dimension of God's justice.

About the Passages

Genesis 3 and 4 reappear. The point here is what the stories say about God. God demands obedience, but Adam and Eve are not destroyed. Cain is punished, but he is protected from the violence he has initiated. The view of God held by the people who handed on the stories is also important.

The Psalms strongly reflect ideas and attitudes about God, for they are expressions of worship directed to God. The Psalms are closely studied in Theme 9, but they are appropriately utilized from theme to theme. Here Psalm 73 bears heavily upon our question.

Jonah has suffered from too much association with the *large fish*, a.k.a. "the whale." God is almost amusingly patient with the prophet's refusal to do as he is told. Jonah is allowed to pout, but God arranges a kind of win-win situation at each step of the story. God's concern for all of creation is clear. The session plan shows how to deal with this important little book.

Job presents the most sustained consideration of the nature of God in the Old Testament. This is reason enough to take up the book this early in our program. It will appear again in Theme 8 with Wisdom Literature, but its concentration on our question makes it valuable here. God's justice is under examination—the theological term is "theodicy." God's love is only implied. After all the complex discussions with the friends and after Yahweh's rather lengthy response, the final point is really simple: God is God! (You may remember that J. B. Phillips wrote a book with the provocative title *Your God Is Too Small*.).

About Satan and Evil

Give some thought to the question of Satan and evil, for it is likely to come up. Again a session plan is provided to help you deal with it. Popular views about the evil one are usually derived more from Dante and Milton than from the Bible. There is very little precise information about the evil one in Scripture, but it will not do to read into the Bible ideas from pagan mythology or even from later Christian poets.

A common argument for the existence of a personal devil is that Jesus apparently believed in one. In response to this, it is most important to keep in mind that Jesus' humanity was real (check the creeds!). His contemporaries accepted Satan as a spiritual power. This was at least partly a consequence of Jewish contact with dualistic Middle Eastern religions. If Jesus had undertaken to argue that the monotheistic sovereignty of God calls into question the existence of an embodiment of evil over against God, he would have stepped out of his location in history. Besides, *the large crowd* that listened to him *with delight* (Mark 12:37) would probably not have known what he was talking about. We ought not to be surprised that Jesus spoke in terms his hearers understood. This was part of God's real involvement in humanity's real situation (this anticipates Part 3).

On the other hand, we ought not to insist that all of Jesus' first century ideas must be included as an element of our faith in him. It is a strange piety that makes articles of faith out of everything Jesus accepted in his cultural setting. Jesus rode donkeys, but we ride in automobiles. Jesus commended footwashing because it was an appropriate social practice in his time and place. We wear foot coverings that make such a practice inappropriate. We can recognize first century ideas without requiring them in our time.

Jesus' words about Satan are always in terms of victor-versus-vanquished. Satan is no longer a serious threat even if one insists upon his existence. To this may be added what Revelation 12:9, 10 implies (and see 13:4 and 20:2, 3, 7-10). All manifestations of evil directed against God and God's people are one. This means that Satan is not *the* personification of evil but *a* personification. The difference is radical, like the difference between *a* God and *the* God.

The absolute reign of God and the victory of Christ must not be compromised. The evil in our lives is set against God's sovereignty and is a denial of Christ's triumph. It is *our* evil, and we are accountable. We laugh at the comedian who excuses his action by saying, "The devil made me do it." Christian faith utterly rejects such an alibi.

Emphasizing the Central Issue

Be sure you are clear about the issue. If God loves persons who do evil, does this mean God lets up on the requirements of justice and righteousness? If God is absolutely consistent in handing out justice, and people show a persistent propensity for not measuring up to divine requirements, how can God deal in love toward them?

In the story of Jonah God shows care for the prophet. At times it is almost tender and borders on good humor. Jonah would not have called it love, but he does not accuse God of injustice. Evidence of God's love appears in the final concern for the people of Nineveh. It is *Jonah's* sense of justice that is offended. Perhaps the story means that God's love and justice are so intimately bound together that they cannot be separated. In Jonah 4:1-4 the prophet's reflection upon Exodus 34:6, 7 shows that he is unable to bring justice and love together in his own life.

God does not abandon Job. Indeed, God treats him with remarkable consideration and dignity and in the end showers him with good things. God's love is never unjust, and the divine justice always operates in a framework of love. As God is one, so God's love and justice are inseparable.

Part 3 develops some New Testament aspects of this theme. It is tempting to move ahead here, but we cannot do everything in every part. Nearly all Scripture reflects thought about God, so we are not done with this question. We shall deal with Paul, who has a great deal to say about righteousness and justice but who also calls love the greatest spiritual gift.

Supplementary Reading

The introductory articles on Job and Jonah in the *New Oxford Annotated Bible* will be helpful. Consult also a Bible commentary on Genesis 3, 4 and Exodus 34:6, 7 and a Bible dictionary on Satan and evil.

SESSION PLANS

Learning Objectives

This session is intended to enable participants to:

1. Describe why the question of how God can be both just and loving arises as a problem in the Old Testament.

2. Summarize briefly how the following Old Testament materials deal with this problem:

   Genesis 3, 4.
   Exodus 34:6, 7.
   Jonah.
   Job.

3. State their own view of this problem and compare it with the biblical materials.

Resources You May Need

   Chalkboard and chalk
   Newsprint and markers
   Newspaper stories, slides or pictures depicting injustice in life
   Script of Genesis 3
   Index cards with Scripture references for reading Job
   Copies of a closing hymn

Leadership Strategy

<u>SETTING THE STAGE</u>

1. Add any questions left from the previous session to the Loose Ends list and decide when to address them in this part.

and/or

Summarize stories from a current daily newspaper, project slides, or display mounted pictures depicting vivid contrasts of plenty and need in our world. For example, compare a family around a well-laden dinner table with children suffering from malnutrition, or people in a mansion with those in a tiny hovel. Point out that one of the theological issues that has plagued believers through the centuries is how a loving God can permit such inequities. Explain that although there is no easy answer to this dilemma, this part traces the struggle with the issue through the Old Testament and analyzes some of the responses provided there.

or

Ask the group members if they have experienced the difficulty of being both loving and just as parents, friends, employers, or workers. Invite participants to discuss an example from their own lives or one that you offer. Ask how they deal with the conflict between love and justice in such instances. Indicate that this struggle is similar to the issue concerning God's love and justice studied in this part.

or

Read Exodus 34:6, 7 aloud to the group. Ask them to help you list all the words or phrases that speak of God's love. Put them on a chalkboard or newsprint. Then list those which mention God's justice. Point out that this part is focused on portions of the Old Testament that deal with how God can be loving and just at the same time.

<u>EXPLORING THE SCRIPTURE</u>

1. Give a brief presentation summarizing the meaning of the Fall in Genesis 3. Focus your remarks on what we learn about God's love and justice from this material. Ask how this story about Adam and Eve answers the question about the origin of the difficulties humans experience in life. In what ways do members of the group agree or disagree with this answer? Both *Understanding the Old Testament* and *Introducing the Old Testament* provide helpful information which sets the story of Genesis 3 in the context of Israel's understanding of herself and history.

or

Create a dramatic reading of the story of the Fall. You will need a narrator and a cast including Eve, the Snake, God, and Adam. The narrator might begin with Genesis 2:15-17 and 3:1 to set the stage. Assign the verses from 3:2-19 to the respective characters beforehand, or type up a script. A suggested breakdown is as follows.

Narrator	2:15-17; 3:1	Adam	3:10
Snake	3:1	God	3:11
Eve	3:2, 3	Adam	3:12
Snake	3:4, 5	God	3:13a
Narrator	3:6-9a	Eve	3:13b
God	3:9b	God	3:14-19

At the close of the reading discuss:

a. What does the story tell us about God's love and justice?

b. What does the story tell us about the origin of the problems of humankind?

c. In what ways is this story our story?

or

Divide the group in half. Have one half read Psalm 73:1-14 and be prepared to summarize for the group the writer's complaint about the prosperity of the wicked. Ask the other half of the group to review Psalm 73:15-28 and report how these verses provide a different perspective.

Discuss what changed the writer's view and whether the second half of the psalm is more an affirmation of faith or a reasoned response to the issue.

2. Summarize the story of Jonah by going around the group asking persons to contribute a sentence or two to the plot. Make certain to include:

• The assignment God gave to Jonah

• Jonah's response

• God's reaction to Jonah's disobedience

• Jonah's mission to Nineveh

• Jonah's feeling about this mission's success

• God's final word to Jonah

Discuss with the group why Jonah was angry with God. In what way did he antici-pate that God's justice would be displayed? How is God's love portrayed in the book? What might have been the original purpose of this story? What does it say about God's love and justice?

or

Ask the group to construct a brief outline of Jonah, either as individuals or in small groups, without using their Bibles. They are to end their outline with a sentence beginning "The main point of the Book of Jonah is . . ."

Invite several persons or groups to share their outlines and compare them. Compare also their analyses of the main point of the book.

and/or

Briefly review the background of Jonah, with special attention to the relationship between the Hebrews and Nineveh. Ask the group to substitute for Nineveh the name of a contemporary group or nation about whom they do not feel kindly. When they now review the story, in what way, if any, does their understanding of its message change?

3. Ask nine persons, who prepared ahead of time, to summarize the following aspects of the Book of Job:

   a. Job's sufferings and the reason for them

   b. Job's expectations of how God should exercise justice

   c. Bildad's argument

   d. Zophar's argument

   e. Eliphaz's argument

   f. Elihu's argument

   g. Yahweh's answer to Job out of the whirlwind

   h. Job's final response in 42:1-6

   i. What happens in the epilogue of 42:7ff.

Discuss with the whole group how Job's outlook changed during the course of the book. What is their evaluation of Job's final answer to God?

or

Assign the following roles and passages to persons in the group and read an abbreviated form of the story of Job in the following segments:

  a. Narrator (Chapters 1, 2)

  b. Job (3:3-5)

    Eliphaz (4:2-9)

    Job (6:2-7)

  c. Bildad (8:2-7, 20)

    Job (9:2-4, 20)

  d. Zophar (11:2-6, 13-15)

    Job (12:2-4)

  e. Narrator (32:1-6a)

    Elihu (35:2-13)

  f. the LORD (38:2-11)

    Job (42:2-6)

After the reading discuss how Job's "friends" understood the relationship of God's love and justice. To what extent was Job's early viewpoint similar to theirs? How does his final conclusion indicate a change in his thinking? Ask participants to summarize in one or two sentences what the Book of Job tells them about how God can be both just and loving. What is their evaluation of this message?

4. If the question of the personification of evil arises, respond with a brief presentation on Satan and dualism, using material from your Bible dictionary and incorporate into your remarks Dr. Walther's comments concerning the Bible's emphasis on the supreme power of God.

or

Assign three persons to read:

    Job 1:6-12   Matthew 4:1-11   Revelation 12:7-12

After each passage is read, discuss what it implies about the position and power of Satan and the supremacy of God. Regardless of what view of Satan persons hold, it is important for them to see that the Bible stresses that God is in control.

CLOSING

Invite a few persons to share their own struggles with God's love and justice and how they have resolved them or learned to live with them. Close by reciting or singing a hymn of patient faith, such as "Be Still My Soul."

Looking Ahead

Item #4 in Exploring the Scripture in the next session suggests that four persons each prepare on newsprint a summary of how God's will is revealed to Paul, Ananias, Peter, or Cornelius in Acts 9 and 10.

PEOPLE REFLECT
ABOUT GOD

THEME
3

*Knowing the
Unknowable God*

PART
3

NOTES FROM THE AUTHOR

Ways of Knowing God

In this part we concentrate on how we know God and on the related subject of divine revelation. The study should show at least four ways by which the people have come to know God. (1) An anthropomorphic stage, when theophany is the mode of revelation. (2) A stage when transcendence and immanence are in tension and mediators function—messengers, angels, prophets. (3) The total transcendence of God, when cultic activity is the supreme interpreter. (4) The unique revelation in Jesus Christ. "Spirit of God" may relate to any or all of these.

At least three subjects that recur in the Old Testament are very important.

(1) Messengers make God known, but their role is not always clear. Traditional ideas about angels fall into this area and need to be put into proper perspective. It seems that only in visions were the messengers different from human beings. The place of angels in other-worldly settings is not under consideration here.

(2) The prophets assumed a special role as messengers. They spoke for God. *Thus says the LORD* most commonly introduces prophetic messages. *The word of the LORD came* occurs again and again. This word in a sense expresses God's presence (see 1 Kings 19:9). Recall the creative power of God's word in Genesis 1.

(3) The role of the Spirit in the Old Testament is not easy to trace. "Spirit of God" often stands for what humans can apprehend of the being of God. The Spirit does not appear in a consistent manner. The New Testament marks a change beginning from the time of Pentecost.

About Scripture

Scripture as a way of knowing God should be kept quite separate from the subject of inspiration. A canon of the Old Testament as we know it was not finally set until the end of the first century A.D.. The written documents are instruments for God's message, and the authority of the message does not depend upon the words of the written form. The code in Exodus 20-23 is early, and its influence on national life preceded the form in which it was finally recorded. Some form of what became our Book of Deuteronomy figured prominently in Josiah's reform (2 Kings 22:3-23:5). Jeremiah's scroll was burned by Jehoiakim and was rewritten by Baruch the scribe. The distinction between form and authority is a fine one, but it is important.

Texts in the New Testament cite passages in sacred Scripture (our Old Testament) as authority, often with an introductory formula such as *it has been written*, but the emphasis is upon the message being conveyed by the passage, not upon the character and context of the passage itself. The form of Paul's quotations is evidence that it was the Word behind the word that carried the authority. There are instances where we cannot trace the exact origin of the wording of his quotations. The use of sacred Scripture by New Testament writers is extensive and authoritative, but the revelation is understood to come from God, not from the text itself.

Along with a warning not to get away from your session plan onto theological debate, I want to remind you that what is an immediate problem for your group may be more important at the moment than what you or I have prepared and consider essential. Many dull and fruitless group sessions have developed when a leader has forced an agenda that ignores the group's current concern. Postscript: be sure it is a group concern, not the hobby of one vocal member.

Knowing God through Jesus

The central affirmation of the New Testament is that God has become known in a unique and definitive way in Jesus Christ. Therefore the focus of this part is on Jesus Christ. In a sense this means that instead of starting with our idea of God and trying to relate Jesus to it, we should rather start with Jesus as revealed in the New Testament and discover what this shows us about God. The New Testament says in various ways that Jesus Christ is the ultimate revelation of what God can be in human frame.

This came as a surprise in the first century world, and even Jesus' followers were slow in comprehending it. We have noted how the Gospels took form backwards. That is, the resurrection reversed the judgment of the cross, and cross plus resurrection gave lasting meaning to Jesus' teaching and deeds. Then some Christians delved into his background and went on to reflect on the eternal significance of his whole career.

Early Christians faced this problem from a perspective quite different from ours. They lived in the time when eyewitnesses testified about the man Jesus, so their difficulty concerned what we may call his divinity. Many centuries of Christian belief in Jesus' divinity separate us from the first century, so our difficulty is with Jesus' humanity. It is not easy for us to believe that the transcendent, unknowable God actually became known in real, human form. We have trouble getting behind the resurrection to accept Jesus' words and deeds as part of God's ultimate self-revelation.

Jesus' Titles

Our problem is reflected in the ways Jesus was regarded by his contemporaries, at least as the Gospels report them. He was considered a prophet, healer, wonder-worker, teacher (including "rabbi," a rough equivalent), and Son of God (in John, *the Son*). People wondered whether he was the Messiah, and occasionally he was called by messianic titles including "son of David" and "king of the Jews." Remember that "Christ" is the Greek equivalent of "Messiah" (= "anointed one") and so is usually inappropriate as a title during Jesus' ministry (so Matthew 16:15-20 NRSV). The slow or mistaken responses to Jesus are a clue to understanding how radical his revelation was.

The Gospels report that Jesus called himself *the Son of Man*. The *Resource Book* presents basic references and observations. Synoptic parallels and differences are not mentioned, for this quickly becomes technical. The possible Old Testament sources are more difficult to trace in the newer versions where they have been relegated to footnotes in the interest of inclusive language. Psalm 8:4 (note NRSV footnote) demonstrates that "son of man" can be a way of saying "I." Yahweh frequently addresses Ezekiel as *son of man*, and Jesus felt a deep kinship with the prophets as God's designated messengers. The apocalyptic use in Daniel 7 introduces a corporate note, and Jesus probably sensed that he would be humanity's representative with God.

Many people are tempted to explain "son of man" in an oversimplified way that is not acceptable. The title is not a term that refers to Jesus' human nature in contrast to his divine nature designated as "Son of God."

The prologue to Hebrews (1:1-4) is a very helpful way to think about God in "son" terms. Jesus and the early Christians called God "Father," so "Son" suggests the closest possible relationship. The key to most of Hebrews is in this title. By the self-revelation in Jesus as Son, we see more of who God is and does than we can from any other way by which God has been revealed.

John and Paul

The prologue to John (1:1-18) is one of the best known New Testament passages that reflect about God. The parallel to Genesis 1:1 is important. The opening phrase in each verse is the same: "in beginning"—no definite article, for God has no beginning. Each book opens with a beginning when God spoke. The beginning for humans is when God first communicated. This communicated word is identified with God (John 1:1), and then in John 1:14 it is identified with Jesus, the Word become flesh. Jesus embodies all God said before. Jesus is the only way to see God (verse 18). The Son Jesus *has made* God *known*.

John 1:1 and 1:18 both affirm the distinction between Jesus and God but also maintain their oneness. This is the problem the theologians of the early Christian centuries wrestled with. In the fourth century the Nicene creed used the term "only begotten" in an effort to affirm both the distinction and the equivalence. The term is still in use, but it is more of an anthropomorphic paraphrase than a translation of the original Greek word. Emphasis should fall on the Son's uniqueness rather than on how he became God's Son.

Paul had to come to terms with the question of how Jesus revealed God. He was certain that in Christ he arrived at an entirely new knowledge of God. He had a very high regard for what he had known as a Jewish leader (see Philippians 3:4-6), but Romans 8:3, 4 indicates how far he had moved. The sermon in Acts 17 begins with remarks about God that are unique in the New Testament, but when Paul begins to preach about Jesus and the resurrection, his audience shuts him off. Philippians 2:5-11 is instructive; for it begins with *equality*, moves to the radical separation, and returns to unity.

The Spirit

Genesis 1:2 introduces the relation of breath-wind-spirit. In both Greek and Hebrew one word may bear any of the three identities, depending on the context. In John 3:8 Jesus uses this overlap of meaning. The identity of breath and wind is easy to grasp. Perhaps in antiquity someone observed that when breath (or wind) left the body, essential life (= "spirit") was gone, and so the additional identity was added. It is a worthwhile word study.

The Spirit changes from the Old Testament to the New in two special ways. (1) In the Old Testament God's Spirit does not appear in any consistent manner. In the New Testament the Christians have a unique experience of the Spirit at Pentecost, and from then on the Spirit is a constant factor in their experience. (2) It is hard to identify the Spirit in the Old Testament and to discover a pattern of relationship with God. In the New Testament God's Spirit plays a strong role in the life of Jesus and after Pentecost is identified with the revelation in Jesus. It is perhaps not surprising that *Holy Spirit* occurs more often in Acts than in any other book.

The connection of the Holy Spirit with Jesus is important as a way to keep trinitarian theology from turning into belief in three Gods. The exaltation (or ascension) of Jesus ordinarily does not keep us from thinking of him as present with us. Since he is not present in the same way as during his earthly ministry, it becomes imperative to associate his presence with the activity of the Holy Spirit. We noted in Part 1 how Jesus affirmed his Jewish faith that *the Lord is one* (Mark 12:29). In any case, you should not give a theological lecture on the nature of the Trinity. That is, after all, a task for systematic theologians. For Jesus and the New Testament writers it seems to be a matter of dealing with how God's revelation continues—"Knowing the Unknowable God."

Supplementary Reading

Review some of the most common titles for Jesus in a Bible dictionary. Articles on the Spirit of God, Holy Spirit and Paraclete will also be valuable. A good commentary on John will prove useful in preparing for the activity on the prologue to this Gospel (1:1-18).

SESSION PLANS

Learning Objectives

This session is intended to enable participants to:

1. Cite at least three ways by which people come to know God and God's will in the Old Testament and suggest one biblical reference to illustrate each way.

2. List three titles or phrases by which Jesus is designated in the New Testament and describe what they tell us about how Jesus reveals God.

3. Compose a brief paragraph on the work of the Holy Spirit in the New Testament.

4. Reflect on the means by which God's will is known to us as individuals and the church today.

Resources You May Need

Chalk and a chalkboard
Newsprint and markers
Bible dictionary and concordance
Prints or slides of artists' paintings or sculpture depicting Christ
Index cards or slips of paper for the activity on the Holy Spirit
Copies of a closing hymn

Leadership Strategy

SETTING THE STAGE

1. Record any questions from the previous session or the preparation for this meeting on the Loose Ends list and determine when to take them up.

and

Ask people to form pairs. In these twosomes, partners are to ask each other to respond with one word or idea to the question "Who are you?" This question is to be asked again and again until each person has heard seven responses. Reassemble in the total group to share insights and make the point that knowing someone else is an ongoing discovery and there are many levels to knowing another person.

or

Choose a public figure everyone knows, such as a national leader or entertainer. Ask the group to list seven or eight facts about this person. Place these on a chalkboard or newsprint and note next to each item the source of this information. In a brief discussion emphasize that the data comes from different sources, that some people have more information than others, and that genuine knowledge of a person is an ongoing process.

or

Read Isaiah 6:1-8 aloud to the group. Point out that this classic text illustrates an unresolved dilemma of the Old Testament: God is beyond our comprehension, yet God is made known to us in various ways. Ask the group to point out parts of the passage that emphasize God's "otherness." Then ask how God's will was made known to Isaiah. This dual emphasis on transcendence and immanence is central to this part of Theme 3.

EXPLORING THE SCRIPTURE

1. If the group made a list of the ways in which God is revealed in the Old Testament in the closing section of Part 1 of this theme, have them review it now. Add any new suggestions. From memory, or using a concordance or Bible dictionary, attach Scripture references to the items on this list. Compare the list with the ways Dr. Walther mentions in "Notes from the Author" (theophany; mediators such as messengers, angels and prophets; cultic activity). What additional categories, if any, has the group listed? How is the Spirit of God related to any or all of these categories?

or

If a list was not made in Part 1, either in the total group or in smaller groups of six to eight, brainstorm instances of God's revelation in the Old Testament. List these on newsprint and attach Scripture references to the items. Display the list(s) for the whole group to see and encourage the participants to note similarities among the items. Ask the group to pick out the primary ways by which God was known. Compare these with Dr. Walther's summary and note any differences.

2. To begin a consideration of how Jesus reveals God to us, point out Dr. Walther's statement in "Notes from the Author" that "instead of starting with our idea of God and trying to relate Jesus to it, we should rather start with Jesus as revealed in the New Testament and discover what this shows us about God." Ask the group to think of the most common titles for Jesus used in the New Testament. List these on newsprint. Then discuss what each of these titles tells us about Jesus and about God. (You will probably have to do some research about the most difficult titles, such as Son of Man, in preparation for this activity.)

or

Display several prints or slides of artists' paintings or sculpture depicting Jesus. Choose several different styles of art. Ask persons to select one to which they react favorably, and to explain why. Discuss what the various interpretations say about the artists' understanding of Jesus and his relationship to God.

and

Have the group members turn to John 1:1-18. They are to read the passage, noting every word, title, or phrase referring to Jesus. List these on a sheet of newsprint. If you choose the first activity above, place the two sheets of newsprint side by side. Ask what the items on the second list reveal about Jesus and God.

or

Deliver a brief presentation on the prologue to John (1:1-18) using information from a good commentary. Analyze the various terms by which Jesus is designated and comment on John's choice of words and phrases. What do they tell us about how Jesus reveals God?

3. Distribute index cards or slips of paper to everyone, asking them to write down at least three words or phrases that come to mind when they think about the person and work of the Holy Spirit. Go around the room sharing these impressions. Then see if the group can draw some conclusions concerning the way they perceive the activity of God's Spirit. If so, record them on newsprint.

and

Summarize the information on the word *Paraclete* from a Bible dictionary. Ask the group what this definition adds to their understanding of the Holy Spirit. Then have the group review Ezekiel 37:1-14. Discuss in what way the operation of God's Spirit is portrayed differently in the Old and New Testaments.

or

Divide the group into three sections and assign one of the following passages to each section: John 14:15-26; John 16:7-15; Acts 16:6-8. Each section is to read its passage and prepare answers to two questions on newsprint:

a. What is the relationship of the Holy Spirit to Jesus, according to this text?

b. What is the task of the Holy Spirit, according to this passage?

Have the sections report their answers to the whole group and display their newsprint in a prominent place. Discuss the similarities and differences among the answers. How does the information gleaned from this exercise compare with the students' previous impressions of the Holy Spirit?

4. Have four persons who prepared ahead of time each present a summary on newsprint of how God's will was revealed to one of the following in Acts 9 and 10: Paul, Ananias, Peter, and Cornelius. Note similarities in the reports. Ask the group how God's will is known to individuals and groups today. Compare these responses with the means reported from the New Testament.

For further discussion analyze how your congregation sought God's direction in a recent decision, such as calling a new leader, developing a new program, or enlarging its mission activity.

and/or

Summarize Paul's argument in his sermon to the Athenians in Acts 17. If you or someone else has a talent for drama, develop a brief paraphrased monologue of this material. At the conclusion of the presentation point out to the group how Paul's approach on this occasion differs from the usual style of sermons in Acts. Ask what kinds of sermons they prefer to hear. Compare these with Paul's style in Acts 17 and elsewhere. Discuss how they see the Spirit of God at work in the preaching and teaching ministries of their congregation today.

1. Have someone who is a good reader close the session by reading Philippians 2:5-11 in a meditative style.

or

Read or sing a hymn about the Holy Spirit, such as "Spirit of God, Descend Upon My Heart" or "Gracious Spirit, Dwell with Me."

and/or

Have each person complete the statement, "The most important thing I learned about God in this theme is . . . ."

Looking Ahead

Item #2 under Setting the Stage in the next session suggests that a member of the group describe the geography of the Holy Land. It is also suggested that someone give an illustrated tour of the Holy Land. A third suggestion is that a knowledgeable person give a report on archeology and the Bible or that several persons report on archeological discoveries in the Ancient Near East.

Item #2 under Exploring the Scripture in the same session suggests that two persons make presentations on Israel's mission to other nations as described in Isaiah 40-55 and Jonah.

PEOPLE LIVE IN GOD'S WORLD

Views of the World in the Hebrew Scriptures

PART 1

NOTES FROM THE AUTHOR

Geography and Archeology

The religion of Israel is indissolubly connected with history, and history takes place in geographical settings. Before we go further, we shall study the world in which God's people live. You will have to balance physical facts about that world and the influence of that world upon Israel's life and faith.

If you are not familiar with the geographical situation of the Holy Land and the location of selected cities and natural features of that land, you must remedy that lack at once. Your personal library should have a good Bible atlas.[1] A set of large maps is practically indispensable and should be in every church library. Good pictures of the physical features of the land are also useful. As we move into themes where history is more prominent, you will find repeated occasion to refer to the physical settings.

This is also an appropriate point to introduce archeology. The supplementary reading will be helpful, and you will also find much valuable information in your Bible dictionary. Again, you may have access to people who have had first hand experience. Archeology has attracted much popular attention and interest, so you will have to be alert to the temptation to pursue it as a fascinating sidetrack.

Be careful to avoid the idea that archeology "proves" the Bible. Many details in Scripture have been illuminated and corroborated by archeological research, but it is a false lead and bad theology to interpret this as "proof." Faith in the Bible must not depend upon whether a destruction level in the walls of ancient Jericho coincides with the period of Joshua. Such simplistic connections are misguided and lead to superficial views of the nature of Scripture.

---

1 *The Harper Atlas of the Bible* (New York: Harper & Row, 1987) is large, comprehensive, and up-to-date; it is also expensive. Other good atlases are available.

International Relations

The geographical location of Israel made constant contacts with surrounding peoples and nations unavoidable. The biblical records make many references to these interrelationships, and occasionally foreign records refer to Israel. It is striking that in the face of such contacts the Hebrew people were able to maintain their social and religious individuality.

According to W. F. Albright, Abraham was probably a caravaneer, and he would wander about a large area of the ancient Near Eastern world. Three generations later, Joseph became closely involved with the government of Egypt. Exodus 1-4 intimates that it was Moses' reluctance to be connected with Egyptian officialdom that led indirectly to his participation in the Hebrew exodus.

Life under the judges, Saul and David was somewhat rustic and provincial. With the accession of Solomon the outside world was brought abruptly into the life of God's people. Solomon's political alliance with Egypt and his business and cultural associations with Phoenicia (Tyre) are part of the evidence. This and the subsequent involvements of the kings of Israel and Judah with surrounding nations are summarized in Theme 6.

The period of exile began a dispersion of Jews that persistently affects their later story. When a remnant returned to Judea, constant difficulty arose from both political and social realities: Neighboring princedoms interfered with the resettlement, and intermarriage was a threat to the religious and cultural separateness of the Jews. Again, these matters appear in later themes.

The intertestamental period and the deuterocanonical books are relevant and not well known. Alexander the Great was *the* political figure of the times, and he is introduced in 1 Maccabees 1. The outside world intruded radically into Jewish life in the person and policies of Antiochus IV, as we noted in Theme 1, Part 2. Israel's century of independence following the Maccabean rebellion came to an end with the Roman conquest of the Middle East. Israel could not escape from the political and social environment.

The World of Nature

"The world" in the Bible is multidimensional. Here we have dealt mostly with political and social aspects. In the Hebrew Scriptures the world of nature is also everywhere present. This natural world may be viewed from three different perspectives: God, humankind, and nature itself. These three need to be carefully distinguished.

If we raise questions about God's relationship to nature, we must remember that Yahweh is Creator and Sovereign, and there can be no room for a real dualism. Questions about humankind in relation to nature are appropriate to all our themes, but care should be taken not to confuse the focus; e.g., in the flood story, nature is not really vindictive but humankind is reprehensible.

When we turn to nature itself, again we must avoid dualism. Nature is not in evil rebellion against Yahweh God, with a titanic struggle in the balance. If we begin with the scriptural premise that humankind is, in a primitive and ultimate sense, the originator of human woe, and if we follow this with the scriptural theme of God's determination to save the people, most of the problems about nature will be resolved.

Sometimes natural forces seem to be out of control, but nowhere does the Old Testament picture God as imperfect in power and will. Both Amos (Amos 1:1) and Zechariah (Zechariah 14:5) mention an earthquake, but Isaiah declares that earthquakes and storms may be agents of Yahweh (Isaiah 29:6). Yahweh insists to Job that all natural forces are under divine control (Job 38-41). Random natural destruction is not considered.

Natural Religion

The Hebrew people did not accept "natural" religion; that is, they did not consider that people should find their way to God through observation of nature. The Hebrew religion depended thoroughly upon revelation. Natural evidence is adduced to comment upon God and to understand the divine majesty. This occurs especially in the Psalms (see Psalms 8; 19:1-6; 24:1, 2; 46:1-3). Only *fools say . . . "There is no God"* (Psalm 14:1). The fool has not failed to observe natural evidences of God but has deliberately ignored wisdom that comes from God (see Psalm 92:5-8; also Proverbs 17:24; 18:2).

Scripture interprets nature. Remember Elizabeth Barrett Browning's lines: *Earth's crammed with heaven, And every common bush afire with God; But only he who sees, takes off his shoes, The rest sit round it and pluck blackberries . . . .*[2] God gave revelation through the writers of Scripture.

Israel's Dual-Directional Role

God's people live in a world that touches them with religious, political, and social pressures, and they are affected by forces of nature. It is in the former arena that they find the greatest challenges. On the one hand, they are to be in a positive relationship with the world. The outcome of God's covenant with Abraham is that *in you all the families of the earth shall be blessed* (Genesis 12:3).[3] On the other hand, they are to remain distinctive and in a real sense apart (see 1 Kings 8:53; Ezra 10:11; Psalm 4:3).

---

2 *Aurora Leigh*, Book vi.

3 Or *by you all the families of the earth shall bless themselves* (see NRSV footnote). Also see Genesis 22:17, 18.

The latter prophets try to deal with this balance of privilege and responsibility. Amos, for example, affirms the uniqueness of Israel's position (Amos 3:2), but he also declares that Yahweh is concerned for the other nations (Amos 9:7). The Book of Jonah provides a striking statement of this concern. (Notice also the details about nature and animal life in Jonah 4:6-11.) The message is clear that the world is to be a mission field for God's people.

A climax to this challenge is reached in the second part of Isaiah (40-55).[4] The opening verses proclaim comfort and hope to God's people (Isaiah 40:1-11). Then in Isaiah 41:1-5 Yahweh's rule over the farthest lands is announced (see also Isaiah 45:22). Even the exile did not teach Israel that exclusivism and the call to be a universal blessing were contradictory. The unique relationship of total commitment to God's sovereignty in no way diminishes the divine concern for the rest of creation. Indeed, this increases human responsibility. For Jonah it meant rejection of personal preference and safety. Isaiah 49:6 and especially Chapter 53 assign to Israel a role of suffering *servant* whereby blessing will come to the world (see also Isaiah 55:5). This was a difficult role for Israel. This section of Isaiah is a natural bridge to Part 2, but do not cross it now.

Endnote about Nature

You will have already discovered that this theme carries several loads. The place of Israel and the world of nations will appear again. This theme is the principal spot to emphasize the relation of faith and revelation to the world of nature. Israel remembered her nomadic days. Though David was the great king, he was also the shepherd boy. Indeed, Ezekiel has an extended passage (Chapter 34) in which the relationship between Yahweh, king, and people is cast in the sheep-shepherd figure (and you will immediately think of Psalm 23).

Hope for the future was often bound up with restoration of the bounty of nature (see Ezekiel 34:25-31; Amos 9:13-15). God's cosmic rule is declared in some of the psalms we have noted, and it is broadly portrayed in Job 38-41. See also Isaiah 40:21-26. The modern application of this is evident in concern for the environment.

Supplementary Reading

In addition to a Bible atlas, there are several good books on the geography of the Holy Land. The *New Oxford Annotated Bible* also has a useful article on the geography, history and archeology of the Bible lands. In addition, you will find helpful information on archeology in the *Lion Encyclopedia of the Bible* and *Introducing the Old Testament*.

---

4   This is not the place to discuss the multiple sources in Isaiah. There will be a better occasion later.

SESSION PLANS

Learning Objectives

It is intended that this session will enable participants to:

1. Describe the major geographical features of the Holy Land and locate the majority of the cities listed in the Research section of the *Resource Book.*

2. Outline the interaction of Israel with other nations during several major periods of biblical history.

3. Summarize God's relationship to the world of nature according to the Old Testament.

4. Discuss Israel's responsibility to other nations according to Isaiah 40-55 and Jonah.

Resources You May Need

Chalkboard and chalk
Newsprint and markers
Map of the Ancient Near East
Maps and the Chronology of the Bible Chart from the *Resource Book* Appendix
Slide or film presentation on the Holy Land
Overhead, opaque, and slide or movie projectors
Copies of the statements concerning God's relationship to creation
Copies of Psalm 19:1-4 or 139:7-12
Slides of nature and a recording of "This is my Father's World"

Leadership Strategy

SETTING THE STAGE

1. Review your Loose Ends list, add new items from this week's preparation and determine when to discuss these questions.

2. Using a large map of the Ancient Near East or an overhead or opaque projection of one, point out the strategic location of Israel at the crossroads of three continents. Then have class members turn to the maps of the "United Israelite Kingdom" and "Palestine in the time of Jesus" in the Appendix of the *Resource Book.* Locate as many of the cities Dr. Walther mentions in the Research section as you can. Use the mileage scale to find distances between the most familiar cities and estimate walking

and driving times. You or a member of the group selected ahead of time may then want to describe the geography of the region using information from a Bible atlas and other reference books.

and/or

Invite a member of your congregation or community to give an illustrated tour of the Holy Land. If this is not possible you may be able to borrow an appropriate slide or film presentation from your local library, a religious film library, or a nearby resource center.

and

Ask an interested participant or another knowledgeable person to prepare a report on the way archeology helps to interpret the Bible. You will find useful information in the *Lion Encyclopedia of the Bible*, and *Introducing the Old Testament*. You may want to supplement this report by having other persons give brief presentations on specific discoveries such as the Lachish Letters, the Mari Tablets, the Nuzi Tablets, the Moabite Stone, the Dead Sea Scrolls, the Nag Hamadi Library, the Ebla Tablets, etc. Information about many of these discoveries can be found in entries in a Bible dictionary. *Biblical Archeology* by G. Ernest Wright and the periodical by the same name offer additional information.

3. Display the following statement on newsprint:

The Fertile Crescent was a busy highway carrying ideas and conquerors through the Middle East. The Hebrews, therefore, did not live in a vacuum, but shared the views, traditions, and thought forms of the people among whom they lived.

Invite the group to recall periods in history when the interaction between Israel and the surrounding cultures was especially significant. List these on a chalkboard or newsprint and then, with the help of the group, arrange the periods in chronological order. Then invite participants to comment on the impact of other cultures on the political and religious life of Israel in the various periods.

or

The Chronology of the Bible Chart in the Appendix of the *Resource Book* is divided into ten major sections:

The Beginnings

The Ancestors of the Israelites

The Israelites in Egypt

The Conquest and Settlement of Canaan

The United Israelite Kingdom

The Two Israelite Kingdoms

The Last Years of the Kingdom of Judah

The Exile and the Restoration

The Time between the Testaments

The Time of the New Testament

Divide into ten small groups and assign each group one section of the chart. The groups are to discuss how Israel was involved with other nations during their period. Each group is to report its findings to the whole group.

EXPLORING THE SCRIPTURE

1. Distribute sheets of paper on which the following statements are printed to members of the group:

   a. God created a good world.

   b. God gives people charge over certain parts of nature.

   c. The world becomes the arena for evil.

   d. God brings judgement on wrong human choice.

   e. God maintains control over creation in spite of human actions.

   f. The God of Israel is superior to other gods.

   g. Nature is a witness to God's power and rule.

   h. God uses nature to bless the people.

   i. The final destiny of all creation is under God's control and purpose.

Divide into pairs and assign each pair one of the statements. The pairs are to use the sections in the *Resource Book* entitled "Small World/Large World," "Israel and the

Promised Land," "Nature and World View" to locate at least two biblical references that support their statement. After the pairs have read the references they are to summarize their findings for the group. As people listen they can fill in information about the statements they were not assigned.

or

Invite participants to review the material in the three sections of the *Resource Book* mentioned above. As they read they are to look up passages which refer to God controlling or manipulating nature. Ask members to share their findings and record their statements of how God is related to the natural world. Then lead the group in formulating a summary of God's control of the world according to the Bible references mentioned.

2. Divide the group in half. Select three or four of the following passages to read aloud. As you read, one half of the group is to list what the Scripture says about God's relationship to the Hebrew people, and the other half is to listen for what is said about the relationship of God or the Hebrew people to other nations.

Genesis 12:1-3	Isaiah 49:5-6
Isaiah 19:23-25	Isaiah 65:17-25
Isaiah 42:1-4	Amos 3:2
Isaiah 45:1-13, 22, 23	Amos 9:7

After the passages have been read have the two groups share their findings while you list the responses on two sheets of newsprint. Discuss the statement that Israel was chosen by God to be a channel of grace to all nations. Ask how the message of the book of Jonah is related to this idea.

or

Invite two persons who were selected ahead of time to make brief presentations summarizing the message of Isaiah 40-55 and Jonah regarding Israel's responsibility to other nations of the world. (Jonah was a Basic Bible Reference in Theme 3, Part 2. There the emphasis was on the question of how God can be both just and loving. Here we are concerned with the mission of Israel to other nations.) Helpful information can be found in the introductions to the the Books of Isaiah and Jonah in the *New Oxford Annotated Bible* and the supplementary reference books.

and/or

Divide into four groups and assign each group one of the following passages:

Isaiah 42:1-4	Isaiah 50:4-11
Isaiah 49:1-6	Isaiah 52:13-53:12

Ask each group to read its assigned passage and reflect on these questions:

    a. Who do you think is the servant?

    b. What is the role of the servant?

    c. To what extent is Jesus a fulfillment of this expectation of a servant?

    d. What is the significance of the concept of the servant?

Reassemble the participants and ask each group to report. Compare notes and discuss the concept of the suffering servant.

CLOSING

1. Sing "He's Got the Whole World in His Hands" and invite the group to suggest verses to add to the song.

or

Do a unison reading of Psalm 19:1-4 or 139:7-12

or

Show slides of nature, while playing a recording of "This is My Father's World," or read Psalm 24 during the slide show.

Looking Ahead

Item #3 under Exploring the Scripture suggests that four persons give brief reports on the significance of four "landmark events" in the growth of the early church.

NOTES FROM THE AUTHOR

There is less text in the *Resource Book* for this part than for Part 1, but the readings in Basic Bible References are substantially greater. The references are diverse, and some of them could lead away from the main directions of the theme. Our principal concern is the interaction of the world environment with the faith and early growth of the new Christian communities.

The World

World was used in more than one sense in Part 1. The range is even greater in the New Testament, so some vocabulary study cannot be avoided. The session plans provide an entry for this.

The most common word for *world* in the Greek New Testament is *kosmos*, the root meaning of which is associated with "order" and usually refers to the *created* world. Another word, *oikoumene*, from which we get "ecumenical," refers to the *inhabited* world. A third word, *aion*, from which we get "aeon," indicates the *experiential* world. It may be translated "age." Each of these words may occur with either a neutral or a negative connotation, which may be discovered from the context.

Two other modifications appear, not directly connected with the dictionary meanings. Sometimes *the world* is an entity in distinction from God without particular emphasis upon its moral or religious values. When the evil aspect of these values is stressed, then *the world* may become a demonic force and may reach a degree of intensity where it seems to be a threat to God's rule over the world. On page 100 of the *Resource Book* the idea of cosmic dualism is touched on, and footnote 9 there refers to our previous meeting with the concept. It is important to stress again that the Bible does not countenance a dualistic view of God's world.

Jesus and the World

In dealing with the Gospel records about Jesus, keep in mind that our theme appears there in more than one guise. Jesus' frequent references to nature always include the implication that it is responsive to and under the particular control of God. The so-called "nature miracles" are not introduced in the *Resource Book*, but they may be interpreted in this light. The stilling of the storm demonstrates that nature responds to the command of one who speaks with the authority of the Creator, and more importantly it teaches human dependence upon that authority. The cursing of the fig tree is an acted parable in which again nature is forced to recognize the power of one who embodies the humanity nature serves.[1]

The temptations of Jesus (Matthew 4:1-11, the parallel in Luke 4:1-13, and the shorter version in Mark 1:12, 13) connect several aspects of this theme. The temptation about the stones and bread suggests a misappropriation of a divinely given, natural resource. The words about jumping from the Temple may be read as defiance of a natural law (which is, after all, built in by the Creator). The offer about *all the kingdoms of the world* explicitly includes the lands outside Israel, but Jesus affirms God's priority. Jesus' view of the non-Jewish religious, cultural, social, and political environment is often implied where it is not explicit.

The Gentile world was not Jesus' primary field of mission; that move remained for Paul. This must not be interpreted as narrow provincialism on Jesus' part. It was rather that he was establishing a base for the church. The outward movement was inevitable, and Jesus, who was an astute student of the Old Testament prophets, knew this. It was necessary, therefore, that Jesus carry out his ministry within the Jewish tradition as a precondition and basis for the saving program of God in the rest of the world.

Is it God's intention to save the whole world? The *Resource Book* introduces John 3:16, 17 and puts it in the Memory Bank. Verse 18 gives the other side of the story: God does not violate the prerogative of decision that is a part of being human. It is evident, however, that God's desire includes all the world.

Evil

The problem of evil surfaces again. We have already emphasized that precisely in Jesus' ministry and mission the ultimate power of evil has been defeated. This is what is implied by Jesus' response to the charge that he was in league with Beelzebul, *the ruler of the demons.* [2] The saying about binding *the strong man* and plundering *his house* surely means that in his ministry Jesus is overcoming the power of the evil adversary.

---

1 The converse responsibility of humanity for the preservation of nature is, of course, not in view in such incidents. In Matthew 6:30 and 10:29, Jesus calls attention to God's care for nature.

2 The *Resource Book* gives the reference in Luke; the parallels are Mark 3:22-27 and Matthew 12:24-29.

Do not be misled by the vivid, oriental imagery. By now the point should be well established that Jesus was true to his Near Eastern heritage, and his proclamation was couched mostly in picture language rather than in rational argument. He followed the prophets and wisdom teachers rather than philosophers.

Two further observations may be helpful regarding evil. Most obvious—and most difficult—is the final fact that God is transcendent and sovereign. If it is claimed that this is a cop-out, recall that this is precisely where Job wound up when he wrestled with the problem. Such a conclusion is ultimately a decision of faith. The second observation is in a sense the flip-side of the first: If God immediately eliminated to our satisfaction everything we consider evil, what would become of our identity as sensitive, responsive, willing persons? Probably this, too, cannot be understood without faith.

Paul's View of the World

Paul's situation differed from that of Jesus in a number of respects, including at least the following:

- The critical events of the crucifixion, resurrection, and ascension had taken place.

- Paul's background differed from Jesus' because Paul grew up in Diaspora Judaism and was a Roman citizen.

- Paul's formal training was different from and more extensive than that of Jesus. Paul was at home in Greek language and literature.

- Paul's ministry extended a generation into the time of the early church.

- Paul regularly dealt with people of diverse ethnic and religious cultures.

- Paul was widely traveled.

Paul understands that forces are at work in the world in opposition to the good news about Christ. He does not entertain any possibility that Christ's victory is ultimately in danger from the power of evil, but he recognizes that there is superhuman opposition to his mission and to the church. He writes bluntly that Satan is working against him (2 Corinthians 12:7; 1 Thessalonians 2:18), but he is never in doubt about the future outcome (2 Corinthians 4:7-12).

The idea that the power of evil exercises a time of rule in the world is difficult to handle, and it is only a step away from a dualistic view of Satan's place in the scheme of things.

Phrases like *the god of this world* (2 Corinthians 4:4) lend support to such thinking. This and related ideas will all become clearer in later themes, and they are best resolved in the final discussion of the Revelation of John (Theme 10).

The words translated *rulers and authorities*[3] in Colossians 2:15 occur seven other times in the New Testament. Probably Paul is thinking of supra-human forces working through powerful human authorities. The phrase occurs in Luke 12:11, where the human element is clear. Compare also 1 Corinthians 2:8, where *the rulers of this age* evidently refers to the authorities responsible for Jesus' crucifixion. The Colossian church was dealing with heretical ideas that were probably influenced by pagan religions. It is beyond the scope of our study here to deal with them. Paul did not maintain the clear-cut distinctions we make between the physical and the spiritual realms. See also Ephesians 3:8-10.

The relationship of Paul and the early church to civil authorities is important. Romans 13:1-7 is a key passage. Jesus' relationship to Herod and Pilate is part of the picture. So is Revelation, but at this point its contribution is confined to assurance that evil government will finally fail. As long as civil government does not interfere with his Christian mission, Paul seems willing to accept the authorities as compatible with God's rule. He utilizes his Roman citizenship and even expresses confidence in Roman justice (Acts 25:10, 11). We do not have his final assessment, of course, but if 2 Timothy 4:6-8, 16-18 preserves his late view, then he is not bitter.

The Future of the World

This subject can hardly be avoided in this theme, yet substantive discussion in the *Resource Book* is postponed until Theme 10. Some of the material has already been introduced in Theme 1, Parts 3 and 4, so the material here is reinforcement. The focus is on how the earliest Christians related to the world about them and what this means for our living and responsibility in our world.

Paul does not hold to the nationalist hopes that are so prominent in the Hebrew Scriptures. The future for him does not embrace land and progeny but the emergence of a new people of God in Christ. Though his view of the future is to a degree otherworldly, he never loses interest in or concern for this world. Compare Philippians 3:20 with 4:11, 12, and note 2 Corinthians 5:1-10. Other relevant passages are Philippians 2:9-11; Colossians 1:19, 20; 1 Timothy 4:10.

---

3 NRSV. In RSV and the older versions this was *principalities and powers*, two terms that required considerable explanation. In this context, the new rendering probably needs some interpretation, too. In Luke 12:11 RSV reads *the rulers and the authorities*.

Supplementary Reading

Most Bible dictionaries will have helpful information about the various meanings of "world" in the New Testament. A good one volume commentary will provide additional background for interpreting specific texts, such as Luke 11:15-22; John 3:16, 17; Romans 13:1-7 and Colossians 2:15.

SESSION PLANS

Learning Objectives

This session is intended to enable participants to:

1. List at least three ways "world" is used in the New Testament.

2. Summarize Jesus' attitude toward the world of nature, humankind, and the power of evil.

3. Compare Jesus' and Paul's understandings of the world and their mission.

4. Name at least three major events that helped the young church spread its message to Gentiles.

5. Describe a vision of the world as it will become through Christ.

Resources You May Need

Chalkboard and chalk
Newsprint and markers
Hymnals
Directions for reviewing Jesus' attitude toward "the world"
Chart(s) for comparing Jesus and Paul
Overhead projector and transparencies
Directions for the role play on conflict in First Church
Directions for creating symbols of the "new world"
Mission Yearbook of Prayer
Missionary or fraternal worker

Leadership Strategy

SETTING THE STAGE

1. Review the major points of Part 1 of this theme, add new issues or questions to your Loose Ends list, and decide when to take these up.

2. If you did not use "This is My Father's World" in closing the last session, sing it now. Ask the class to locate two different ways the "world" is referred to in the hymn. Then lead a discussion about the ways "world" is used in the New Testament.

or

Make a brief presentation on the ways "world" is used in the New Testament. In "Notes from the Author," Dr. Walther mentions the following:

    a. the world of nature

    b. the inhabited world, especially the non-Jewish world

    c. the forces of evil

    d. a time, age, or eon

Additional material is available in most Bible dictionaries.

EXPLORING THE SCRIPTURE

1. To begin the discussion of Jesus' attitude toward nature, the power of evil and humankind, divide the group into three sections. If possible, find a place for each section to meet alone. Provide newsprint and markers and a set of directions:

Group 1

    a. Read Matthew 6:26-30 and Luke 12:54-56.

    b. Discuss the question "What is Jesus' attitude toward nature in this story?"

    c. Recall other times Jesus spoke about nature.

    d. Summarize Jesus' attitude toward nature as demonstrated in these stories and sayings.

e. Together create a poster that will help you share this summary with the group. You may use words, symbols, and drawings.

f. Decide how to present your summary to the whole group.

Group 2

a. Read Luke 4:5-8 and 11:15-22.

b. Discuss the question "What is Jesus' attitude toward the power of evil?"

c. Recall other times Jesus spoke about evil.

d. Summarize Jesus' attitude toward evil as demonstrated in these stories and sayings.

e. Together create a poster that will help you share this summary with the group. You may use words, symbols, and drawings.

f. Decide how to present your summary to the whole group.

Group 3

a. Read Matthew 28:16-20 and John 3:16-17.

b. Discuss the question "What is Jesus' attitude toward all humankind?"

c. Recall other times Jesus spoke about the Gentile world.

d. Summarize Jesus' attitude toward the world as depicted in these instances.

e. Together create a poster that will help you share this summary with the group. You may use words, symbols, and drawings.

f. Decide how to present your summary to the whole group.

Gather together and share the summaries through the use of the posters.

or

Write the above sets of Scripture references on separate sheets of newsprint. Read each reference and comment on how it reveals Jesus' attitude toward nature, humankind, or the forces of evil. Invite members of the group to recall other instances when Jesus spoke about these subjects. Then lead the group in formulating summary statements of Jesus' attitude toward each of the topics. Write the statements on the newsprint sheets.

2. As Dr. Walther points out, Paul's situation was different from that of Jesus in several ways. This is especially evident in the scope of their travels and the people among whom they worked. Prepare the following chart on a transparency, newsprint, or chalkboard.

	Jesus	Paul
Birthplace		
Citizenship		
Education		
Occupation		
Language Spoken		
Cities/Countries Visited		
Target Population for Mission		
Cause of Death		
Summary of Message		

Invite participants to share information they have about these items. Fill in the chart with their answers. You may want to refer to the maps in the Appendix of the *Resource Book*. Ask the group to suggest reasons why Jesus chose to remain close to home while Paul journeyed far and wide.

or

Divide into two groups. Have one group compile the information about Jesus needed for the chart while the other group works on Paul. Then reconvene, share information, and complete the chart.

or

Provide the group with copies of the chart. Ask them to fill in as much information as they can and then in twos or threes share information.

and

Lead a discussion about the ways Paul's situation was different from Jesus.' There are helpful suggestions in "Notes from the Author."

3. Divide the participants into two sections. Ask one half to re-read the material on page 97 of the *Resource Book* entitled "The Early Christian Mission." Each person is to list the situations that enlarged the early church's vision of mission and at least skim the important Bible references.

The other half should re-read the material on pages 97-98 of the *Resource Book* entitled "Paul's Mission." They are to list the situations where Paul acted to spread the gospel and review the most important references.

Then reconvene the group and lead the two sections in reporting their findings.

or

Have four participants who have prepared ahead of time give brief reports on the significance of these "landmark events" in the spread of the Christian message to non-Jewish people:

> Pentecost - Acts 2
> Philip's evangelistic work - Acts 8:4-40
> Peter's visit to Cornelius - Acts 11:1-18
> Paul's first missionary journey - Acts 13:1-3, 44-48

or

Summarize the same material yourself and use the maps in the Appendix of the *Resource Book* to trace the spread of the Christian faith around the eastern rim of the Mediterranean Sea.

4. The subject of the relationship of the church to civil authority was raised in item #2 of Exploring the Scripture in Theme 1, Part 4. If you did not have an opportunity to discuss the matter then, the following activities are appropriate for this session.

Read Romans 13:1-7 and 1 Peter 2:13-17 aloud. After reading each passage discuss these questions with the group:

> What was the situation when these words were written?
> What did these words mean then?
> What is the situation of Christians now with regard to civil authorities?
> What do these words say to us as Christians today?
> In what sense are the governing powers today part of the "world?"

and/or

Ask for six or eight volunteers to role play this situation:

> The members of First Church are being divided by a disagreement about the place of the American flag in the sanctuary. Half of the members feel that the flag belongs on display in the sanctuary. The other half feel just as strongly that the flag does not belong there.

The group (half of the volunteers) that speaks for the placement of the flag in the sanctuary can refer to the Scripture passages above. The other group may want to refer to 1 Peter 4:12-19, and recent developments in the relationship of church and state. After five or six minutes of debate, invite everyone to join the discussion. When the discussion winds down debrief the role play.

Discuss questions such as the following:

a. How did the two groups use the Bible in their remarks?

b. How appropriate was this use?

c. In what ways did the two groups move closer together or farther apart during the discussion?

5. The final section in "Notes from the Author" is entitled "The Future of the World." To engage members of the group with this material, distribute a sheet of construction paper and a marker to each person along with these instructions:

The New Testament writers have a vision of the world as it will become through Christ.

• Work alone or with another person.

• Read either 2 Corinthians 5:17-20; Romans 8:18-23, 38, 39; or Revelation 21:1-5.

• Reflect on what these verses are saying to you about the future of the world.

• On the construction paper draw a symbol or symbols that can convey this meaning to others.

Reconvene the group and ask volunteers to share their drawings.

or

Write the phrase "New World through Christ" at the top of a chalkboard or sheet of newsprint. Ask the participants to read 2 Corinthians 5:17-20; Romans 8:18-23, 38, 39 and Revelation 21:1-5 and select three to five adjectives that describe this new world. Then call for volunteers to list their choices and write them on the board or newsprint. When the suggestions run out, lead the group in discussing the progress that has been made toward the realization of this vision.

CLOSING

1. Once again read the Great Commission in Matthew 28:18-20. If your denomination has a *Mission Yearbook of Prayer* or some similar publication, share a reading with participants.

and

Discuss the ways your congregation is attempting to fulfill the Great Commission.

or

Invite a missionary or a person involved in the mission program of your church to talk about how the Great Commission is being carried out today.

2. Sing "To God Be the Glory."

and/or

Have the group repeat together John 3:16, 17 and close with prayer.

Looking Ahead

Item #2 of Exploring the Scripture in the next session suggests that nine participants present brief magazine articles nominating various Old Testament characters for the "Leader of the Year Award." The leaders are Joseph, Moses, Joshua, Deborah, Samson, Samuel, Saul, David and Abigail. Bible dictionaries will be useful for this activity.

*Early Leaders in the
Rise of the Nation*

NOTES FROM THE AUTHOR

Your Leadership

Themes 1 through 4 include diminishing amounts of story material. Themes 5 and 6 offer more, so they provide a change of pace. If you have bogged down, here is a new start to give you momentum. The increase in story material brings some increase in the Basic Bible References.

Remember that the primary purpose of this program is to develop useful mastery of the contents of the Bible. I say *useful* because we must admit that some sections of Scripture do not readily translate into spiritual nurture, and some sections are practically trivia. The most ardent believers in the inspiration of every verse of the Bible do not give equal attention to all passages. Isaiah's vision in the Temple is incomparably more useful as biblical knowledge than the commands about bodily *discharges* in Leviticus 15. Your leadership in emphasizing, reviewing, and supplementing is vitally important, for there is a tremendous amount of material for your group to master.

Some material is repeated in several themes, usually with varying emphases. For example, Moses appears again in this theme, now stressing how he functions as a leader. David reappears here, and he is important also in the next theme. Such repetition is one indication that the material is particularly useful.

No leader's guide, however thorough, can anticipate the needs of every group. Both leader and group must develop skill in sensing what must be accomplished in each session. Don't worry if some well-prepared supplementary material does not get used. Seize the moment and the momentum. Do well what you do together. A jumbled mass of uninteresting information will not produce a useful structure, but a solid foundation and framework will support and shape later study.

Leaders in the Bible

All along we have been dealing with the people of God, and we know that in every group of people some invariably become leaders. We are devoting a theme to the leaders of God's people, for much of the story line of the Bible moves along as the story of these leaders. Twice in the New Testament there is a roll call of Old Testament leaders: In Stephen's speech, Acts 7, and in Hebrews 11. The most extensive roster is in Sirach (Ecclesiasticus) 44-50.

Biblical leaders function by virtue of a special relationship to God. They hear and obey the word of God. Often, the word *hear* is associated with obeying or answering—as a parent today may say, "Now you listen to me!" Sometimes the leaders present God's word to the people. Sometimes they lead by example, as in the case of Joshua. The greatest leaders combine functions, as did Moses. The greatest task of leaders is to inspire followers. Biblical leaders discern God's will and inspire followers to know and to do it.

Patriarchs

Abraham, Isaac, and Jacob were leaders in the limited sphere of family and clan. Joseph became an international figure, and we have material to see how this leader developed. His integrity is emphasized, and his loyalty to his Jewish heritage makes him a link between the patriarchal age and the time of the exodus.

Moses

The *Resource Book* refers to a great amount of material connected with Moses' career. The most important passages here are those that highlight his qualities as a leader. It is hard to balance his reluctance to become a leader (Exodus 4) with his effectiveness before Pharaoh and in the wilderness years. Numbers 12:3 says that *the man Moses was very humble,*[1] *more so than anyone else on the face of the earth*, but contrast the testimony of Numbers 12:6-8.

The stature of Moses is emphasized by how important he is in the New Testament. He appears at Jesus' transfiguration, and Luke 9:31 refers to Jesus' ultimate mission in terms of "exodus" (the Greek word; NRSV *departure*). Check your concordance. Moses is mentioned in Revelation 15:3, and shortly afterward the world suffers plagues like those in Egypt.

---

1 NRSV footnote gives an alternate translation *devout*; KJV and ASV read *meek*.

Joshua, Judges, Ruth

In connection with the Joshua stories you may want to check archeological information related to the conquest of Canaan. The biblical records have somewhat glamorized the period, beginning with the battle of Jericho. Your task is not to attack the biblical narratives but to be prepared to interpret them accurately.

Our first meeting with a judge was in Theme 1, where we studied Gideon as an agent of God's saving action. Note that the enemy was Midian, and four tribes were rallied initially to aid Gideon (Judges 6:35). Typical of the period, the Ephraimites are angry that they were not called until later (Judges 8:1).

The story of Deborah is selected to emphasize the role of women in Scripture. Samson is chosen because at least parts of his story are well known. Probably you should have in hand a list with data about each of the other judges in case a trivia-minded member of the group brings up some detail. The story of Jephthah and his tragic vow is interesting but has difficult details (Judges 11:1-12:7). Once again the Ephraimites are miffed.

Ruth, while not technically a leader, is important at least because a biblical book bears her name.[2] She is probably best known for her loyalty to Naomi. The social and religious implications of her life are more important for our study. Hebrew marriage customs, which seem uninteresting in code form, come to life in Ruth's story. Deuteronomy 25:5-10 gives instruction concerning "levirate" marriage, i.e., the responsibility of a brother to produce children by the wife of his childless brother. In Ezekiel 16:8 Yahweh treats Jerusalem with the marriage symbolism Ruth addresses to Boaz in Ruth 3:9. Leviticus 25:23-25 tells of the responsibility of next of kin to keep property in the family. The background of Ruth's gleaning is in Leviticus 19:9, 10; 23:22; and Deuteronomy 24:19-22. The fact that Ruth was not Jewish has more importance in other themes.

Samuel

Samuel's role as king-maker is enough to guarantee his place in the story line of the Old Testament. His part in instituting the monarchy comes to the fore in Theme 6. He is the key person in the transition from tribal confederacy to monarchy.

This change is foreshadowed in the call of Samuel. It is easy to miss the importance of Samuel by failing to see that the sweet boy grew up into a tough leader. His ministry is summed up in 1 Samuel 3:19-4:1a. There is a disaster in 1 Samuel 4-6; the Philistines

---

2   Esther also bears a woman's name. Her leadership is dealt with in Theme 9.

capture *the ark of God*. One of Samuel's first public achievements is setting things right after this event (1 Samuel 7:3-14). The etiology of *Ebenezer* (7:12) is worth noting.

Saul

The career of Saul gives us glimpses of how the early Hebrews observed character. Woven into his story are curious details about religious practices such as sacrifices, anointing, clairvoyance, and charismatic frenzy. We also read about social customs, eating and sleeping, farming, and choosing by lot. There are popular sayings. We must not forget that these stories were recorded in the light of their outcome, but details that are not reflected in later events should be assumed to be traditional recollections.

The chief qualification that led to the choice of Saul as king seems to be physical (1 Samuel 10:2-24). His eventual downfall is attributed to his failure to obey Yahweh, but it seems clear that some instability of character contributed. The pathetic story of Saul's consultation with the medium at Endor may raise questions related to present-day interest in the occult. The head-on response is that the Bible is unequivocally opposed to any such practice. Your concordance will quickly show you the references. The only New Testament reference is in Paul's list of *the works of the flesh* in Galatians 5:19, 20 (NRSV *sorcery*). The story in 1 Samuel 28 is unique in the Bible. Details are shadowy. Saul does not actually see Samuel; he identifies him from the medium's description. Samuel's message to Saul is bad news. As a dramatic prelude to Saul's death, the story is surely gripping.

The record says that Saul himself *had expelled the mediums and the wizards from the land* (1 Samuel 28:3), yet he consults one. He first *inquired of the LORD*. Apparently there were lesser prophets than Samuel available (28:6). *Dreams* are also a way in which Yahweh might have answered. A third way is *by Urim*. (If you did not do Research 2 in Theme 3, Part 3, check your Bible dictionary for details and see 1 Samuel 14:36-42). In any case, sorcery constitutes an affront to God's complete control of all events and a failure to deal directly with God regarding human destiny.

David

David's early career overlaps Saul's kingship, and it is impossible to separate them in many of the passages. There would be ample material to take up a whole theme with David. The slaying of Goliath is too renowned to omit. The friendship with Jonathan is too complex for brief summary and is not directly relevant to the subject of leadership.

Abigail (1 Samuel 25:2-42) is included because of her extraordinary character and initiative. Consider the ethics of the story, the social commentary, the religious overtones (*the* LORD *struck Nabal, and he died*). Again we have a notable instance of the importance of women in early Israelite times.

The formation of David's character interests us here. You should note his magnanimity in sparing Saul's life twice (1 Samuel 24, 26). We return to David the king in Theme 6 and to the psalmist in Theme 9.

Supplementary Reading

The best source for summaries of the life and work of the leaders mentioned in this part is a Bible dictionary or the *Lion Encyclopedia of the Bible*. More extensive data will be found in the other supplementary books on the Old Testament.

SESSION PLANS

Learning Objectives

This session is intended to enable participants to:

1. Locate these Old Testament characters on a time line: Joseph, Moses, Joshua, Deborah, Samson, Samuel, Saul, David, Abigail.

2. Name at least one event in the life of each of these persons when they exercised leadership, and describe their behavior.

3. Retell the story of Ruth.

4. Compare the qualities of leadership in the Old Testament with those sought in church leaders today.

Resources You May Need

Newsprint and markers
Chalk and a chalkboard
Chronology of the Bible chart from the Appendix
Worksheets for creating profiles of Old Testament leaders

Leadership Strategy

SETTING THE STAGE

1. Add new questions from this week's preparation to your Loose Ends list and decide when to respond to them.

2. Place three sheets of newsprint before the group with one of the following questions on each sheet:

　　a. What qualities of leadership do we look for in candidates for public office?

　　b. What criteria do corporations use for selecting management personnel?

　　c. What leadership skills or traits are sought in leaders of our congregation?

As each question is discussed, list the responses on the newsprint. Compare the answers to the three questions and note similarities and differences.

or

Ask for persons in the group to name their favorite character in the Bible or public life and describe why they find this person attractive. Note on newsprint the names and qualities mentioned.

EXPLORING THE SCRIPTURE

1. During this session you will find it helpful to refer to the Chronology of the Bible in the Appendix or the time line you began in Theme 1. Using these visual aids, read each of the following names to the group and ask participants to place the leaders in their appropriate historical context.

Joseph	Deborah	Saul
Moses	Samson	David
Joshua	Samuel	Abigail

or

Place the names of the following major periods in the Old Testament history on a chalkboard:

The Patriarchal Period
The Exodus
The Conquest

The Tribal Confederacy

The Monarchy

Summarize the political situation of Israel in each period in three or four sentences. Then ask the group to place the leaders named above in the appropriate period.

2. Create "profiles" of the above leaders by using the following questions: (These should be listed on a chalkboard or newsprint or copied on worksheets for participants.)

   a. During what period did this leader live?

   b. How did this person rise to a position of leadership?

   c. What problems or challenges did this leader encounter?

   d. How did this person provide leadership (by example, physical courage, delivering God's word, etc., or some combination of these)?

   e. What were his or her major accomplishments?

   f. Describe any significant personality traits of this leader.

This task may be carried out by having each participant or small groups of two or three select one of the leaders or by drawing the leaders' names from a hat.

The profiles are to be completed from information in the *Resource Book* and the Scripture references listed there. (If there is a Basic Bible reference for a leader be sure to include the information found there.) The profiles are then to be presented to the whole group.

or

Divide into nine small groups and assign each group one of the above leaders. Each group is to write a newspaper obituary for its leader, briefly outlining the events and leadership qualities that made him or her important. These are then to be read to the whole group.

or

Have the persons selected the previous week present their articles for B.C. magazine, nominating one of these leaders for the "Leader of the Year Award." The group may ask questions of those making the presentations and may then be polled to determine the most popular leader.

and

Discuss the similarities and differences between the qualities of the leaders just researched and those mentioned under Setting the Stage.

3. Summarize the Book of Ruth for the group, using material from *Today's English Version*, the *New Oxford Annotated Bible* or a Bible dictionary. Be sure to mention that Ruth is included in David's and Jesus' family lines (see Matthew 1:5).

or

Divide the participants into four groups and assign each group a chapter of Ruth to summarize for the entire group in no more than five sentences.

and

Compare the qualities exhibited by Ruth and Naomi with those noted about Deborah and Abigail. Discuss one or more of these questions:

   a. How different are the roles played by women and men leaders in the Old Testament?

   b. What indications are there, if any, that women are subordinate to men in the Old Testament?

   c. What bearing does this information have on your understanding of the leadership to be expected from women and men in the church today?

CLOSING

1. Have someone read the roll call of the faithful in Hebrews 11:17-34, or ask four persons to read a paragraph each.

and/or

Discuss the question of the extent to which Old Testament leaders can provide role models for us today.

2. Close with thanksgiving and prayers for the leaders of your congregation and the church around the world.

Looking Ahead

Item #4 of Exploring the Scripture in the next session suggests that four persons each prepare to represent one of the major sects of first century Judaism (Pharisees, Essenes, Sadducees and Zealots) in a panel discussion.

GOD'S PEOPLE HAVE LEADERS

Prophets and Later Leaders

PART 2

NOTES FROM THE AUTHOR

The Early Prophets

Be sure you are familiar with the *Resource Book* material on Elijah, Micaiah, and Elisha, including all references. Names are important: Elijah means "My God is Yahweh" and Elisha means "God is salvation." The Bible tells about Elijah's encounters with Ahab and Jezebel in great detail. Jezebel is a formidable leader, but she is on the wrong side. She frightens Elijah. His subsequent meeting with Yahweh at Horeb deserves careful attention. It can be related to Theme 3, Part 1.

Micaiah appears only in 1 Kings 22 and the parallel 2 Chronicles 18. We wish we knew more about him. He seems to be all the more striking because his story comes in the midst of Elijah's time. What can you make of the character of Jehoshaphat? The court-guild prophets come off as a sorry bunch of establishment actors. Micaiah's vision in 1 Kings 22:19-22 may remind you of the prologue of Job.

The view of God's Spirit in that time is dramatized in 1 Kings 22:24. Zedekiah and Micaiah both claim to be speaking Yahweh's word, but obviously only one truly is. Zedekiah bluntly asks how *the spirit of the LORD* passed from him to Micaiah. (Such a simple-minded view, of course, is not limited to this story.) Micaiah's reply is like a word of Jeremiah: *When the word of that prophet comes true, then it will be known that the LORD has truly sent the prophet* (Jeremiah 28:9). This incident may recall our study of the Spirit in Theme 3, Part 3.

We do not hear how matters turn out for Micaiah. The narrative is concerned with the justification of Yahweh's word through the prophet concerning the destiny of Ahab, who was rated a very bad king. We like our stories neat and complete. The writer here is concerned with a greater matter: How God's rule is faring with the people.

The Writing Prophets

The great writing prophets did not leave such fine stories as occur in Samuel and Kings. Their messages are greater in scope and depth and require careful study. Their relation to their times is not always easy to perceive. We are concerned here with their impact upon national life rather than their theology, so their location in the time line is important.

The *Resource Book* suggests that Amos did not make a lasting impact upon Israel's life, but his boldness and strength of character have given him a firm place among the prophets. In Amos 4:1-3 he apparently addresses the wives of prominent men of Samaria. Is it any wonder he was unpopular?

Obviously we cannot spend as much time on any of the latter prophets as we might wish. A good picture of the history of the period and the parts played by the great prophets in key events will help you handle any questions that may develop in the session. These prophets are extraordinary leaders who bring God's message to bear upon national and personal situations. This concern outweighs for now the natural desire to have extensive biographical details.

Special Issues in Isaiah

In previous themes the second part of the Book of Isaiah was to the fore. Here we deal with the first part, Chapters 1-39 (with a few omissions). You are probably aware that biblical scholars speak of "First" and "Second" Isaiah. Some treat Isaiah 56-66 as "Third." The reason is plain. Chapters 1-39 are concerned with the career of Isaiah ben-Amoz, whose ministry was before the exile. Chapters 40-55 reflect conditions in the exile and hopes for its end. Chapters 56-66 may be concerned with religious life in Judea after the return from Babylonia but are in the same spirit as 40-55.

Controversy about the unity of the book is counterproductive here. I have found that if I speak of the "parts" of the book rather than "First" or "Second," problems are less likely to appear. You must not, however, compromise your understanding of what the texts say. For example, it is really impossible to take the reference to Cyrus in Isaiah 45:1 as coming from before the exilic period, for Cyrus' edict releasing the Jews is to be dated about 538 B.C. Since the details about Isaiah's political action are all in the first part of the book, the problem of unity really need not arise.

The *Resource Book* makes no mention of the parts of Chapters 7, 9, and 11 that contain what are sometimes called "messianic prophecies." They properly belong to Theme 10 on "Hope," and it is best to defer discussion. Isaiah 7:14 has caused a great deal of disputation, for it has traditionally been regarded as a prediction of the virgin birth of the messiah.

The Hebrew word translated *virgin* in KJV means "a young woman of marriageable age," and Hebrew has another word for "virgin." The Septuagint, however, translates the Hebrew by a Greek word that does mean "virgin." NRSV and NJB have notes to this effect and translate *the young woman*. The point here does not concern the Gospels' testimony about the virgin birth of Jesus but rather forthright and honest treatment of Old Testament prophecy. The simple distinction between "forthtelling" and "foretelling" is valid here.

Ezekiel

Ezekiel often receives less study than his importance for the New Testament merits. This is partly because of some of his strange prophecies and his eccentric actions. To connect him with today, note the mention of *Tel-abib* in 3:15, from which modern Tel Aviv takes its name. Ezekiel was a priest, and this is reflected in parts of his book.

One translation detail should be noted. Over ninety times in the book the prophet is addressed by a particular term that in KJV, RSV, NJB, and NAB is translated (literally) *son of man*. This is a Hebraic phrase that is equivalent to "man" (see Psalm 8:4 RSV), the translation REB uses. TEV renders *mortal man*. NRSV has *mortal* throughout Ezekiel. In Daniel 7:13, where the comparable phrase in Aramaic occurs, NRSV has *human being*. In the New Testament, however, where the Greek equivalent occurs over sixty times in reference to Jesus, it is translated *Son of Man*. These variations must be borne in mind when the relationship among the texts is studied.

After the Exile

We have not done much with Chronicles. A comparison with Samuel and Kings would require an additional—and somewhat technical—study. Chronicles in the Hebrew canon is one of the Writings and stands last. This must have been so in Jesus' time (see Matthew 23:35 and Luke 11:51, an incident referring to 2 Chronicles 24:20-22). The end of Chronicles and the beginning of Ezra overlap, but the collection of material in Ezra-Nehemiah differs from Chronicles in focus and organization.

The circumstances of Judah at this time are a factor in several developments. There was an increased emphasis on individual piety, the synagogue came into being and spread its influence, and there was a growing interest in apocalyptic. The Maccabean period brought special hopes and effects, among them the growth in the power of the priesthood.

Bridge from the Old to the New Testament

Additional material on the parties, sects, and other leaders that reach from the intertestamental period into the New Testament may be found in a Bible dictionary and in the other supplementary books. Notice where the rigid differences were and where the lines were fluid. Scribes are perhaps the most difficult to identify. "Rabbi" can be an honorific title. Recall that it was occasionally applied to Jesus, who as far as we know, had no special training and no party affiliation.

The oral law was codified and written down in the second century A.D. and became known as the "Mishnah." These laws in turn were elaborated by commentaries and other material and several centuries later became two collections known as "Talmud."

The Essenes continue to excite interest today, particularly because of the Dead Sea Scrolls. There is no general agreement as to how much influence they had on John the Baptist or Jesus. The Zealots interest biblical scholars. Jesus' developing career would likely attract their attention for its potential as a revolutionary movement.

Supplementary Reading

Once again a Bible dictionary will be an important source of information about the leaders in this part. You will also find valuable insights in the introductions to various books of the Bible provided in *Today's English Version*, the *New Oxford Annotated Bible* and other study Bibles.

SESSION PLANS

Learning Objectives

This session is intended to enable participants to:

1. Define in their own words the task of a Hebrew prophet.

2. Describe at least one occasion on which each of the following prophets was involved in influencing the political life of Israel/Judah: Micaiah, Elijah, Elisha, Amos, Isaiah, Jeremiah, Ezekiel.

3. Summarize in a paragraph the leadership roles Ezra and Nehemiah played during the restoration.

4. List at least two major characteristics for each of the four groups active in the intertestamental period (Pharisees, Essenes, Sadducees, Zealots).

Resources You May Need

Newsprint and markers

Chalk and chalkboard

Scripts and nametags for the play about Micaiah

Map of the Divided Kingdom

Copies of questions for discussing 1 Kings 22:1-28

Copies of questions and Bible references for the activity on the prophets

Construction paper

Chronology of the Bible chart

Hymnbooks

The Apocrypha

Leadership Strategy

SETTING THE STAGE

1. Add any questions left over from the previous sessions to your Loose Ends list and decide when you will take them up.

2. Have the group recall the names of the leaders discussed in Part 1.

and

Ask the group for names of people who have played a "prophetic" role in contemporary society. List their names on newsprint and beside each name add the qualities the group feels made them leaders.

EXPLORING THE SCRIPTURE

1. Use the script found at the end of these session plans on pages 175-177 to present the story of the prophet Micaiah found in 1 Kings 22:1-28. The material is based on *Today's English Version*. You will need copies for all members of the group. There are six major parts. It might be helpful to use large nametags for these speakers. The rest of the group is to read the part of the four hundred prophets. Introduce the play with a few brief remarks about the political situation in Judah and Israel during this period of the Divided Kingdom. The map in the Appendix will be helpful in setting the stage for the story.

At the conclusion of the reading, discuss:

a. Why do you think King Jehoshaphat suggested another prophet be consulted? (see verse 7)

b. If you had been in Micaiah's place, what thoughts would have been going through your mind as you spoke with the kings?

c. What reason, if any, do the kings have to believe Micaiah rather than the other prophets? What means do you suggest be used to make distinctions between false and true prophets?

or

Divide into groups of six to eight persons. Ask everyone to read 1 Kings 22:1-28 silently. Have each group appoint a recorder to lead a discussion of questions such as those listed above. (The questions should be placed on newsprint or given to the recorders.) Then reconvene the whole group and the recorders will report the responses. Follow up by discussing any contrasts among the groups' answers.

2. If you used a map to introduce the story of Micaiah, continue to refer to it for this activity on the prophets.

Divide into six groups. Assign the prophets listed below to different groups and ask them to provide the following information for their prophet:

a. Approximate date of his work

b. Name of king(s) and kingdom(s) where he was active

c. Description of the historical situation

d. Style of leadership used (direct action, example, preaching, etc.)

e. Task performed or message given

The Scripture references, the Chronology and other material provided in the *Resource Book* will help the groups find the data requested. You may want to give each group a list of these references and the five items of information requested or display them on newsprint.

Elijah	1 Kings 17:8-24; 18; 19
Elisha	2 Kings 3 (skim), 4:38-44; 5:1-16; 6:8-23; 9:1-3
Amos	Amos 1:1; 5:10-15, 18-27; 7:10-15

Isaiah   2 Kings 18:1-8, 9ff. (skim); 19
Jeremiah   Jeremiah 1; 19:14-20:6; 26
Ezekiel   Ezekiel 1:1-3; 4; 24:1, 2

After the groups have completed their work, they will report their findings. Form a large wall chart from this information. To do this provide the groups with sheets of construction paper and ask them to write the information for each item on a separate sheet. As the reports are given, place the names of the prophets in a column and to their right place the sheets with the appropriate information in rows to form a grid similar to the following:

Name	Date	King(s)	Situation	Style	Task/Message

or

Using the same group divisions as above, assign each group the task of creating a banner or coat of arms for one of the six prophets. Have large sheets of paper and markers available. Ask participants to use the above Scripture references and the *Resource Book* to recall what is distinctive about their leader and to represent this visually. Then the groups will describe their work and display their creations around the room.

or

Direct each of the six groups to work with one prophet and to prepare an interview with that prophet using the five categories of information listed above. All group members will provide information, but one person will take the part of the prophet and one person will take the part of the interviewer. Then enact the interview for the whole group.

3. Using material from a Bible dictionary, *Understanding the Old Testament* or *Introducing the Old Testament*, give a brief presentation summarizing the work of the Chronicler and the roles of Nehemiah and Ezra during the restoration.

or

If you used a time line or the Chronology of the Bible chart in Part 1 of this theme, display it again and introduce this section with a few comments on the situation of the Hebrew people in Babylon and later under the Persian rulers.

Read Ezra 1:1-8 to the group and encourage members to imagine the feelings of the exiled Jews as they hear the passage. (The exiles have been away from their homeland so long they know Jerusalem only from the stories of their parents. The city lies in ruin, the return journey will be difficult, only the unknown lies ahead.) Discuss the emotions being felt by the class.

Divide the group into pairs. Assign half of the pairs Ezra and the other half Nehemiah. The pairs are to use the following references and material from the *Resource Book* and/or supplementary resources to create a "help wanted" ad for the position of leadership filled by their person. When they have finished, ask for volunteers to read their ads. Compare other ads which include additional information.

Nehemiah		Ezra	
Nehemiah	1:1-4	Ezra	1:1-8
	2:1-6		7:1-10
	6:1-16		
	8:1-12		

4. Using the *Resource Book* and material from the supplementary resources, give a brief presentation summarizing the major characteristics of the Pharisees, the Essenes, the Sadducees, and the Zealots.

or

Invite the persons selected ahead of time to represent the four religious sects on a panel. Each person is to give a two or three minute presentation on his or her sect. After all the presentations have been given, the group may ask questions of the panel.

or

Divide the group into four "political parties" representing the Pharisees, Essenes, Sadducees, and Zealots. Each party is to develop a platform and political slogans to be used in a campaign to attract additional recruits. A representative of each party is to present these materials to the group, which may then ask questions.

CLOSING

1. Recite or sing a hymn, such as "God of the Prophets" or "For All the Saints."

or

Read Ecclesiasticus (Sirach) 44:1-15 while the group prayerfully meditates on male and female religious leaders who have been important in their lives.

Looking Ahead

Item #3 of Exploring the Scripture in the next session suggests that twelve persons each be prepared to give a two to three minute report about one of the disciples. You will have to make a choice about which names to include in your list. See the chart in the Appendix of the *Resource Book* and a Bible dictionary for assistance.

Item #5 in the same section suggests that four persons each present a five to seven minute summary of one of Paul's missionary journeys.

MICAIAH
(I Kings 22:1-28)

The script is based on the text of the *Good News Bible, the Bible in Today's English* Version. Copyright © American Bible Society, 1976. Used by permission.

Cast: King Ahab, King Jehoshaphat, Zedekiah, the prophets (a group of 400 court prophets), court official, Micaiah, Narrator

Narrator: There was peace between Israel and Syria for two years, but in the third year King Jehoshaphat of Judah went to see King Ahab of Israel. Ahab called his court officials to him.

Ahab: Why is it that we have not done anything to get back Ramoth in Gilead from the King of Syria? It belongs to us! King Jehoshaphat, will you go with me to attack Ramoth?

Jehoshaphat: I am ready when you are, and so are my soldiers and my calvary. But first let's consult the Lord.

Narrator: So Ahab called in the prophets, about four hundred of them.

Ahab: Should I go and attack Ramoth, or not?

Prophets: Attack it. The Lord will give you victory.

Jehoshaphat: King Ahab, isn't there another prophet through whom we can consult the Lord?

Ahab: There is one more, Micaiah son of Imlah. But I hate him because he never prophesies anything good for me; its always something bad.

Jehoshaphat: You shouldn't say that!

Narrator: Then Ahab called in a court official and told him to go and get Micaiah at once.

The two kings, dressed in their royal robes, were sitting on their thrones at the threshing place just outside the gate of Samaria, and all the prophets were prophesying in front of them. One of them, Zedekiah son of Chenaanah, made iron horns and spoke to Ahab.

Zedekiah: This is what the Lord says: "With these you will fight the Syrians and totally defeat them."

Prophets: March against Ramoth and you will win. The Lord will give you victory.

Narrator: Meanwhile, the court official sent to get Micaiah reached him. He decided to give Micaiah some helpful advice.

Official: All the other prophets have prophesied success for the king, and you had better do the same.

Micaiah: By the living Lord I promise that I will say what he tells me to!

Narrator: Micaiah was taken by the official to the place that the kings had set up their thrones.

Ahab: Micaiah, should King Jehoshaphat and I go and attack Ramoth or not?

Micaiah:	Attack! Of course you'll win. The Lord will give you victory.
Ahab:	When you speak to me in the name of the Lord, tell the truth! How many times do I have to tell you that?
Micaiah:	I can see the army of Israel scattered over the hills like sheep without a shepherd. And the Lord said "These men have no leader; let them go home in peace."
Ahab:	King Jehoshaphat, didn't I tell you that he never prophesies anything good for me? It's always something bad!
Micaiah:	Now listen to what the Lord says! I saw the Lord sitting on his throne in heaven, with all his angels standing beside him. The Lord asked, "Who will deceive Ahab so that he will go and be killed at Ramoth?" Some of the angels said one thing, and others said something else, until a spirit stepped forward, approached the Lord, and said, "I will go and make all of Ahab's prophets tell lies." The Lord said, "Go and deceive him. You will succeed." This is what has happened. The Lord has made these prophets of yours lie to you. But he himself has decreed that you will meet with disaster.
Narrator:	Then the prophet Zedekiah walked up to Micaiah and slapped him in the face.
Zedekiah:	Since when did the Lord's spirit leave me and speak to you?
Micaiah:	You will find out when you go into some back room to hide.
Ahab:	Officer! Arrest Micaiah and take him to Amon, the governor of the city, and to Prince Joash. Tell them to throw him into prison and to put him on bread and water until I return safely.
Micaiah:	If you return safely, then the Lord has never spoken through me! Listen, everyone, to what I have said.

NOTES FROM THE AUTHOR

John the Baptist

The time of John's ministry is probably A.D. 26-27. Herod the Great, who rebuilt the Temple, died in 4 B.C., and his kingdom was divided. Antipas and his brother Philip ruled two of the four divisions and are sometimes called "tetrarchs" (KJV and the NRSV footnote at Luke 3:1). They ruled under Roman authority. Herod Antipas was the antagonist of John the Baptist.[1]

It is important to grasp John's role in renewing the prophetic presence. His popularity with the masses and the suggestion that he might be Elijah reincarnated presented problems to the authorities. His descent from a priestly family does not fit with his unusual ministry. It has been suggested that John in some way became associated with the Qumran community, but he certainly turns out to be a unique individual.

Jesus' baptism by John would hardly have been recorded if it were not firm in the tradition, for the Gospels are concerned to prove Jesus' superiority to John. Jesus spoke of John in the highest terms (see Luke 7:18-35). Jesus' career in a sense picked up where John left off, but we know that groups of the Baptist's followers continued through the apostolic era. Thus Apollos at Ephesus about twenty-five years later *knew only the baptism of John* (Acts 18:25; see also 19:1-5).

Jesus

The kinship of Jesus and John is an unresolved problem. Elizabeth is descended from Aaron (that is, Levite). Mary, her *relative* (Luke 1:36) would then seem to be Levite. But Jesus, to be David's descendant, must be of the tribe of Judah. This was Joseph's lineage, and of

---

1   See Map 13 in *The New Oxford Annotated Bible*.

course Jesus was considered to be Joseph's son during his public ministry. The Gospel writers were not concerned with giving us the details we should like to have to resolve such questions.

This is the part of our program where the life of Jesus is considered, that is, what we can know of his biography as separate from the purpose of the Gospels as proclamation. In modern times this is the distinction made between the Jesus of history and the Christ of faith. This distinction is important, but it is probably too technical to deal with here. We are all deeply indoctrinated by centuries of faith, so it is extremely difficult to appreciate clearly how Jesus' contemporaries felt about the man of the Galilean ministry and the leader who chose the way of the cross.

I do not share the skepticism about the Jesus of history that has characterized some modern schools of thought. It is true that the early church sorted its traditions according to the needs they faced a generation or so after Jesus' life, but that does not mean that the traditions were unreliable or that the church fabricated material to meet its needs. After all, we have four Gospels, each with particular views of the Christ event. The differences in particulars and the details that created problems in the church could have been avoided if the church had chosen to manipulate the traditions.

I think it is important to understand that Jesus was *at least* a great leader appointed by God. The extraordinary things he said and did during his ministry are explained by some people as having been doctored by the church in the light of resurrection faith while others see them as evidence that he was somehow a divine being all along. Neither alternative is necessary.

The role of Mary is a case in point. Since we know how the whole story turned out, we must exercise great care to understand Mary's situation with imagination and sympathy. Luke writes that the young mother *treasured all these words and pondered them in her heart* (Luke 2:19) and that she *treasured all these things in her heart* (Luke 2:51). She seems to be the only person who has an inkling of Jesus' destiny from the beginning. Confessions made by others during Jesus' ministry turn out to be something less than they first appear, for the cross and resurrection catch them all by surprise.

There are only a few firm pegs upon which to attach an outline of Jesus' public life. The fourth Gospel tells that Jesus had a short ministry in Judea before he began his principal work in Galilee, and John spreads that Judean ministry over a longer period than appears in the synoptics. This makes sense. The Jewish authorities are concerned early with the activity of the country preacher, but the evolution of the challenge surely took more than a few months. All the Gospels find a turning point in the feeding of the five thousand and the disciples' confession of faith shortly afterward. John's details are different (John 6), but the general points match the others. The principal part of each Gospel is the narrative of the passion and resurrection.

The clearing of the Temple presents some problems. The different location in John may be addressed by the expedient of alternatives. (1) The Synoptics are right. (2) John is right. (3) It happened twice. (4) Its part in the development of Jesus' public career has led to its use in two different spots. With regard to (4) note that in the Synoptics it is part of the trigger that brings the final confrontation with Jesus' enemies, while in John the raising of Lazarus plays that part.

This leads to several observations about Jesus' role as a religious leader. (1) He took on an air of authority. (2) His striking deeds and words had profound religious overtones like those of the ancient prophets. (3) Details were remembered though sometimes the settings were forgotten or ignored. (4) It can be disconcerting and unproductive to press details in some passages. Although we cannot reconstruct a biography of Jesus, we may speak assuredly about the force of his character, the power of his leadership, and the effect of his words.

The Twelve

There is not much to say about most of the Twelve. A Bible dictionary will tell you what is recorded in the Bible and some later traditions. Jesus undoubtedly intended the group to be the leaders of the church he was establishing. Acts 1 implies that the earliest church assumed the number twelve should be continued. The comparative list in the Appendix suggests that either the number did not always include exactly the same persons or else some of them went by more than one name.

Peter is the most interesting of the Twelve, and he receives most attention in the texts. The *Resource Book* implies that his nickname today might be "Rocky." In Matthew 16:17 he is called *son of Jonah*—KJV, *Bar-jona*. The modern equivalents are seen in Mac<u>don</u>ald, O'Hare, Mendels<u>sohn</u>, Ivan<u>ovich</u>, and David<u>son</u>; so Bar-jona today might be "John<u>son</u>!"

John, Mary, James, and Others

The relationship of the apostle John to the five Johannine books is best passed over at this point. The arguments are too complex for discussion here. In his *Anchor Bible* commentary Raymond Brown traces the beginning of Johannine traditions to the apostle but makes it clear that there is much further development in the literature that carries John's name.

Mary certainly merits more consideration than non-Catholic writing has given her. This is an opportunity to put her in the very important place the New Testament implies. I think the suggestion that she is the first disciple is quite reasonable.

James, the leader of the Jerusalem church, is important. Peter must have been accorded a position in a circle wider than that. Here we can see the place of the "mother church" in the developing mission that was reaching out beyond Jewish territory. Paul, who is the main leader in that movement, maintained a concern for the Jerusalem church and urged the new churches to send support to Jerusalem, since life appears to have become difficult for the Christians there.

Paul

Based upon the amount of canonical literature related to him, Paul is the most prominent leader in the New Testament Christian movement. The *Resource Book* introduces a great deal of material, so you will need to give extra diligence to session planning. Paul is the key figure in the spread of the Christian faith from Jerusalem to Rome, and the letters attributed to him are the richest mine for digging out what the churches believed in that primary period.

About the middle of the second century a book called *Acts of Paul* circulated in Asia Minor. This describes him as *a man small in size, bald, bow-legged, sturdy, with eyebrows meeting and a slightly prominent nose, full of grace*. His letter to Philemon provides our only casual glimpse of the man, and here, reading between the lines, we find reasons why he was so popular. For example, the letter is full of affectionate terms.

The details of Paul's final arrest and trials are complicated and incomplete. The strength of his character and faith is nowhere more evident than when he is confronting high government officials, military officers, and, we must add, the forces of nature. The tradition that he died a martyr may be accepted though details are lacking.

Supplementary Reading

Preparation for the activities in this part will provide basic information about the many leaders who are mentioned. Since this is the session in which the life of Jesus is considered, you may want to spend some time reviewing the outline of Jesus' public ministry as it is presented in the synoptics and John. In addition to *Understanding the New Testament* and *Introducing the new Testament*, consult *Jesus Through Many Eyes*.

SESSION PLANS

Learning Objectives

This session is intended to enable participants to:

1. Summarize the message of John the Baptist and describe in two or three sentences how he led the way for Jesus.

2. List at least four different ways in which Jesus displayed his leadership in the New Testament and illustrate each way with a story or incident.

3. Name at least eight of the twelve disciples and describe four of them with a sentence or two.

4. Create a one paragraph synopsis of Paul's career, indicating at least three reasons why he was such a prominent leader in the early church.

Resources You May Need

Newsprint and markers

Chalk and a chalkboard

A recording of *Godspell*

Four different colors of construction paper cut into 9" x 3" strips

Profile sheets for the disciples

Bible dictionaries or copies of the material on the disciples found in a
Bible dictionary

Maps or overhead transparencies of Paul's missionary journeys

Hymnals or songsheets

Leadership Strategy

SETTING THE STAGE

1. Ask for questions left over from Part 2, add them to your Loose Ends list, and decide when to respond to them.

2. Play the song entitled "Prepare Ye The Way of the Lord" from *Godspell* and ask the members of the group what their impressions were of John the Baptist as they listened to the music.

or

Ask the group to create a "word picture" of John the Baptist by responding to questions such as the following:

    a. What does he wear?

    b. What does he eat?

    c. Where might he live?

    d. How would you describe his body?

    e. What is his hair style?

    f. How does his voice sound?.

or

Display a list of the following items on newsprint. Invite the group to provide answers as a brief review of John's life.

Father's name

Father's occupation

Mother's relative mentioned in the Bible

Important events in his parents' lives preceding his birth

Unusual manner of choosing his name

Vocation

Cause of death

EXPLORING THE SCRIPTURE

1. Ask everyone to read silently Luke 3:1-20. Half of the group is to imagine they are followers of John. They should concentrate on John's message. The remainder will compose questions to ask John's "disciples" about his life and message.

Conduct a discussion between the two groups. Any disciple who feels comfortable answering a question can do so spontaneously. You can act as the moderator of the discussion. If your group is too large for this format, select four or five volunteers from the "disciple" group to field questions as a panel.

or

Divide the participants into three groups. Assign Luke 1:5-25, 57-80 to the first group; Luke 3:1-20 to the second group; Mark 6:14-29 to the third group. Instruct each group to compose on newsprint four or five "headlines" that will help review John's life and message. Have the groups share their work with everyone and display their headlines in a prominent place.

and

Brainstorm a list of leadership qualities displayed by any of the prophets you studied previously. Then discuss the ways that John resembles these former prophets. Note similarities and differences between the messages, styles, and results. Then discuss John's role in preparing the way for Jesus.

2. Invite members of the group to suggest words that describe Jesus' unique leadership. As each word is suggested write it on newsprint and ask the group to relate a story or incident that illustrates this quality of Jesus' leadership.

or

Divide the participants into four groups and assign one of the following passages to each group.

Mark 1:16-20	Mark 11:1-19
Mark 8:27-30	John 2:1-11

While they are reading, members of the small groups are to jot down words they feel describe Jesus' personality as shown in the passage being read. Then they are to discuss the words they have chosen. After eliminating the duplicates, have a group "scribe" write each word on a 9" x 3" strip of construction paper (use a different color for each group). Next, the strips should be attached to a large chart that you have prepared. The title of the chart is "Jesus: A Unique Leader." Taking turns, have the groups explain their choice of words.

or

Using the same divisions and Scripture references, ask the four groups to dramatize their passages for the rest of the members in ways that show Jesus' leadership ability.

3. Have the twelve persons chosen the previous week present two to three minute reports about individual disciples.

or

Create a profile sheet to be completed for each disciple. Some items to use are:

> Name
> Birthplace
> Occupation before being called
> Major contributions to the group
> Three words that describe the disciple

Distribute these sheets to all the participants. Invite people to choose their favorite disciple or randomly assign a disciple to them. Have them work alone or in pairs to complete the profile sheets and then share the results with the whole group.

In addition to directing attention to the appropriate Scripture references for this activity in the *Resource Book*, use several Bible dictionaries or copies of the information in a Bible dictionary about each of the Twelve.

or

Use the above procedure to link members of the group with one of the Twelve. Each person or pair is to compose a cinquain poem about their disciple.

Cinquain poetry follows a distinct form.

> Line 1 Title (a noun: one word)
> Line 2 Describes the title word (two words)
> Line 3 Action words or phrases about the title (three words)
> Line 4 Describes a feeling about the title (four words)
> Line 5 Refers to the title (one word)

Example:

Peter
Bold Disciple
Proclaimed Jesus Messiah
Faith Gave Him Strength
Rock

After the poems are finished ask participants to share them with the group.

and

Define the words *disciple* and *apostle*. Then, direct the participants to read Acts 1:15-26, about the choosing of Matthias to replace Judas as the twelfth apostle. Discuss the reason for keeping the number at twelve, the requirements for being chosen, and the manner of the choosing.

4. With the assistance of the group quickly review the life of Paul up through his conversion, as found in Acts 22:3-21.

   Since there is so much material to cover about Paul and his missionary journeys, this may be an appropriate time to use a lecture format. A wealth of information can be found in *Harper's Bible Dictionary* as well as *Understanding the New Testament* and *Introducing the New Testament*. The maps of Paul's journeys in the Appendix of the *Resource Book* will also be helpful. Be sure to incorporate the other Basic Bible References about Paul into your presentation.

   or

   Have the four persons selected last week present five to seven minute summaries of Paul's missionary journeys. The books mentioned above as well as the Bible references and maps found in the *Resource Book* will be helpful.

   and

   When the presentations are finished, ask the group to relate any favorite stories they care to share about Paul. Discuss why Paul is considered the foremost leader of the early Christian church.

CLOSING

1. Since you have just completed the theme on leadership, ask participants to list their favorite leaders of the Bible. Place their names on a chalkboard or newsprint. Close with a prayer of thanks for these former leaders and a commitment to the tasks to which we are called today.

   or

   Lead a discussion of one of the questions for reflection in the *Resource Book*.

   or

   Adjourn by singing one verse of "On Our Way Rejoicing" or another parting song your congregation uses.

Looking Ahead

Item #3 of Exploring the Scripture in the next session suggests as an option that two participants prepare three to four minute summaries of the reign of Solomon. One person is to focus on Solomon's achievements and the other on his failures as a monarch.

GOD'S PEOPLE HAVE RULERS BUT ONE SOVEREIGN

Yahweh, Kings, and a United Kingdom

NOTES FROM THE AUTHOR

The Nature of Kingship in Israel

It is important to have a clear picture of the special nature of the monarchy in Israel. The constant point of reference is the conviction that Yahweh is the ruler of the people. The phrase *The LORD is king!* occurs often, particularly in Psalms 93, 95-99 (KJV, *The LORD reigneth*; NJB, *Yahweh is king*; REB, *The LORD has become King*).

If Israel's demand for a king is related to its experience with neighboring kingdoms, it follows that the Israelite monarchy develops further from such experience. There is little theological reflection on human kingship as vice-regency for Yahweh—perhaps some verses in the royal psalms and in Ezekiel 34. The king's religious standing is mostly determined on a pragmatic level: How well did the king keep Yahweh's statutes and how well did he carry out cult responsibilities? A "royal theology" did develop, but the focus was on the king rather than on Yahweh.

No doubt the steps to the monarchy seemed natural enough to the people who were involved. If we take the stories one by one, the steps appear to follow a fairly obvious development. What Samuel and the later prophets saw so clearly was that the unique importance of Yahweh was at stake. That should be the point of reference in this theme.

The contrast between what is natural enough and what is theologically difficult confronts us in the decision to make Saul king. The steps in the texts appear to be contradictory. On the one hand, Samuel proclaims flatly that the demand for a king is a rejection of Yahweh's sovereignty. On the other hand, the human ruler was an idea whose time had come in Israel, and Yahweh directs Samuel in choosing a king for the people. The record is no doubt influenced by the way history turned out. However clearly Samuel sees the dangers ahead, he cannot withstand the demand for a king, and Yahweh helps him through the crisis.

Saul

The character of Saul as presented in 1 Samuel is closely related to the character of the monarchy in its first stage. Rule is subject to the feelings of the ruler, and Saul is somewhat charismatic. Many of the stories in these chapters are popular, but they present a clear enough picture of psychological failure.

The overlap of Saul and David presents a few difficulties. The two stories about how David came to Saul's attention are not easy to reconcile (1 Samuel 16:14-23 and 17:55-58). This illustrates well the composite nature of the records.

David

The *Resource Book* uses some of the better-known stories about David and some that affect the development of the monarchy. A side theme is David's involvements with women. The story of Bathsheba is best known, but his relationship with Abigail is more to David's credit. His marriage to Saul's daughter Michal was stormy.

David's unification of the kingdom was a great achievement. The settlement of the land and the period of the judges are evidence of how fragmented politically the people really were. The machinations of Joab and Abner are fierce. The way David handles the death of Abner apparently helps to unite the kingdom (2 Samuel 3:31-39). His treatment of the remaining family of Saul is sensitive and skillful, and no doubt this is a factor in eliminating resistance in the north. The story of little lame Mephibosheth is a sentimental favorite (2 Samuel 9).

Yahweh's promise that David would have a lasting dynasty is important because it shows up in so many subsequent contexts. The character of David is surely somewhat idealized in the records. The line of rulers in his family dynasty contrasts with the instability of the throne in the Northern Kingdom. We meet David again in Parts 2 and 3.

Solomon

The narratives about Solomon's rule are complex. The building of the Temple is of permanent importance, and his political achievements are impressive. It is clear, however, that the seeds of the dissolution of the United Kingdom are sown in his reign.

Solomon's reputation for wisdom is proverbial. The background is in 1 Kings 3:5-14. Notice the mixed assessment of Solomon's life and rule. The alliance with the Pharaoh looks like an astute political move, but the evaluation in 1 Kings 11:1-8 from the writer's viewpoint is different. Wisdom is considered in detail in Theme 8; a summary is given in 1 Kings

4:29-34. Best known stories are those about the prostitutes' babies (1 Kings 3:16-28) and about the Queen of Sheba (1 Kings 10:1-13).

The organization of Solomon's kingdom is a formidable accomplishment. There is substantial archeological evidence (see Research 3). His international relations are sophisticated for his day. Economic development is extensive though its cost raises questions. To achieve such a contrast from Saul's day must have imposed a tremendous tax burden, and it certainly is the background for the failure of Solomon's sons.

Solomon's influence upon the religion of the Jews is important. The Temple becomes the focus of the cult until the exile, and it is the ideal by which subsequent reconstruction is judged (see Haggai 2:3, 9). The dedicatory prayer (1 Kings 8) is a devotional treasure, but it is more appropriately considered in Theme 9. When international skills and material are imported for work on the Temple, it becomes symbolic that Israel-Judah is to be the center of the world.

Solomon's palace, *the House of the Forest of the Lebanon* (1 Kings 7:2) is larger than the Temple and took longer to build. Influence of Egyptian architecture is evident, and Solomon builds a separate *house . . . for Pharaoh's daughter*, one of his wives (7:8). Criticism of this extravagance appears later.

The Division of the Kingdom

Unrest in the kingdom rises even while Solomon is at the zenith of his power. Details of Jeroboam's revolutionary activity and the role of Ahijah are cryptic, but Jeroboam becomes an exile in Egypt (1 Kings 11:26-40). The succession at Solomon's death offers an occasion for change, and Jeroboam comes forward again.

The text of 1 Kings 12 implies that if Rehoboam had been willing to negotiate grievances, the division might have been avoided. The counsel of *the older men* (1 Kings 12:7) might be interpreted as the conservatism of age, but it is more likely that it reflects the judgment of those who can compare the state of Solomon's government with earlier years when national integrity was emphasized and the religion of Yahweh was the arbiter. Ahijah's prophetic performance suggests that Solomon's religious achievements were not completely acceptable.

It appears that Jeroboam did not succeed in avoiding all of the mistakes that caused the rupture of the United Kingdom. Since he had the political support of his constituency, however, the revolt was permanently successful. Shechem, his capital city, had a long and distinguished history and was in a strategic location. (Modern archeology has studied it extensively.) Establishment of worship centers at Bethel and Dan (1 Kings 12:29) is politically motivated. The *two calves of gold* are probably not a complete rejection of Yahweh-worship. They may be intended as a cult focus for the God who cannot be seen, perhaps as some sort of substitute for the cherubim in the Jerusalem shrine. The connection with the calves at Sinai, however, is explicit, and Jeroboam becomes stigmatized as the one *who caused Israel to sin.*

About Chronicles

Parallel references between Samuel-Kings and Chronicles are usually not given in the *Resource Book* or the *Leader's Guide.* They are easy to come by, and your preparation should include some study of these parallels.

I have passed over Chronicles here as a matter of brevity and convenience. This does not reflect a value judgment. The Chronicler adds important information and perspective to the Samuel-Kings material. All the same, we should remember that Chronicles is written from a different point of view and is accorded different status in the Jewish canon.

Supplementary Reading

In addition to the usual articles on the major leaders considered in this part (Samuel, Saul, David and Solomon), review material on the theology of kingship in Israel. *Harper's Bible Dictionary* and *Understanding the Old Testament* both have useful information.

SESSION PLANS

Learning Objectives

This session is intended to enable participants to:

1. Trace the steps by which Israel became a monarchy.

2. List at least four major events in the lives of Saul, David, and Solomon, and discuss how these events reveal Israel's understanding of kingship in relation to the authority of God.

3. Retell the story of the division of the kingdom under Rehoboam and Jeroboam.

Resources You May Need

Newsprint and markers
Chalkboard and chalk
Sets of index cards listing events from Saul's life
Blank sheets of paper
Photocopies of 1 Kings 12:1-17
A list of questions regarding Jeroboam's reign
Map comparing the territory under control of Saul, David and Solomon

Leadership Strategy

SETTING THE STAGE

1. Ask the group for suggestions to add to the Loose Ends list and discuss any that seem especially appropriate now.

2. Write on newsprint or the chalkboard a list of some past and present monarchs. Ask everyone to brainstorm a list of these rulers' characteristics (character traits, political powers, abilities, etc.). List these on the board or newsprint beside the list of rulers. Explore with the group how these characteristics compare with the view of kings portrayed by the biblical writers.

and/or

Divide the group in half. Ask one half to suggest the reasons Israel wanted to have a monarch and be "like the other nations." Have a scribe list these on a chalkboard or newsprint. The other half of the group is to do the same thing with the reasons Israel should not have asked for a king. Compare the two sets of reasons. If it has not been referred to in the discussion, read 1 Samuel 8:4-9 and discuss how it portrays Israel's desire to have a king. Use the story of Abimelech in Judges 9 to illustrate the ambivalent feelings Israel had about human kingship.

EXPLORING THE SCRIPTURE

1. Ask members of the group to name important events in the life of Saul. Make a list of these events on the chalkboard or newsprint as they are mentioned. Have persons individually or as a group arrange the events in chronological order to create an outline of Saul's life. If participants have trouble naming events, the leader may suggest ones from the list below.

or

Divide the group into three or four small groups. Give each small group a set of index cards, with each card bearing the name of one of the following events from the life of Saul:

> Saul meets Samuel
> Samuel anoints Saul
> The Spirit of God possesses Saul
> The people proclaim Saul king
> Saul defeats the Ammonites
> Saul disobeys God at Gilgal
> Saul battles the Philistines
> Saul takes spoil from the Amalekites
> God regrets making Saul king
> Samuel anoints David
> Saul takes David to be his servant
> Saul becomes jealous of David
> Saul attempts to kill David
> David spares Saul's life
> Saul consults the medium
> Saul dies on Mt. Gilboa

The small groups are to arrange the events in chronological order. The subheadings in 1 Samuel 8-30, which *Today's English Version* and many other Bibles have, will be helpful in this task.

and

Once the order of events has been agreed on, have the small groups note those where Saul is acting with God's blessing and those where he is not. Discuss the possible correlation between Saul's obedience to God and his success as a king.

2. David's relationship with each of the following people is significant for his career as king and his role as God's servant:

> Saul
> Jonathan
> Nathan
> Bathsheba (and Uriah)
> Absalom
> Joab

Divide the group into at least six small groups and assign one of these people to each small group. The small groups are to review the relevant biblical references and material in the *Resource Book* to answer the following questions:

a. What are some of the significant events in the development of this relationship?

b. What does this relationship reveal about David's character?

c. In what ways does this relationship lead David to obey or disobey God?

Have the small groups each report their answers to the whole group.

or

Use the same small groups and biblical characters as above. Ask the groups to select a significant episode from David's relationship to their assigned character and work up a brief dramatization of this event to present to the whole group. Following the presentations discuss with the members of the group what the episode reveals about David's character.

or

Have the participants create a human time line of David's life. This can be done by asking persons to recall events from the life of David. As an event is named, the person who suggested it goes to the front of the room to represent the event. The person who names the next event goes to the front and stands to the right or left of the first person, depending on whether the new event occurs before or after the first one mentioned. Each person who names an episode then comes to the front of the room and stands for that event. Participants should arrange themselves in order or the leader or members still seated may amend the order by changing people's positions. Those in the time line should be prepared to repeat their event as often as necessary for others to remember the sequence. Continue until you run out of events or people.

After the human time line is completed give the following instructions to the participants. "If you feel that your event reflects David acting in obedience to God, remain facing the group. If your event reflects David in disobedience to God, turn away from the group. If your event is neutral (reflects neither disobedience or obedience), sit down." Discuss any comments or questions participants have about particular events. Conclude the activity by inviting members of the group to offer summary statements about David's role as a political and religious leader.

or

Present a mini-lecture summarizing David's rise to power and his accomplishments as a ruler. A Bible dictionary, *Understanding the Old Testament* and *Introducing the Old Testament* provide the background information you will need.

and

Read 2 Samuel 7:4-16 aloud to the group. Ask each person to write a paraphrase of the promise God made to David. Ask several persons to share their paraphrases with the group.

3. Ask everyone to list five characteristics of Solomon's personality. Then invite volunteers to share their lists with the group and create a master list. Lead the group in a discussion of how the various characteristics aided or hindered Solomon in his position as a leader.

You may also want to compare this list of Solomon's characteristics with the one created in *Setting the Stage*. How does Solomon fit the image presented there?

or

Have two people selected at the close of the previous session present three to four minute summaries of the reign of Solomon. One is to focus on his achievements as monarch, the other on his failures.

or

Examine Solomon's career in terms of his ongoing relationship with God. To do so give each person a blank sheet of paper to graph Solomon's religious development as shown below.

The baseline of the graph represents neutrality. Events listed above the line show Solomon in close relationship with God. Events below the line are those where Solomon pulls away from or disobeys God. The leader may begin a simple graph on the chalkboard. Participants may include events of their own choosing on their graphs.

Solomon builds the Temple

Solomon asks God for
wisdom

Solomon burns incense in the
high places

Solomon marries
many foreign women

4. Select persons to play the roles of Rehoboam, Jeroboam, "old" advisors (three to five persons), "young" advisors (three to five persons), and the people of Israel (the remainder of the group). Provide copies of 1 Kings 12:1-17 and ask everyone to read the passage silently. Then, with the leader acting as narrator, present the passage as a dramatic reading.

and/or

Divide the group into clusters of three or four. Instruct the clusters to read 1 Kings 12:25-33 and discuss the following questions:

a. What problems did Jeroboam face?

b. What options did he have?

c. What did he decide to do?

d. Why do you think that he chose this approach?

e. If you were Jeroboam, what do you think you would have done? Why?

Gather as a whole group and share the ideas discussed.

CLOSING

1. Sum up the changes that took place during the early monarchy by reading 1 Kings 10:23-29. You may also want to use a map comparing the territory under the control of the three major kings. Some editions of *Today's English Version* contain such a map.

and/or

Ask the group to share any thoughts they have about the rule of God as their king, or as our nation's king. Do they think of God in this way? Why is it appropriate or inappropriate in this day?

and/or

Read Psalm 93, Psalm 95, or another of the songs celebrating Yahweh's rule.

Looking Ahead

Item #1 of Exploring the Scripture in the next session suggests that three members of the group present brief reports on 1 Kings 21:1-26; 2 Chronicles 22:10-23:21; 2 Chronicles 34:14-33. See the description of the activity for details.

Item #2 of the same section suggests that twenty persons present one or two minute reports on important characters of the Old Testament. The names are listed in the activity.

Item #4 of the same section also suggests that two persons prepare brief remarks on two topics. One is to speak on the meaning of "messiah" as found in a Bible dictionary. The other's subject is Israel's hope for a restoration of the Davidic line in the post-exilic period.

GOD'S PEOPLE HAVE
RULERS BUT ONE
SOVEREIGN

THEME
6

*Rulers and the
Divided Kingdom*

PART
2

NOTES FROM THE AUTHOR

About Too Many Details

The records of the two kingdoms are diverse and extensive. An Old Testament study may founder at this point from insisting on too many details and too many kings. I have tried to cut through this danger, but you will have to add your judgment and ingenuity to avoid the trivia sidetrack. The persons singled out in the *Resource Book* are noteworthy for one reason or another.

It is important to remember that the prolific narrative details move toward an end, the working out of God's sovereign will in the national life of the people. The religious assessment of the kings, which is integral to this end, sometimes obscures their political importance. The chronological chart in the Appendix is useful here. You may suggest annotating the chart as an aid to keeping details in order.

Omri and Jeroboam II

Omri is a good example of how difficult it is to get a balanced view of this history. He appears to be the first Israelite king mentioned in outside historical sources. He is named twice on the Moabite Stone:

> *Omri, king of Israel, oppressed Moab for many years, because Chemosh was
>   angry with his land . . . .*
> *Omri took possession of the entire land of Medeba . . . .*

An Assyrian obelisk of Shalmaneser II mentions the later King Jehu, and calls him the son of Omri (which he wasn't). So Omri was very important to non-Israelite contemporaries even though the writer of Kings notes him only briefly and negatively.

Moving the capital to Samaria was strategic, for the location was much easier to defend than Shechem. Archeology has uncovered part of the wall of Omri's palace. The city remained important after Israel's collapse. Much later, Herod the Great built extensively there.

The reign of Jeroboam II illustrates again the religious purpose of the writer of Kings. Only by reading between the lines do we discover the political significance of his reign. It is ironic that the height of Israel's national fortunes came not long before her final fall.

Ahab, Jezebel, Jehu, and Yahweh's Will

The evil pair Ahab and Jezebel would probably have received scant attention were it not for Elijah. We may also say with regret that Ahab is overshadowed by Jezebel. 1 Kings 21 illustrates this. The rape of Naboth's vineyard violated family property rights, which were guaranteed by divine covenant.

The writer of Kings is a good observer of character. The superficial cleverness of Ahab's arrangement to let Jehoshaphat be the sole king-figure in the battle at Ramoth-gilead tells something about both men. The writer says that the bowman who killed Ahab *unknowingly struck the king of Israel* (1 Kings 22:34). A writer with a more fatalistic view might have said that Yahweh directed the arrow, but here the narrative is content to imply that Yahweh's will as predicted by Micaiah comes to pass in the ordinary process of events.

So also for Jezebel's end. She faces Jehu with wicked cunning and steely determination and also with physical wiles. Other kings succumbed to female beauty and seduction, but not Jehu. So again Yahweh's will, told through Elijah, is carried out in the details of a vivid story.

Here is commentary upon how these Old Testament writers viewed divine destiny. Often they are content to recount the traditions of what happened and to observe that Yahweh's way prevailed. They do not suggest that Yahweh rigs events in a mechanical manner. People live out their lives, consistent with their character, and Yahweh's word comes to pass.

There is a strong political undercurrent in this part. Elisha anoints kings. Jehu continues the battle against Baal, but it is associated with the transition from the rule of Ahab (2 Kings 10). Jehu is a clever strategist. His dynasty is the longest in the Northern Kingdom, a line of five kings. Nevertheless, the writer is dissatisfied with the religious accomplishments of Jehu and his line.

The influence of Ahab and Jezebel reaches into Judah. Athaliah is an exceptional figure even though evil. Her rule, which broke the succession of kings, invites comparison with the Egyptian queen Hatshepshut, who ruled in the early years of the fifteenth century B.C. and broke the succession of Pharaohs. Her elaborate palace near Thebes has been restored.

Kings of Judah

Asa has a long reign, and he passes the religious test. But he begins the policy of appeasement, which ultimately has disastrous effects in both kingdoms. Buying off an enemy seems innocuous enough the first time. But, like paying blackmail, there is no end to it.

Joash, the boy king, has been a popular figure in Sunday School lessons. A priest Jehoida played a crucial role in bringing Joash to the throne (2 Kings 11) and his further influence upon Joash is noteworthy (see 2 Kings 12:2). (In Greece the philosopher Aristotle influenced Alexander, and in Rome Seneca was a good influence upon Nero until the philosopher's death.) The money chest has often been imitated in church financing. The statement about the honesty of Joash's workmen, 2 Kings 12:15, is truly a "golden text."

Josiah is related to the outside world in Research 5. You should familiarize yourself with the history mentioned there.

The end of Judah is somewhat complicated. A first group of exiles went to Babylon about 597 B.C. Ezekiel was probably among them. When Jerusalem fell a decade later, most of the people that the conquerors considered important were deported. Some Jews, however, were left in Judah. Later a group went to Egypt and became a significant colony in Alexandria.

Israel's Deportation, the Samaritans, and the "Ten Lost Tribes"

After the fall of Samaria, leading citizens were deported, but the future of the land was determined by the resettlement of foreigners among the Israelites who were left. Religious consequences of this are given in some detail in 2 Kings 17:24-41. Israel never revived. The postexilic Jews in the south shunned the "Samaritans" with deeper feeling than had separated the tribes earlier. Religious differences were emphasized, and past ties were ignored.

The Samaritan canon is limited to the Pentateuch in a version somewhat different from the one we know. A Bible dictionary will give you basic information. A few thousand Samaritans survive today in and around Nablus, a town between the sites of Shechem and Samaria. They still celebrate the Passover on Mount Gerizim. Information and pictures may be found in the public library file of *The National Geographic.*

Avoid the question of the so-called "lost tribes" if you can. There are two modern points of reference. A movement called "British Israel" believes legends that some of the dispersed Israelites eventually found their way to Britain and a place in the ancestry of the British people. Latter Day Saints (Mormons) believe that a remnant of one of the tribes came to America and became the ancestors of pre-Columbian civilizations referred to in *The Book of Mormon*. Both of these ideas are fruitless digressions from our study.

The Postexilic Period

The *Resource Book* locates the beginning of messianic expectation during the exilic period. At this point any discussion of this expectation should be limited to its relationship to political reality, especially the absence of a Davidic ruler.

Likewise for the Daniel stories. Their point here is how the supreme, sovereign power of God strengthened Daniel and his friends, and how this same power strengthened Jews under oppression, first in the exile, but particularly in the Syrian period in the second century B.C.

The restoration under and after Nehemiah and Ezra give no support for royal pretensions. The rebuilding of the city and especially the Temple suggested that Yahweh was again king in the Promised Land. This was also the beginning of the period in which the documents that became the canon were being edited and were taking on sacred authority. Ezra is credited with fixing the place of the Pentateuch in the national life (fifth century B.C.). Perhaps this also contributed to the strengthened role of the priesthood.

The Outside World

About the time of Jeroboam II, Greeks held the first Olympiad, 776 B.C. Shortly after that, the city of Rome was founded, 753 B.C., a decade before Isaiah's Temple vision. Mesopotamia and Egypt were already old, and they left many records, but the western world was just emerging into recorded history. Carthage had been founded during the time of Joash of Judah, but it was not prominent until its later struggles with Rome. This all tells us that we have a remarkable amount of information about Israel and Judah when we consider how early the period is.

Scholars are not in exact agreement about some dates. The reason for this is that dates in ancient times were reckoned quite differently from the way we reckon them today. (Recall that there are two different dates for George Washington's birth.) If we can date a biblical event with a variation of only one year, that is remarkable precision.

Supplementary Reading

In addition to gathering information on the many leaders included in this part, it will be useful to review material on the perspectives from which the writers/editors of Kings and Chronicles view the history of the two kingdoms. The introductory articles in your study Bible and several of the supplementary books contain sections on this topic.

SESSION PLANS

Learning Objectives

This session is intended to enable participants to:

1. Summarize the method used in 1 and 2 Kings to evaluate the rulers of Israel and Judah.

2. Identify at least six of the kings of the divided kingdom with two or three statements about each one.

3. Describe how Israel's faith in God's sovereignty was kept alive in the exilic and post-exilic periods by a) hope for a future Davidic ruler, and b) stories such as those in Daniel 1-6.

Resources You May Need

Newsprint and markers
Chalkboard and chalk
Stories from newspapers and magazines concerning nations or people living in exile
Chronology of the Bible listing the kings of Israel and Judah from the *Resource Book*
Overhead projector and transparencies of the Chronology of the Bible
Strips of different colored construction paper
Pictures of the stories of Daniel

Leadership Strategy

SETTING THE STAGE

1. List any questions or issues left over from the previous session on your Loose Ends sheet and decide how to incorporate them into this session.

2. The author (editor) of 1 & 2 Kings employed a single-minded approach when evaluating the reigns of the kings of Israel and Judah. Political accomplishments or their lack were disregarded. Instead, the merit of each king was measured by how well he kept the covenant with Yahweh and how much his rule reflected the ultimate kingship of Yahweh. (See 2 Kings 22:2 for the "good king" formula and 2 Kings 14:23-24 for the "bad king" formula.) Discuss this type of evaluation with the group. What are the strengths and weaknesses of this approach? Do we ever use this criterion when we evaluate our "rulers"?

and/or

The biblical material for this session describes the crises Israel and Judah faced as their land was overrun by foreign powers, their governments toppled and their people carried into exile. Search current newspapers and magazines for stories of nations confronted by hostile powers or people in exile, and present summaries of the stories to the group. Discuss possible parallels with the biblical material for this part.

EXPLORING THE SCRIPTURE

1. If you wish to cover the biblical material in a brief, selective fashion, the activities that follow immediately are appropriate.

From the time when the nation divided, until 722/721 B.C., when Israel fell to Assyria, the moral situation of the Northern and Southern Kingdoms changed very little, at least for any length of time. In this activity you will compare the situation under King Rehoboam, the first king of Judah (1 Kings 14:22-28) with that of King Hoshea, the last king of Israel (2 Kings 17:1-24). Draw the following chart on the blackboard or newsprint and have members of the group complete it individually or together, using the above Scripture references.

King	Rehoboam	Hoshea
Kingdom	Judah	Israel
Political Situation		
Religious Situation		

Discuss any comments or questions raised by members of the group during the activity.

and

To highlight some of the events which occurred in this period invite the three persons selected at the last session to report on the following Basic Bible References: 1 Kings 21:1-29; 2 Chronicles 22:10-23:21; 2 Chronicles 34:14-33.

They should include in their reports answers to:

a. Who was the king/queen and what kingdom did he or she rule?

b. What was the political situation, either internal or external?

c. What was the moral/religious situation?

d. What evaluation is made or implied about the ruler by the writer?

e. What insights did you receive from this passage?

or

Divide the group into three sections. Assign one of the passages above to each section. Tell them to read the passage and then prepare a way of sharing the story with the members of the whole group. Some suggestions are: Role play, TV news broadcast, newspaper editorials, acrostic poetry, cartoon strips, and pantomime of the story using a narrator. Reconvene and have the sections make their presentations.

2. If you have time to review the material of this part more extensively, assign each of the following names to a member of the group. (This assignment may have been made at the close of the previous session.) Ask the participants to scan the *Resource Book* and the relevant biblical material and present a one or two minute report on their respective persons. It may be helpful to keep your time line or the Chronology of the Bible from the Appendix in the *Resource Book* before the group while the reports are presented. The chart could also be made into a transparency and projected on a screen.

Asa	Joash	Tiglath-Pileser
Omri	Jeroboam II	Sennacherib
Ahab	Hoshea	Nebuchadnezzar
Jezebel	Hezekiah	Cyrus
Jehoshaphat	Josiah	Belshazzar
Jehu	Zedekiah	Darius
Athaliah	Zerubbabel	

or

Divide the group into two teams. Play a game similar to a spelling bee. Each team in turn is given a name from the list above to identify briefly. If the person whose turn it is cannot do it, the question is given to the next person on the other team. The first team to answer correctly wins a point. Play until all names are used up. The team with the most points wins.

3. The Davidic covenant promised that Judah's throne would always be occupied by a descendant of David. Ask the group to imagine they are the people of Judah who have been exiled to Babylon. Have one person read aloud Jeremiah 52:1-16, which tells about the last Davidic king and the fall of Judah. Have another person read Psalm 89:19-21, 35-40, 46, 49. Ask persons to share their feelings about Yahweh's judgment and their hopes and fears about the future.

or

Read the Scriptures listed above. Make available a variety of strips of different colors of construction paper. Invite the group to choose colors that represent how they would feel if they were the Babylonian exiles who had seen their Davidic monarchy end. Ask several persons to share why they chose the color they did.

4. Introduce the two persons who agreed at the last session to make brief presentations on:

   a. The meaning of the term "messiah" as found in a Bible dictionary.

   b. A discussion of Israel's hope for the restoration of the Davidic line of kings in the post-exilic period.

and/or

Divide the group into three sections and ask each section to create an informal dramatization of one of the following scenes from Daniel's life:

   a. Daniel and his friends keep kosher (Chapter 1).

   b. Daniel and his friends in the fiery furnace (Chapter 3).

   c. Daniel in the lion's den (Chapter 6).

After the dramatizations have been presented, discuss how this book interprets God's kingly power in a time when the Jews have no king.

or

Display around the room pictures of Daniel and his friends from your church school's teaching picture file and reconstruct one or two of the above stories using the pictures to illustrate your remarks. Discuss what the stories say about God's kingly rule.

CLOSING

1. Read aloud Psalm 132:11-18, indicating how it reflects the hope for a Davidic ruler developed during this historical period and prevalent at the time of Christ.

or

Compose a summary of God's faithfulness to Israel during the exilic period and the following centuries, and have the group say it in unison. On the following page you will find a sample of such a statement from "A Declaration of Faith," which was adopted for study by the 1977 General Assembly of the Presbyterian Church in the United States. This selection is from Chapter 3, "God and the People of Israel."

God Did Not Forsake the People

God restored some of the people to their land and left others

scattered over the earth.

In a time of exile and alien rule, the Jews survived and multiplied.

They enriched the whole world:

They compiled the Scriptures, preserving God's Word to them;

They sang their songs of praise and lamentation;

They sought wisdom, examining God's ways in the world;

They searched the mysteries of rising and falling kingdoms and set

their hope on the kingdom of God.

We testify that God is faithful.

Even when we are faithless, God remains faithful.

The Lord still brings from oppressed and uprooted peoples riches of

insight and daring visions that can judge and bless the world.

We can have confidence in God's coming kingdom even in the darkest times.

GOD'S PEOPLE HAVE RULERS BUT ONE SOVEREIGN

Jesus and the Kingdom of God

NOTES FROM THE AUTHOR

Interpretations of "The Kingdom of God"

We may be fairly certain that it was Jesus who gave the term "the Kingdom of God/Heaven" currency and lasting importance. It was not common in the Old Testament, but it did appear in some nonbiblical Jewish literature of the intertestamental period. Only Matthew credits John the Baptist with using the phrase. Against the background of Parts 1 and 2 we may say that by "Kingdom of God/Heaven" Jesus means that God is sovereign over the people and that expectations about an earthly Davidic monarchy are reinterpreted and fulfilled in Jesus' person and mission.

A primary datum about the Kingdom is that it refers first of all to the fact of God's rule, not to the place or realm. This does not preclude consideration of the "where" of the Kingdom. A contemporary comedian says, "Everybody gotta be some place," and we really cannot think about God and people without localizing the relationship. Indeed, Jesus emphasizes that God's rule makes demands upon the people wherever they are. Old Testament people usually thought of God in terms of concrete activity, so "Kingdom of God" in the Old Testament may be equivalent to the declaration *The LORD is king!* (Psalm 97:1; 99:1; etc.).

In the first half of the twentieth century there was a lot written about the Kingdom, and it centered on eschatology, that is, the "when" of the Kingdom. Albert Schweitzer emphasized the future dimension. C. H. Dodd stressed the "already" aspect. Others have tried to do justice to both elements by speaking of "inaugurated eschatology." It boils down to how one views the significant point of God's activity for the people. If one concentrates on the incompleteness of God's rule today, one will probably stress the future. If one concentrates on God's victory in Jesus Christ, one can emphasize God's sovereignty in present experience and deal with the future in terms of what has already happened. In any case, God's sovereign rule must be affirmed.

Matthew's use of "heaven" calls attention to the independence of the Gospel traditions. One old study Bible claimed that "Kingdom of Heaven" meant something different than "Kingdom of God," but that is not tenable. The Jewish practice of avoiding the name of God is probably part of the explanation, but this must be modified by noting that on occasion Jesus did not hesitate to speak of God on most intimate terms. In any case, I think that Jesus probably did not say "Kingdom of *God*" in his native Aramaic. More likely he would speak of "the Kingdom of the Lord." As far as we can tell, the Jews of that time substituted "Lord" rather than "God" for the divine name "Yahweh," which was never used in ordinary speech. It was the church in the Greek-speaking missions that came to use the phrase "Kingdom of God." Perhaps the most we can say here is that according to the Gospel records, Jesus was quite flexible in his approach to different people, so both Gospel traditions can be correct.

In the third century Origen called Jesus *autobasileia*, "himself the Kingdom." God's sovereign rule entered history in a unique way with the mission of Jesus. *Is at hand* (KJV) does not mean "is somewhere far future"; NRSV is better, *has come near*. The force of Jesus' teaching is that the Kingdom "is breathing down your back." Something decisive about God's rule is taking place in and through Jesus.

Parables and the Kingdom

Here and briefly in Theme 8 parables are studied. Notice two important things. First, parables are a most appropriate form for teaching about God's rule. The Old Testament insists that God is not directly observable, and this is echoed in John 1:18, *No one has ever seen God*. It is therefore very fitting to speak of how God exercises rule, what it *is like*. Second, insofar as Jesus embodies God's rule, we can observe how God is acting in the human situation. It is therefore possible to think of Jesus' deeds, especially what we call miracles, as acted parables.

In the context of the *secret of the kingdom* (Mark 4:10-12) the purpose of the parables is addressed with a difficult quotation from Isaiah 6:9,10. Four comments are appropriate here. (1) It is difficult to speak about God. (2) The freedom of God's activity requires that it be spoken about with flexible language. (3) Jesus says things about God that must have been radical to many of his hearers, and therefore an indirect approach is desirable. (4) A pronouncement may be abruptly rejected, but a story is easily remembered for further thought and possibly later acceptance.

Jesus' attempt to reinterpret the messiahship was so new that even his intimate circle of friends did not comprehend it. So he spoke in parables. The Gospel traditions are evidence that his parables were carefully remembered, and since they were somewhat open-ended, their real significance dawned upon the disciples later. *Then they remembered his words* (Luke 24:8) is a commentary on the Gospel traditions.

In interpreting parables we must not make a hasty identification of each detail with something else. In Matthew 13:45, 46 the Kingdom is not really *like a merchant* nor like the *one pearl of great value*, but rather it is like the point of the whole parable. Here the rule of God requires a response of total commitment. We may paraphrase, "The rule of God is like a situation in which . . . ." Occasionally, a parable includes instruction as to how some details should be understood, and then there is warrant for specific identification (see Mark 4:13-20; Matthew 21:45).

John's Gospel and the Kingdom

Although the phrase "Kingdom of God" occurs seldom in John, the concept of God's rule is there quite substantially. John is attached to his own body of tradition, which frequently follows a line different from that of the Synoptics. John stresses a series of "signs" that focus on actions of Jesus. As we have noted, these often have a symbolic value that may be thought of as parable in action.

John knows that Jesus used the phrase *kingdom of God*, for it appears in the unique story about Nicodemus (John 3:1-10). John's vocabulary about God, however, emphasizes other relationships than that of rule. There are notably the "life/eternal life" passages (see especially 11:25). Jesus' role is cast in the association of "Father-Son." "Messiah" is considered in a long passage, John 7:25-44, but the tone is one of questioning, not declaration. In a parallel to Peter's confessing the Messiah at Caesarea Philippi, John's tradition has, *Lord, to whom can we go? You have the words of eternal life . . . you are the Holy One of God* (6:68, 69).

Paul and the Kingdom

Paul seems to develop his own tradition. It is not likely that he would avoid "Kingdom of God" because of its Old Testament background. It has been suggested that the political situation of the church would keep him from using royal terminology, but Paul looks forward to the triumph of God's rule (as in 1 Corinthians 15:24-28). Like John he probably preferred other ways of expressing the relationship of God and people. Since Jesus' mission on earth was completed, it was clear that he was the key to the God-people relationship.

The phrase *in Christ* becomes central for Paul. He sees that the relationship of God-Christ-people is greater than any one way of describing it, even including tradition from the teaching of Jesus. Thus he develops the metaphor of "the body" and applies it to the church.

The church, the body of Christ in the world, thus becomes the sign of God's sovereignty in the present age.

The short consideration of "The Kingdom Forever" in the *Resource Book* is primarily for the sake of completeness. The future Kingdom must be part of the theme here, but full consideration of eschatology and particularly apocalyptic is reserved for Theme 10.

Supplementary Reading

Several books mentioned as supplementary resources contain information on the "when" of the Kingdom. *Introducing the New Testament* is especially helpful, but other volumes also take up the topic and point out the different ways the Synoptics, John, and Paul speak about God's rule.

SESSION PLANS

Learning Objectives

This session is intended to enable participants to:

1. Summarize Israel's hope for a king at the time of Jesus' ministry.

2. Formulate at least six statements about Jesus' teaching concerning the Kingdom of God/Heaven.

3. Recall the terms Paul and John use to describe the Kingdom.

4. Discuss how the Kingdom arrived in Jesus and is still coming in the future.

Resources You May Need

Chalkboard and chalk
Newsprint and markers
Slips of paper with Bible references about the Kingdom
Pictures from magazines that have potential for metaphor
Recording of the Lord's Prayer or "The Hallelujah Chorus"

Leadership Strategy

SETTING THE STAGE

1. Add any questions the group has from previous sessions or the present reading to the Loose Ends list and decide when to cover them.

2. Give a brief presentation reviewing the political situation in Israel from the beginning of the Roman occupation to the ministry of Jesus.

or

Invite members of the group to imagine they are residents of Jerusalem in 30 A.D. Conduct a series of "on-the-spot" interviews, asking participants what they think about the promised coming of a messiah. Do they expect this leader soon? How will they recognize the anointed one? What will the messiah do? You may want to prepare some comments for members of the group to rehearse or have participants *ad lib* their own responses.

EXPLORING THE SCRIPTURE

1. Write several statements about the Kingdom of God on individual slips of paper along with the biblical references for each. Here are some examples:

   "The time is fulfilled, and the kingdom of God has come near; repent, and believe in the good news."   Mark 1:15

   "When Jesus realized that they were about to come and take him by force to make him king, he withdrew again to the mountain by himself."   John 6:15

   "Your kingdom come. Your will be done, on earth as it is in heaven."   Matthew 6:10

   ". . .unless your righteousness exceeds that of the scribes and Pharisees, you will never enter the kingdom of heaven."   Matthew 5:20

   "Not every one who says to me, 'Lord, Lord,' will enter the kingdom of heaven, but only the one who does the will of my father in heaven."   Matthew 7:21

   "Let the little children come to me; do not stop them; for it is to such as these that the kingdom of God belongs. Truly, I tell you, whoever does not receive the kingdom of God as a little child will never enter it."   Mark 10:14-15

"How hard it will be for those who have wealth to enter the kingdom of God!"

Mark 10:23

". . .no one can enter the kingdom of God without being born of water and Spirit.

John 3:5

". . .anyone who hears my word and believes him who sent me has eternal life, and does not come under judgment, but has passed from death to life."   John 5:24

Have individuals or small groups take one reference and spend ten to twelve minutes finding out what the passage says about the Kingdom. Include an examination of the context of the passages and a comparison of parallel texts. Then have the findings shared with the whole group.

or

Invite volunteers to read aloud: Mark 1:15; John 6:15; Matthew 6:10; Matthew 5:20; Matthew 7:21; Mark 10:14-15; Mark 10:23-25.

Ask each person to make a list of five words or phrases that describe the Kingdom of God based on passages just read. Then invite several persons to share their lists, creating a master list on the chalkboard or newsprint. Ask the group if they can think of any additional descriptive phrases that contribute to their picture of the Kingdom and add these to the list.

2. Divide the group into five sections. Assign each section one of the following passages which contain metaphors for the kingdom of God:

Mark 4:26-29   Matthew 13:47-48
Matthew 13:44   Matthew 13:52
Matthew 13:45-46

Ask the sections to read their passages and prepare brief interpretations focusing on the meaning of the Kingdom. Share the interpretations with the whole group.

or

Make a collection of magazine pictures of people, objects, scenes, buildings–anything that catches your eye and seems to have potential for metaphor. Display these pictures around the room. Direct participants to work in pairs and to select one picture and use it as a basis for creating an original metaphor or parable about the Kingdom of God that is consistent with Jesus' teaching. Ask the pairs to share their creations with the group.

3. Jesus' interpretation of messiahship and kingship, especially in Matthew 22:1-14, 41-46, and John 18:33-38, was surprising to his hearers. Divide the group into three sections and ask each section to study one of these passages. For each passage they are to:

a. State to whom Jesus was speaking.

b. Explain the ideas about God's "Kingdom" with which Jesus seems to be disagreeing.

c. State the point that Jesus appears to be making about messiahship/kingship or the Kingdom.

Reconvene in order for the sections to present their findings to each other.

4. The phrase "the Kingdom of God/Heaven" is not used by all of the biblical writers. Instead they use other terms to express the same concept. List the following texts on the chalkboard or newsprint:

John 3:16   Romans 12:5
John 5:24   2 Corinthians 5:17
John 20:31

Divide the group into pairs with these instructions:

a. Together select two or three of the passages above and read them.

b. Identify the phrase(s) you believe mean the same as the "Kingdom of God/Heaven."

c. Discuss why you think the author used a different phrase in this instance.

d. Decide which phrase or term expresses the idea best to you.

e. Be prepared to share your ideas with the whole group.

or

As a whole group read the above passages aloud. As they are read, ask persons to identify the phrase that is used to mean the Kingdom of God/Heaven. Which terms do they find the most useful or enlightening? Why do they think the author chose that way of expressing the idea?

5. Ask the group to re-read the section entitled "Paul, the Kingdom, and the Christ" in the *Resource Book*. After they have read this they are to summarize the points that trace the biblical understanding of kingship in the final paragraph of the section. You may want to list these points on newsprint. Review the material for this theme by asking persons for two or three summary statements for each of the major points you have listed.

and/or

In the *Resource Book*, Dr. Walther says that God's reign has been established in Christ, but God's sovereignty does not yet appear complete in the world. Assign the following passages to be read aloud. After each text has been read, ask the group to point out how it illustrates this dual nature of God's reign.

Mark 1:15	1 Corinthians 15:20-28
Matthew 16:28	Revelation 11:15-17
Luke 9:27	

Then discuss questions such as the following:

a. In what ways do you think of the Kingdom of God as present? As future?

b. How do you reconcile these two aspects of the Kingdom?

c. How and when does one enter the Kingdom?

CLOSING

1. Lead the group in reciting the Lord's Prayer or meditate as a recording of the Lord's Prayer is played.

or

Listen to a recording of the "Hallelujah Chorus" from Handel's *Messiah*.

Looking Ahead

Item #3 under Exploring the Scripture in the next session suggests that three members of the group be asked to prepare presentations on the background and content of the three law codes.

GOD DEMANDS A RIGHTEOUS PEOPLE

The Law of God

NOTES FROM THE AUTHOR

Law and Righteousness

In the pilot program, over twenty years ago, this subject was treated in two themes: "God's People Have Laws" and "God's People Must Be Righteous." It immediately became clear that the two cannot really be kept apart. Biblical law calls for certain patterns of response, and righteousness presupposes certain prescriptions from God. These are two sides of one coin. In modern terms we are dealing with law and ethics.

This theme in the previous edition of this program bore the title GOD'S LAW DEMANDS A RIGHTEOUS PEOPLE. During a discussion of biblical themes in a colloquium one member, a rabbi, raised the point with me that it is really *God* who DEMANDS A RIGHTEOUS PEOPLE. The Law is a gift of God to show people a way to be righteous. Before you jump too quickly to a New Testament distinction between Law and grace, remember that Law is viewed by Jews as a gracious gift of God. God's people are answerable to a loving God, not to books of legal codes. So the theme title is revised.

It is important that the terminology be kept straight. Torah is a part of the canon of the Hebrew Scriptures, but the term is also used to refer to the laws that are a prominent feature of the Pentateuch. In the New Testament "the law" is often used to refer to the Pentateuch. Take care that Paul's negative statements about the law are not allowed to become the group view of the law. When it suits his argument, Paul writes *the law is holy, and the commandment is holy and just and good* (Romans 7:12). It was perversion of the law that gave it a bad image. Torah is Yahweh's gift (see Psalm 1:2). The law for a pious Jew was and is the kind of burden that sails are for a ship.

About the Law Codes

The legal portions of the Pentateuch are not conveniently organized. The codes are collections that have gravitated together, and they are not difficult to identify. The outline form that has been adopted in this part is designed to help in this identification.

The laws appear in the context of Israel's movement from the wilderness of Sinai to the Promised Land. The *Resource Book* points out that many regulations are designed for the time when Israel was settled in Canaan. Scholars generally agree that, since Torah was finally edited no earlier than the time of Ezra, conditions that prevailed in the time of the monarchy are probably reflected in the final form of the codes. This matter should not be raised at this point. Some folks will not be ready to accept this growth process but will be content to believe that all of the details were revealed to the wilderness generation and brought into Canaan. Careful reading may in time make evident at least that there are anachronisms. Each reader will come to deeper understanding at an individual pace.

The Decalogue

The Ten Words mark the start of the legal collections. They almost float in their setting at the beginning of Exodus 20. The context is extremely solemn. The emphasis, however, is upon what Yahweh said rather than upon the setting. This becomes more evident when the words are given again in Deuteronomy 5. Deliverance from Egyptian slavery is the essential setting.

The *Resource Book* urges memorization of the Ten Commandments. This is really a must for biblical literacy. There is something to be said for using the KJV in this instance, for that is the translation in which the Ten Commandments have usually entered our literary culture. Modern translations serve to keep the words from losing their impact due to repetitious familiarity.

Jews treat the introduction, Exodus 20:1, 2, as the first Word, and then verses 3-6 as the second. In pictorial art (stained glass, stone, etc.) the two tablets are sometimes divided 5 and 5, sometimes 4 and 6, or even 3 and 7. The two parts represent duties to God and duties to people according to how the Ten Words are divided in the tradition represented by the art. See Research 1.

The Covenant Code

Exodus 24:3-7 marks the end of the Covenant Code. Note *the book of the covenant* in verse 7. The outline survey shows that there is no more collection of laws in the remainder of the book.

The *lex talionis* (Exodus 21:24) appears to sanction bloody retaliation. In its time, however, it was a distinct improvement on unlimited revenge that was the contemporary practice. The code restricts injured parties to precisely equal satisfaction. The law thus abolished the continuing blood feud. Exodus 22:26, 27 is an excellent example of the humanitarian concern of this code. A business arrangement must not work undue hardship on another Jew. The sex taboos and the Sabbath laws have practical as well as religious aspects. The sabbatical years foster a rotation of crops.

The Holiness Code

The Holiness Code is a collection of laws explicitly calling for a holy life. It covers many of the same areas as the Covenant Code, sometimes more elaborately. For example, the Sabbath regulations are much more elaborate than the simple Word of the Decalogue, but they are not nearly so complicated as the rabbis made them later, prior to New Testament times.

The existence of different codes in such an unorganized arrangement leads to the matter of the final collection and editing. The final forms came some time after the latest code was formulated. It was probably the intention of the editors to play down the differences in origin of the codes. Refinement of dating is unnecessary at this point.

It is best not to become involved at this point in the process that led to the final forms. There is quite enough to study in the texts themselves. If you wish to study for your own information the steps from Sinai to Pentateuch, you will find details in *Understanding the Old Testament*.

The Deuteronomic Code

The narrative in 2 Kings 22, 23 gives this code (Deuteronomy 12-26) an important place in Josiah's time, but of course the material must have been in some written form well before the workman found it.

Beside the code, several details in Deuteronomy related to law are important. The alternate form of the Decalogue is one. Notice Deuteronomy 6:1, repeated in substance at Deuteronomy 12:1. The *Shema* (Deuteronomy 6:4), the central affirmation of Jewish religion, is regularly repeated in modern Jewish liturgies. Perhaps you can learn it in Hebrew or get a recording of it. It is integral to the development of Jewish monotheism, and Jesus' use of it makes it important for Christians.

Biblical Covenants and Blood

The relationship between blood and biblical covenants is a matter of unusual interest and concern to some people. Read Exodus 24:3-8. Sacrificial blood was *dashed against the altar, the book of the covenant* was read, and the people agreed to obey it. Then Moses took *blood and dashed it on the people* (NJB, *sprinkled it over*). The ceremony has a distant connection to Abraham (Genesis 15), but more is involved here than the recovery of an ancient ritual. Leviticus 17:11 declares, *the life of the flesh is in the blood.* The ceremony connects the given life of the sacrifice with the continuing life of the people.

Notice especially that the blood is applied to the people only after they hear and accept the words of the covenant. The New Testament explicitly recognizes Jesus' death as a sacrifice and connects it with this and perhaps other blood ceremonies. The Exodus connection would then demand some acceptance of the new covenant that Jesus was making. The Lord's Supper is considered in detail in Theme 9, but here it may be noted that in 1 Corinthians 11:25 Paul writes, *this cup is the new covenant in my blood.* The covenant blood is on the cross. The cup of wine—no Jew would drink blood (Leviticus 17:10)—is the acceptance of the covenant.

My point is that we impoverish the wealth of associative meaning in many of the great biblical themes if we push one detail until it squeezes out other important matters. Historical theology presents many "theories" of the atonement. Each had its day because each embodied an element of truth. But the whole is greater than any partial perception. So it is with the relationship between God and people as this is reflected in the law and the call for righteousness. This is one reason we stress that we are studying the Bible whole.

Supplementary Reading

It will be worthwhile to review background information on the law and righteousness as well as the major law codes discussed in the *Resource Book*. A Bible dictionary will get you started and both *Understanding the Old Testament* and *Introducing the Old Testament* will provide additional material.

SESSION PLAN

Learning Objectives

This session is intended enable participants to:

1. Describe how the people of the Old Testament viewed the Law of God as a gift rather than a burden.

2. Illustrate the Hebrew understanding of the results of obedience and disobedience to the Law with at least two stories from the early chapters of Genesis.

3. Locate the two versions of the Decalogue in the Old Testament and list the Ten Commandments.

4. Name the three other major law codes of the Old Testament and describe each one of these in two or three sentences.

Resources You May Need

Chalkboard and chalk
Newsprint and markers
Handout of selected verses from Psalm 119

Leadership Strategy

SETTING THE STAGE

1. You are now nearly two-thirds of the way through your study of *Kerygma: The Bible in Depth*, making this a good time to review your progress. One way to do this is to take a few moments to summarize the first six themes, which have dealt with the formation and history of God's people. The remaining themes are concerned with how God's people are to order their lives in response to God's saving action. You may want to offer a brief preview of what's ahead in these units.

2. Write the word "Law" on a chalkboard or newsprint. Divide the group down the middle. One side is to prepare a list of the positive effects laws have in society. The other side is to describe all the potentially negative effects laws may have. If the groups are large, sub-divide further so that participants are working in small groups of three to five members each. A person from each side should present the list from his or her side to the whole group. Following this, make a brief presentation on the Jewish attitude toward the Law. Ask the group to evaluate Dr. Walther's statement, "The Law for the pious Jew was the kind of burden that sails are to a ship." In addition to the information in the *Resource Book*, consult an article on "Torah" in a Bible dictionary.

or

Organize everyone to work in clusters of three or four to draw up a list of the laws they regard as most essential for a well-ordered society. Then have each cluster present its list to the whole group. Note similarities and differences in the lists. Discuss in what ways a community that received such a list might consider it as a gift for ordering its life. (You may want to keep your list to use in connection with activities suggested later in this session and in Exploring the Scripture in Part 3 of this theme.)

EXPLORING THE SCRIPTURE

1. The Old Testament writers believed that God's will had been revealed to the people and that obedience to this revelation would result in blessing. Divide the group into four sections and assign each section one of these passages:

   Genesis 2:16, 17; 3 (Adam and Eve)
   Genesis 4:8-16 (Cain and Abel)
   Genesis 6:5-13; 9:1-17 (Noah)
   Genesis 15:6; 17:1, 2; 22:1-18 (Abraham)

   The sections are to prepare presentations to the group in which they respond to the following questions:

   a. What is the promise/command of God?

   b. What is expected of the person(s) in the story?

   c. What are the consequences of obedience or disobedience for the person(s)?

   and/or

   In the *Resource Book* (p. 145), Dr. Walther says the purpose of the Law is "to produce in God's people a condition that Scripture refers to as 'righteousness'." Leviticus 19:2 stresses the obligation of God's people to be "holy." Using material from a Bible dictionary, summarize the meanings of "righteousness" and "holiness." Indicate how these terms are related to God's intention in the stories from Genesis listed above.

2. Ask members of the group to list the Ten Commandments on a sheet of paper without using their Bibles or the *Resource Book*. Assure them that no one will see their papers. This is not a test, but an exercise to enable them to see what they already know. When they have finished, review the commandments with them.

   and

   Invite everyone to open their Bibles to Exodus 20:1-17. Ask one person to read Deuteronomy 5:6-21 while the rest follow the Exodus passage. Note the differences between the two lists of the commandments and discuss the possible reasons for these. (This activity may also be done in pairs.)

and/or

Assign a different one of the Ten Commandments to each of ten small groups. Each group is to write a paraphrase of the commandment in contemporary language and present it to the whole group on a sheet of newsprint. At the time of the presentation each small group is to indicate what the law meant for Old Testament society and how it might apply to contemporary life.

and

If the group prepared lists of the essential laws for a well-ordered society in the opening part of this session, compare those lists with the contemporary statements of the Ten Commandments.

3. Present a mini-lecture (or introduce the three people who have agreed to make presentations) on the background and content of the three law codes:

> The Covenant Code (Exodus 21:1-23:19)
> The Holiness Code (Leviticus 17-26)
> The Deuteronomic Code (Deuteronomy 12-26)

and/or

Divide the group into seven subgroups and assign material from the law codes to these as follows:

> The Covenant Code
>> Group 1 Exodus 21:1-23:19
> The Holiness Code
>> Group 2 Leviticus 17-21
>> Group 3 Leviticus 22-26
> The Deuteronomic Code
>> Group 4 Deuteronomy 12-15
>> Group 5 Deuteronomy 16-19
>> Group 6 Deuteronomy 20-23
>> Group 7 Deuteronomy 24-26

The assigned passages are to be divided among each subgroup's members. Everyone is to read his or her portion and select at least two passages, laws, or concepts representative of the passage. The subgroups are to make composite charts on newsprint listing these selections from their assigned passages, and present the charts to the whole group for a brief review of the law codes.

CLOSING

1. Distribute a hand-out with the following verses of Psalm 119 on it: 10, 12, 18, 34, 73, 81, 105, and 166.

   a. Line out each verse on the hand-out, allowing group members time to repeat each verse after you.

   b. Invite each member to select one line or phrase to repeat silently several times with eyes closed.

   c. Lead the group in a unison reading of the verses.

2. Ask a person who reads well to assume the role of Moses and read Deuteronomy 6:4-9, 20-25, and possibly 30:11-20 aloud. The members of the group are to imagine that they arc Israel, gathered on the edge of the Promised Land, as they listen.

Looking Ahead

Item #3 under Setting the Stage in the next session suggests that a member of the group read pre-selected portions of the blessings and curses found in Deuteronomy 28.

Item #1 under Exploring the Scripture in the next session suggests that nine members of the group each present two to three minute reports on these prophets: Amos, Isaiah, Jeremiah (two reports), Hosea, Micah, Habakkuk, Zechariah, Malachi. See the description of the activity for details.

GOD DEMANDS A RIGHTEOUS PEOPLE

Prophets' Call for Righteousness

NOTES FROM THE AUTHOR

The Purpose of God's Law

The purpose of Torah is to establish right relations (1) between Yahweh and people, (2) between the individual Israelite and the nation, (3) among individual Israelites, and (4) between Israelites and outsiders. Yahweh's concern for the poor and oppressed is very evident. The relationships are the practical expressions of the covenant in the everyday life of the people. Other ancient peoples associated their deities with their national life, but Israel's ethical monotheism is a towering landmark in the history of humankind.

The prophets' principal purpose was to monitor and react to the outworking of the covenant and the demands of Torah. They were concerned with the breakdown of the relationships however and wherever they occurred. Their assurances of deliverance to God's people when they were oppressed had a counterpart in their denunciation of God's people when they oppressed others.

The prophets speak for God. *Says the LORD* occurs over and over. The term "oracle," as it occasionally occurs in the prophetic books, is simply another term to designate a prophet's message (see Malachi 1:1). The prophets assume that the people are familiar with the law. Failure in the day to day application of the law is a principal target of the words of the prophets.

You will find many connections between this part and parts of other themes. The *Resource Book* occasionally notes such instances. This is a principal way by which we tie together the study of the Bible whole. This part is our main look at the prophets, but we shall see some of them again in Theme 10 on "Hope."

Isaiah

Isaiah ben-Amoz has appeared in most of the themes so far. There is also material from Isaiah of the exile. By now the diversity in the contents of the Book of Isaiah should not be a problem. All parts of the book sound a note of peace and reconciliation. Isaiah 1 begins with a recital of Judah's sins, but quickly Yahweh offers pardon for disobedience: Verse 18 is well known. The metaphors and similes throughout the book are memorable. The law is infrequently mentioned. For examples, see Isaiah 2:3 (*instruction = torah*) and Isaiah 42:21 (*teaching = torah*).

The idea of a *remnant* is introduced in Isaiah 10:20-23. This becomes increasingly important as Judah's political situation deteriorates. Note Isaiah 11:15, 16, where deliverance from the Assyrian threat is promised on the ground of the deliverance from Egypt, and it is *the remnant* that is saved. A revival of *the root of Jesse* is promised in Isaiah 11:10. Since this was a shaky prospect in Isaiah's day, the remnant faith was important.

This is a bridge to the *servant* passages. There is no consensus about the identification of the *servant*. We may agree, however, that a remnant of God's people is called to become identified with the servant in redemptive suffering. This in turn leads to the great call in Chapter 55. The metaphors and similes throughout the book are memorable.

Jeremiah

Theme 6, Part 2, highlights how Jeremiah deals with history. He warns that history teaches lessons and that if the lessons are not learned, trouble is sure to follow. Thus in Jeremiah 8 Judah has failed to keep Yahweh's law (verses 4-9) and refused to face reality (verse 11). Many of Jeremiah's memorable phrases and statements have found their way into our language; "sour grapes" and "teeth on edge" come from Jeremiah 31:29, 30. A story about a potter, Jeremiah 18:1-12, is picked up by Paul, Romans 9:21.

Sometimes words need careful explanation. In Jeremiah 1:11, 12 there is a play on words—it is almost a pun. The NRSV footnotes show how close the Hebrew words for *almond tree* and *watching* are. NAB translates the first word as *watching-tree* and notes that the almond tree is the first to blossom in spring. Figurative language about love, sexuality, and marriage is frequent in Jeremiah. Often it is associated with denunciation of pagan religious rites (see Jeremiah 3:6-10).

Look again at Jeremiah 31:29, 30. The contrast between corporate and individual responsibility is important. We have been stressing corporate righteousness, "a righteous people." A people, of course, becomes righteous as individuals become righteous, but in Hebrew thought—as indeed in Christian teaching—the righteous individual does not appear in isolation. Where the corporate existence of the people is in jeopardy, however, the significance of the individual increases. So when the prophet says *everyone*, it is very important. Ezekiel quotes the same saying and adds, *it is only the person who sins that shall die* (Ezekiel 18:4).

Amos

Theme 5, Part 2, treats Amos as a leader-figure. His lists of Israel's sins are often graphic and pungent. Even Israel's religious observances are unacceptable to Yahweh: *I hate, I despise your festivals, and I take no delight in your solemn assemblies* (Amos 5:21)—these are tough words. The description of the women of Samaria, Amos 4:1-3, is downright scandalous. The connection between "righteousness" and "justice" is nowhere plainer than in Amos.

Amos claims direct connection with Yahweh's intentions: *Surely the Lord GOD does nothing, without revealing his secret to his servants the prophets* (Amos 3:7). Sometimes the prophet intercedes for the people (Amos 7:5, 6), and their condition is not hopeless (Amos 9:11-15).

A play on words—like Isaiah's—occurs in Amos 8:1, 2. The footnotes show the relationship between *summer fruit* and *end*: The *summer fruit* is the *end* of the season. We might play with the English translation and read, "My people Israel is a basket case." You may also notice the reference to star constellations in Amos 5:8.

Micah

Surely Micah is "minor" only in the length of his book. His accusations of evil are vigorous and vivid. He comes down hard on rulers, priests, and false prophets (Micah 3). He uses a court scene in Chapter 6, a device used by other prophets. The Hebrew word *hesed* occurs in Micah 6:8, translated *kindness* (TEV, *constant love*).[1] The figure of *summer fruit* occurs in Micah 7:1.

Habakkuk

This book deals with Job's question: What connection is there between one's righteousness and how one fares in life? *Justice never prevails* (Habakkuk 1:4). Habakkuk's answer is somewhat different from Job's: Be patient and the *vision . . . will surely come* (Habakkuk 2:3).

---

1   HBD lists the word under "loving-kindness," the KJV translation.

Habakkuk 2:4b is important for Paul. His interpretation is not our concern here, but we need to consider the best translation. *Faith* (NRSV) must not be construed in a passive sense. The root is from the Hebrew word that gives us "amen"; it has to do with firmness. REB translates, *the righteous will live by being faithful*. NJB, *the upright will live through faithfulness*. TEV is close to paraphrase: *Those who are righteous will live because they are faithful to God*. The same root is translated *believed* in Genesis 15:6. Consider what Habakkuk is saying in the context.

Malachi and Zechariah

These prophets are from a later period. Malachi says that the people should not expect God to right the wrongs done to them, for they have been unjust to God. *The difference between the righteous and the wicked* is the difference *between one who serves God and one who does not serve him* (Malachi 3:18). Nevertheless, there is hope at the end.

Zechariah looks largely to the future. His visions and oracles stress coming judgment and call for right ways. He is hopeful, so his book appears again in Theme 10. *Even though it seems impossible to the remnant of this people in these days, should it also seem impossible to me, says the LORD of hosts.* (Zechariah 8:6).

Daniel

Again, it is important not to get sidetracked by questions of literary history. The point here is how the stories emphasize the demand for righteousness. In Theme 5, Part 2, the stories were applied to the situation of God's people facing oppression and temptation to apostasy. Here the focus is on how people are to relate to God in order to receive deliverance.

Psalms

The Psalms are the principal content of Theme 9, Part 2, so here there is no need to deal with their literary form(s) nor their place in Jewish worship. Research 3 touches on Jewish worship, but it will be more adequately considered after Theme 9, Part 1. The emphasis on law and righteousness in the Psalms makes it impossible to bypass them here.

Supplementary Reading

In addition to adding details to your knowledge of the various prophets included in this part, it will be helpful to review the relationship of the prophets to the covenant. The indexes of the various supplementary books will lead you to the relevant material.

SESSION PLANS

Learning Objectives

This session is intended to enable participants to:

1. Describe the purpose of the Law in the Old Testament.

2. Explain how the Law is connected to God's saving action and promises in the covenant relationship.

3. Summarize in a paragraph the role of the prophets in calling God's people to righteousness.

4. Illustrate Israel's attitude toward the Law with a poem or poster based on Psalms such as 1, 19, 119.

Resources You May Need

Chalkboard and chalk
Newsprint and markers
Chronology of the Bible chart from the *Resource Book*
Paper and markers for creating posters
Hymnbooks or copies of a responsive reading

Leadership Strategy

SETTING THE STAGE

1. Ask for questions left over from the previous session or generated by the present material. Record them on your Loose Ends list and decide when to consider them in this session.

2. Encourage participants to recall childhood experiences of breaking rules made by parents or teachers. Invite a few volunteers to share their stories. They should describe what happened, including how their relationship with the parents or teachers was affected.

   Then ask members of the group to reflect on the same situation from the opposite perspective by thinking of times when children or students broke a rule they had enforced. Invite a few volunteers to describe how they confronted the offender and what difference this experience made in their relationship.

and/or

Display this information on newsprint or a chalkboard:

The purpose of God's laws is the establishment of right relations:

a. Between Yahweh and the people.

b. Among individual Israelites.

c. Between individual Israelites and the nation.

d. Between Israel and other peoples.

Ask the group to recall from Part 1 at least two laws that are related to each of these four categories. Discuss how the laws fulfill God's purpose to establish right relationships.

3. Have the group read Joshua 8:30-35. Then divide the group down the middle and ask them to imagine the Ark of the Covenant is resting between the two halves of the group. You may be able to find an illustration of the Ark from the Sunday School teaching pictures file to serve as a focus for their imagining. Have both sides of the group face the imaginary Ark while a person reads portions of the blessings and curses found in Deuteronomy 28 which he or she has selected beforehand.

Discuss Israel's understanding of the relationship between God's covenant promises to the patriarchs and Moses, and obedience to God's law.

or

Read aloud the following statement by Dr. Walther, found on page 153 in the *Resource Book*:

We have stressed the importance of the development of monotheism in earliest Hebrew faith. This belief in one God leads naturally to the conviction that God's people are ruled by divine law. This is expressed in a covenant relationship, which God's people accept. This biblical faith is unique in the religions of the world.

Then ask the group to review 1 Kings 2:1-4. Discuss:

a. How does David connect God's covenant promise and law in his charge to Solomon?

b. How does this charge differ from the parting words a king might be expected to give his son under similar circumstances?

c. In what way may Israel's outlook be considered unique?

EXPLORING THE SCRIPTURE

1. Present a brief review of the role of the prophets in the Old Testament, using material from supplementary resources such as the *Lion Encyclopedia of the Bible* and *Understanding the Old Testament*. Refer to the Chronology chart in the Appendix of the *Resource Book* and locate Amos, Isaiah, Jeremiah, Hosea, Micah, Habakkuk, Zechariah and Malachi. Then assign these Scriptures to nine small groups:

   Amos 2:6-8; 5:24; 9:11-15
   Isaiah 1:16-20; 8:16-20
   Isaiah 52:13-53:12; 55:6-9
   Jeremiah 7:1-11; 34:8-20
   Hosea 8:7-9; 12:2-6
   Micah 4:1-4; 6:6-8
   Habakkuk 2:6-20
   Zechariah 7:9, 10
   Malachi 3:16-18

Each subgroup is to read the assigned passages and together compose a summary of the prophet's message in contemporary language. One person from each subgroup is to then read this summary to the whole group. When the summaries have all been read, note similarities and differences among them. Discuss how the prophets' messages are related to their understanding of the covenant. (What did God promise people? What did God expect of them? How will their actions be punished or rewarded? What hope is left for Israel?)

or

Introduce nine persons selected at the previous session to give two or three minute reports about the above prophets. The Scripture references and comments in the *Resource Book* and a Bible dictionary will be helpful.

The reports should include:

    a. The prophet's name.

    b. The historical setting of his prophecy.

    c. A summary of his call to righteousness.

    d. A description of the threat or promise he presents to the people.

or

To understand in more depth the experience and message of one prophet, focus on Jeremiah. His career is discussed in a chapter of *Understanding the Old Testament*. You will also find information in *Introducing the Old Testament* and a Bible dictionary. From these resources develop a brief lecture on the stages of his life which is illustrated with specific passages from the Bible.

2. Divide the group into pairs or small clusters and assign one of the following passages to each subgroup:

    Psalm 1
    Psalm 19:7-13
    Psalm 119:9-11
    Psalm 119:18
    Psalm 119:97
    Psalm 119:105
    Psalm 119:165
    Psalm 119:176

The subgroups are to create posters illustrating the joy found in following God's law, as described in the Bible passages. One person from each subgroup should then describe the poster to the whole group.

or

Using the same assignments as above, have each of the subgroups write on newsprint a cinquain poem about law. The guidelines for cinquain poetry are:

    Line 1 Title (a noun; one word)
    Line 2 Describes the title word (two words)
    Line 3 Action words or phrases about the title (three words)
    Line 4 Describes a feeling about the title (four words)
    Line 5 Refers to the title (one word)

(You will find an example of cinquain poetry in the session plans for Theme 5, Part 3.)

The poems are to be presented to the whole group, and the newsprint displayed where all can see it.

CLOSING

1. Read a unison or responsive reading from your church's hymnbook that includes Psalms 1, 19, or 119.

or

Select one of the prophets studied above and discuss the kind of message he might bring to your church or country today. In connection with this discussion respond to questions 2 and 3 in the "Reflection" section on page 159 of the Resource Book.

Looking Ahead

Item #2 under Setting the Stage in the next session suggests that a group member comment on Jesus' attitude toward the oral tradition of his day, using selected Scripture references.

Item #4 under Exploring the Scripture in the next session suggests that three persons present a dramatic reading of John 3:1-21 or that one person make a presentation on the meaning of being "born from above."

234

GOD DEMANDS A RIGHTEOUS PEOPLE

THEME 7

Jesus and the Law

PART 3

NOTES FROM THE AUTHOR

The Law in Jesus' Day

The religious environment of Jesus' ministry is not easy to assess. Because the oral law ultimately found expression in the *Mishnah* and *Talmud*, we know a lot about the Pharisees. Since the middle of this century, we have learned much about the Essenes. But the largest group remains the least known, the *'am ha-'aretz*, "the people of the land" (see, for example, Jeremiah 34:19; Ezekiel 45:16). Most of what we learn about them we gather by inference from literature written by people who were not of their number. We may be sure that most of Jesus' contemporaries held Torah in great veneration, so it is not surprising that Jesus has much to say about the law and the call for righteousness.

John the Baptist's call to repentance and its consequences led directly into Jesus' public ministry. Be sure the group remembers what has been said about the meaning of "repent"—it requires a whole new mind set. John's particular applications provide some insight into the state of religious practice at that time. He brought the law into the everyday life of his hearers.

The Sermon on the Mount

The Sermon on the Mount is prominent in this part. The Beatitudes are a poetic summary of much of Jesus' ethical teaching. The poetic form gives them a sort of catechetical flavor, easily remembered. *But I say to you* gets to the heart of Jesus' attitude toward the law: The law is basic, but it must be understood in terms of what it implies about motivation.

Sometimes it is argued that Jesus' teachings are too idealistic to be practical. Matthew 5:48 is a case in point. Persons who lightly claim to follow the Sermon on the Mount seldom really wrestle with Jesus' ethical idealism. In this verse *perfect* is a key word. It does not carry the connotation of a philosophical absolute—no one, of course, could be as perfect as God in that respect. The Greek word implies the appropriate end in view. Here the context is the love commandment, so NJB translates, *You must therefore set no bounds to your love, just as your heavenly Father sets none to his.* Those who accept Jesus' teaching are to achieve an ethical level above others, and they are to measure their growth by God's standard. God's goodness always beckons further.

Jesus refers to God as *Father* seventeen times in these three chapters. It is part of the genius of Jesus' theology that God is to be known by the family term. His followers are invited to share that intimacy of relationship that he enjoys with God. It is not unnatural nor unreasonable to expect the child to grow toward the maturity of the father. Overwhelming as it seems, this is what Jesus proposes. It is beside the point here to debate about inclusive language. Jesus certainly would not hesitate to commend the maturity of a girl in terms of the maturity of the mother.

Jesus' Teaching: For Individuals or for Communities?

The Gospels relate many stories in which Jesus meets and ministers to individuals. Nicodemus is an instance in this part. The question may then arise, did Jesus intend to found a church, that is, a corporate body? We have already pointed to the fact that a corporate body is composed of individuals, so perhaps the question should be reframed: What is the relationship of individuals to the body of the church?

Theme 6 discusses the reign of God. God's rule clearly connotes a people over whom God is sovereign. From the exodus on, God's people were a body conscious of national identity. When the nation was in danger of collapse, the prophets laid more emphasis upon individuals. In Theme 9 it is noted that this individual relationship appears in the devotional experience. Jesus comes among a people who have never lost their sense of belonging together but who have uniquely provided for the rights of individuals.

At the outset of his public ministry Jesus forms a close circle of followers and trains them to work with him and with each other. He calls them *little flock* (Luke 12:32). He calls himself *the good shepherd*, and although his parable is about the one lost sheep, there are *ninety-nine* others in the flock. The number "twelve" is significant. As there were twelve tribes in Israel, so the new people of God whom Jesus is gathering begins with twelve men. At the end of his ministry Jesus celebrates Passover, which remembers the moment when God began the deliverance of a people. Jesus gives it a new meaning. Theme 9, Part 3, explores this further.

Jesus' interpretation of the law and the call for his followers to be righteous are much more than laying down detailed regulations for Christians. He is moving from a people of God lost in a wilderness of misunderstanding and failed expectation to a new people who find renewal and hope in following him. They are becoming a church, no less God's people than are the people of Torah. Jesus says, *unless your righteousness exceeds that of the scribes and Pharisees, you will never enter the kingdom of heaven* (Matthew 5:20). It is the believing relationship with Jesus that makes this possible.

Source Criticism

Biblical scholars deal with what they call "source criticism."[1] This is the study of the sources that may lie behind the final (canonical) form of a biblical book. If you have pursued this study, you may be uncomfortable as the *Resource Book* moves easily back and forth among the four Gospels. I have tried to avoid anything that is in clear defiance of the nuances imposed by sources. Of course, you should regularly consult a harmony of the Synoptic Gospels, even when no problem seems to be present. I have avoided material that might put the Synoptics and John in conflict. Two further observations are in order.

Gospel criticism will continue to fall short of coming to unquestionable conclusions until there is agreement about the dating of the Gospels and about their precise relationships. That day has not yet dawned. Meanwhile, I think it makes good sense to attribute to Jesus what the Gospels clearly attribute to him. Matters of precise wording and variations of setting are important only to one who holds a completely mechanistic view of the texts. I think we can place considerable confidence in the oral process of the first Christian generation. This is better than believing in an imprecisely identified community or an equally indistinct editor. At our Kerygma level of study we need to introduce only as much source study as is useful or necessary for our understanding of texts as we go along.

Finally, we are dealing with the canon. The church has developed its theology from the biblical books as we have them, and we are the inheritors of nearly twenty centuries of this process. This is no excuse for ignoring Gospel source-study where it helps to solve problems and illuminates the texts. But finally we have the Gospels as edited and transmitted by the church. Paul's standard of what is right for the church applies here: *Let all things be done for building up...* (1 Corinthians 14:26).

Supplementary Reading

The *Lion Encyclopedia of the Bible* contains a brief introduction to "Biblical Criticism." Both *Understanding the New Testament* and *Introducing the New Testament* add further details. For a practical approach, which shows how the critical efforts of scholars are helpful

---

1   It is awkward that the word "criticism" has been adopted for what German scholars call "history." Criticism in this context is not intended to have a negative connotation.

in understanding particular texts, see the Kerygma Program's course *Interpretation: A Guide to Understanding the Bible Today.*

SESSION PLANS

Learning Objectives

This session is intended to enable participants to:

1. Summarize John the Baptist's message about repentance and forgiveness.

2. Illustrate Jesus' attitude toward the Law with at least three examples from the Sermon on the Mount.

3. State how Jesus summarized the Law in Matthew 7:12 and 22:34-40.

4. Describe how Jesus provides for his followers to become righteous.

Resources You May Need

Newsprint and markers
Excerpts from the Mishnah or Talmud
Copies of an order of worship with a prayer of confession
Construction paper and crayons or markers
Bibles with cross references
Directions for group study of Matthew 5
Outline of the Sermon on the Mount
Scripts for a dramatic reading of John 3:1-21
A recording of "You Are the Light of the World" from *Godspell*

Leadership Strategy

SETTING THE STAGE

1. Ask the group for questions left over from the last session or generated by the new material. List them on your Loose Ends list and determine when to take them up.

2. Invite the group to imagine a situation where they would purposely disregard a social convention or custom. What factors would lead them to make such a choice? Why

would these be important?

Ask people to share their examples. Discuss whether it is ever acceptable to disobey the law. What principles or values or circumstances might be included in the deliberation about this issue? How might such considerations be related to the Old Testament's demand for "righteousness"?

and/or

Make a brief presentation on the attitudes toward the Law among the Sadducees, Pharisees, and Essenes of Jesus' day. Helpful information will be found in *Understanding the New Testament*, the *Lion Encyclopedia of the Bible*, and articles in a Bible dictionary. Draw attention to Mark 7:1-13 as an illustration of the development of oral tradition. Most public libraries have a collection of sayings from the Mishnah or Talmud from which you might read selections to illustrate how the oral material continued to grow.

and/or

Have a person who has prepared in advance comment on Jesus' approach to the oral tradition of his day, using references such as Mark 7:1-13, Luke 11:46, and Matthew 23:2-4.

EXPLORING THE SCRIPTURE

1. Distribute copies of a church bulletin or order of worship containing a prayer of confession. Discuss the significance of confession in worship and in the personal lives of Christians. Then summarize the meaning of repentance as found in a theological wordbook, such as Alan Richardson's *Theological Word Book of the Bible*, and relate this to the practice of confession.

   Now read aloud John the Baptist's call to repentance in Luke 3:7-18. Ask the group to list the "fruits" of repentance John mentions and discuss their relationship to the Jewish Law.

   or

   Distribute sheets of plain construction paper and crayons or markers to the group. Ask everyone to draw stick figure cartoons to illustrate at least one practical effect repentance should have, according to John the Baptist. Depending on the size of the group, have persons share their drawings with the whole group or with small clusters.

Divide the group into five sections. Assign one of the following parts of John's preaching in Luke 3:7-18 to each section. They are to decide to whom John's message might be addressed today when he says:

  a. Whoever has two coats must share with someone who has none.

  b. Whoever has food must share it.

  c. Only collect the appropriate amount of taxes.

  d. Rob no one by violence or false accusation.

  e. Be content with your wages.

Have the sections report their conclusions to the whole group.

2. To begin the discussion of Jesus' attitude toward the law, read Matthew 5:17-20 aloud to the group. Then divide into six small groups and make these assignments:

> Group 1 - Matthew 5:21-26
> Group 2 - Matthew 5:27-30
> Group 3 - Matthew 5:31, 32
> Group 4 - Matthew 5:33-37
> Group 5 - Matthew 5:38-42
> Group 6 - Matthew 5:43-48

Each group will need a Bible containing cross references, a sheet of newsprint, a marker, and these directions:

> Read your assigned Scripture. Using cross references locate the Old Testament law(s) to which Jesus is referring. Divide your sheet of newsprint into two columns. In the left column summarize the Old Testament laws. In the right column summarize Jesus' interpretation of these laws. Discuss what your passage indicates about Jesus' attitude toward the Law. By what authority does he re-interpret the old laws? Choose someone to present a summary of your discussion to the whole group.

Reconvene and have persons from each group display the newsprint and summarize their group's discussion.

or

Have the group develop a summary of the Sermon on the Mount. To do this use an outline you have designed or one found in a Bible dictionary such as *Harper's Bible Dictionary*. Divide the group into the same number of subgroups as there are major sections in your outline. Provide each subgroup with the appropriate Scripture references for a section and ask them to summarize the content of that section on newsprint.

When the subgroups have completed their work, have them report their findings. Then have the whole group evaluate the statement:

> Righteousness is not a matter of rule-keeping, but a total dedication to the will of God.

or

Divide into four groups. Each group is to develop a summary of Jesus' teaching in the Sermon on the Mount on one of these topics:

Family life
Relationships with other people
Worship
Forgiveness

Reconvene and have the groups present their summaries. If you made a list of laws for the ideal society in Part 1 of this theme, compare Jesus' teaching with this list and with the Ten Commandments.

3. Read Jesus' summary of the Law in Matthew 7:12 and Matthew 22:34-40 to the group. Assign each of the following passages to one third of the group: Mark 2:23-28; Luke 10:25-37; Luke 18:9-14. Allow time for the sections to read their passages. Then lead a discussion with the whole group on how these passages illustrate Jesus' understanding of the Law.

or

Make a brief presentation describing the Old Testament roots of Jesus' summary of the Law in Matthew 7:12, Luke 6:31, and Matthew 22:34-40. Illustrate how he lived out his convictions in his association with the unrighteous. See the *Resource Book* for additional Scripture references.

4. Introduce three persons who have prepared in advance to present a dramatic reading of John 3:1-21. One person is to be the narrator, one is to take the role of Nicodemus,

and one the role of Jesus. Instruct the readers to go slowly. The remainder of the group is to listen carefully for the things that Jesus says are necessary to become righteous. At the close of the reading, break into clusters of three and ask each group to list these requirements for righteousness. Then have the clusters share their findings with the whole group.

or

Have a person who has prepared in advance make a brief presentation on being "born from above" as described in John 3:1-21, or make such a presentation yourself, using the supplementary books and commentaries for information. Discuss how Jesus provides for his followers to become righteous.

CLOSING

1. Listen to a recording of "You are the Light of the World" from *Godspell.*

or

Read Matthew 11:28-30 and/or John 13:34, 35 and close the session with a prayer.

Looking Ahead

Item #1 under Exploring the Scripture in the next session suggests that several participants stage a debate on the issue discussed at the Jerusalem Council in Acts 15.

Item #2 of the same section suggests that additional members of the group be included in presenting a summary of Paul's theology.

GOD DEMANDS A RIGHTEOUS PEOPLE

THEME

7

Righteousness in the Church

PART

4

NOTES FROM THE AUTHOR

Our Resources for this Part

Not only are there differences among the Gospels, there are important differences between the Gospels and the other parts of the New Testament. This is remarkable since the Gospels come out of the very churches in which the other literature was produced. The differences raise important questions, but the early acceptance of most of the books by the church suggests to me that we ought to have a high measure of confidence in their integrity.

The bridge between Gospels and epistles is Luke-Acts. Critics are quick to note how the editorial hand of Luke has shaped the material, but it is equally important to observe how the variations in the material point to his use of sources and traditions. The centrality of Jesus, particularly his cross and resurrection, is unquestionable. Problems arise in reconciling details in Acts with data from Paul's letters, but most of them may be ignored without loss in our study.

The Double Task of the New Church

The first task that the earliest church undertook was its outreach mission. The church felt compelled to spread its good news in ever-widening circles. This produced a corollary duty: as the mission entered new religious, political, and social circumstances, the message had to be reconsidered so it would be effective in the changing situations. This was immediately engaged when the mission moved into pagan territory where there was no familiarity with the Hebrew Scriptures.

The second task followed the first. What happens once you have heard and received the good news? The nurture of the church called for guidelines to regulate the life of the Christian community and the lives of the individuals in it. What happens to Torah laws in the Christian setting? How does one live in Christian freedom without losing Christian identity? What relationships are possible with pagan neighbors? How does one relate the personal Christian experience with corporate associations in the church? Wrestling with law and ethics in the New Testament church is a complicated matter.

Galatians

Paul's letter to the Galatians offers a critical entrance to many matters because it contains biographical details from Paul's life, it deals with a basic point in Paul's theology, and it moves to ethical injunction. If problems of the chronology of Paul's life did not come up in Theme 5 Part 3, they need not detain you here. The solutions become quite technical. The date of the Jerusalem Council—usually given as A.D. 49—shows how soon after the resurrection Paul was active in the church and how much had transpired before Paul wrote the letters we have.

Galatians moves quickly from the biographical background to the present situation, which leads Paul to his principal point. Right deeds (*the works of the law*), important as they are, are not the basis of acceptance by God. Rather, they are evidence of a relationship that is established (*believing—faith*) prior to deeds. This relationship is possible because Christ has removed the negative hindrance (*sin*). The language Paul uses to describe this has become traditional in the church—and thus often stereotyped. Notice that he uses several ways to describe the process including some reasoning that seems stretched. Abraham appears several times in illustrations.

We mentioned Habakkuk 2:4 in Part 2. The heart of Paul's use of the quotation is the meaning of *faith*. Is it passive, something simply declared? Or is it active, something that requires doing—that is, *faithfulness*? It is pretty clear that Habakkuk implies the second meaning, but in Galatians Paul implies the first. It is not fair to say that Paul is a bad exegete. He is using Scripture he knows well in the light of the new revelation in Jesus Christ. Paul is surely in favor of faithfulness, as the sequel makes plain. But he is concerned to say that believing is prior to faithfulness. Otherwise, Christ becomes, not the Savior, but the example. In Romans 7 he argues that faithfulness is impossible without believing.

Paul's shift from theological reasoning to practical admonition at Galatians 5:13 is important. Doctrine moves easily and surely into action. *The works of the flesh* break commands of the law, and Paul argues that this cycle is self-destructive. *The fruit of the Spirit* means that faith enables us to be righteous, to get the results the law by itself could not produce. So we can work for the good of all (Galatians 6:10)—even as Jesus went about doing good (according to Peter, Acts 10:38).

Romans

Romans presents in rather orderly fashion what Galatians delivers in a heated situation. Both cite Abraham as a paradigm of faith—or faithfulness, for both nuances are present. We may note in passing how Paul uses Old Testament Scripture. In Romans 3 and 4 he uses a number of verses from the Psalms and lines from Isaiah 59:7, 8.

In Romans 6:1, 2 Paul touches on a heresy that church history knows as "antinomianism." I have not introduced the term in the *Resource Book*, but you should be familiar with it. It is the theme precisely in reverse: God's love brings forgiveness to sinners; therefore sinning gives God's love greater opportunity to be manifest. *Continue in sin in order that grace may abound?* Paul responds, *By no means!*—NAB (1988), *Of course not!* Incidentally, Paul uses this emphatic expression fourteen times in the letters.

Chapters 9-11 call for some further remarks. There are lots of Old Testament quotations, as we might expect. The composite from Hosea 2:23 and 1:10 (in Romans 9:25, 26) is particularly instructive. The metaphor of the olive tree in Romans 11:17-24 is helpful. Throughout, Paul emphasizes the people of God.

The critical verse, Romans 11:26, *so all Israel will be saved*, cannot be referred to the New Israel, the church, as the quotation from Isaiah 59:20, 21 and 27:9 makes evident. Paul's argument is not entirely clear to us, but his certainty is. At the least, we must reject the reasoning that runs thus: Only those who accept Jesus as God's deliverer are saved; Jews do not accept Jesus as their deliverer; therefore, Jews are damned. Such spurious logic breaks up on Paul's emphasis upon God's covenant faithfulness. There is *mystery* involved (Romans 11:25); *how inscrutable his ways!* (Romans 11:33). The Jewish people are in a different category from the rest of the world-apart-from-Christ. We are learning to read the Bible for what it teaches when all the relevant texts are read in the context of each other.

The ethical section, Romans 12-16, begins with the impressive summary appeal to righteousness, 12:1, 2. Chapter 16 contains all the personal greetings. Note the reference to *sister Phoebe, a deacon*, and to *Prisca and Aquila*—why the wife first? There are textual grounds for suggesting that the letter was circulated in copies that went to churches other than the one at Rome.

1 Corinthians

This letter is not organized as systematically as is Romans. The doctrinal and practical matters are interspersed. This is probably dictated by the communications that occasioned the letter. Paul attacks at once the besetting sin of the Corinthian church, divisiveness. This appears repeatedly in the letter. It is the background for his discussion of the church as the body of Christ, and 1 Corinthians 13 is the ultimate antidote. Sin is manifested corporately as well as individually. *You* and *your* in 1 Corinthians 3:16 and 6:19 are plural. Disputes among members of the congregation should be settled in the community of the church (1 Corinthians 6:1-8). Our earliest account of the institution of the Lord's Supper is occasioned by a breakdown in community life among the Corinthian *saints* (1 Corinthians 11:17-29). See also 1:2; 6:1, 2.

Modern curiosity about *speaking in tongues* may surface in the group. Paul is concerned about the divisiveness of this practice. He implies that tongues should be kept as an exercise of private devotion. *Those who speak in a tongue build up themselves, but those who prophesy build up the church* (1 Corinthians14:4). Building up the church is crucial for Paul. *Prophecy* seems to be a kind of informal preaching by members of the congregation, and Paul favors it. Tongues are of no benefit unless they are interpreted, and John Calvin commented that when tongues are interpreted, then there is really prophecy.

Paul's discussion of the resurrection, 1 Corinthians 15, is treated in Theme 10, Part 3. Here we may note a possible problem in Paul's line of argument. 1 Corinthians 15:22 reads, *as all die in Adam, so all will be made alive in Christ.* Without the context, here and elsewhere in Paul's letters, this sounds like a declaration of universal salvation (review 1 Corinthians 6:9, 10). The subject can lead you far astray, and you need to be aware of that so that you can get back on track quickly if it comes up.

Two Final Matters

(1) The *Resource Book* introduces the distinctiveness of the pastoral letters. The problem of authorship is best left untouched. The special character of these letters is important. The authorship and consequent dating, however, do not affect this theme, for in any case the letters intend to give Pauline views. Some matters are best left for more intensive studies of particular books or for advanced courses, especially when those matters are complicated.

(2) How is Jesus effective in making people righteous? This has come up before, and I have noted that New Testament writers take many approaches in their efforts to explain it. Theologically, this concerns theories of the atonement. Each approach surely has a piece of the truth, yet each is inadequate to explain the whole truth. The salvation process (as it may be called) may be analyzed into four steps: (a) the human situation, (b) God's action, (c) the result, (d) human response. The New Testament uses perhaps a dozen or more sets of terms to describe the process. For example, (a) slavery, (b) redemption, (c) freedom, (d) responsibility. The terms do not occur in such neat arrangements. The point is that the truth is always greater than any set of terms employed to describe it. Narrow dogma does not see this glorious greatness in the biblical books.

Supplementary Reading

The Apostolic Council is a critical event in the development of the early church. The supplementary books will provide additional insights. *Introducing the New Testament* has a brief section on it. You may also want to explore the guidelines Paul proposes for life in the Christian community. See the material on 1 and 2 Corinthians in *Understanding the New Testament*.

SESSION PLANS

Learning Objectives

This session is intended to enable participants to:

1. Describe the issue debated at the Jerusalem Council in Acts 15 and tell how it was resolved.

2. Summarize Paul's teaching on the Christian's relationship to the Law and Christian liberty.

3. List at least four qualities that Christians are to embody or four practical ways they are to demonstrate righteousness.

Resources You May Need

Chalkboard and chalk
Newsprint and markers
A list of requirements for membership in your congregation
Directions for the two groups studying Acts 15:1-35
Commentary on Galatians
Copies of the song "They Will Know We Are Christians By Our Love"

Leadership Strategy

SETTING THE STAGE

1. Review your Loose Ends list, add new items from this week's preparation, and determine when to discuss these questions.

2. If your church has a statement regarding requirements for church membership, make copies for members of the group. Distribute the statement for them to read and then ask if they think these requirements are appropriate or adequate. What, if any, additional requirements would they suggest? Are there any guidelines for conduct the participants think all Christians should follow? Relate this discussion to the situation in the early church regarding observance of the Law.

or

Read Galatians 5:13, 14, 22, 23 and James 2:14-17. Ask the group what attitudes toward the Law they see reflected in these two passages. Use this discussion to highlight how the issue of the relationship of the early church to its Jewish heritage was critical in the first century.

or

Summarize in a brief presentation the two directions in which the early church developed, with a conservative Jewish-Christian group in Jerusalem and a more ecumenically-minded group centered in Antioch in Syria. The section in the *Resource Book* entitled "Apostolic Witness" provides basic information. You will find additional material in *Understanding the New Testament* and *Introducing the New Testament*.

EXPLORING THE SCRIPTURE

1. Divide the group in two. One half is to represent Paul, Barnabas and the church of Antioch. The other half is to represent the church in Jerusalem. If possible, have the groups work in different rooms.

Distribute copies of these directions:

Reread the section entitled "Enter Paul" on page 168 of the *Resource Book* and Acts 15:1-35. Then discuss and record answers to these questions:

a. What is the issue at the Jerusalem Council?

b. What is your group's position?

c. Why do you feel this position is necessary?

d. What problems might arise if the other group prevails?

e. What possible alternatives are available?

Choose several people to represent your position in a debate.

Reconvene the whole group and stage a debate between the leaders representing the two sides. When the debate has run its course point out the conclusion reached in Acts 15 and have the group evaluate this resolution of the conflict.

or

Stage the same debate using three or four persons selected the previous week to represent each position.

or

Make a presentation summarizing the issue before the Council in Jerusalem. Trace the course of the debate and indicate how the issue was resolved. Have the group discuss how this solution affected the growth of the early church.

2. On page 169 of the *Resource Book* Dr. Walther mentions three factors that need to be kept in balance when studying Paul's teaching. Place these on newsprint or a chalkboard:

   a. He emphasizes freedom from the law.

   b. He demands righteousness as both a gift and a response.

   c. He insists on regulations for Christian living.

Divide the following passages among individuals or small clusters. After reading the texts they are to summarize them for the whole group and indicate to which of the above three factors their Scripture is most closely related.

Acts 13:38-41	Romans 1:1-17
Galatians 3:1-14	Romans 2:12-16
Galatians 3:15-29	Romans 3:21-31
Galatians 5:1-6	Romans 12:1-13
Galatians 5:13-15	

or

Present a summary of Paul's thinking on the role of the Law. The chapter on Paul in *Understanding the New Testament* has sections focusing on Galatians and Romans and will be helpful in developing your remarks. You may want to have several members prepared to join you in the presentation or have each of them prepare a report on one of the sections of the outline you develop.

3. Draw a line down the middle of a sheet of newsprint. Select two scribes from the group. As you read Galatians 5:16-23 one scribe is to list the "works of the flesh" on

the left hand side of the paper, and the other scribe is to list the "fruit of the Spirit" on the right hand side.

Lead the group in a discussion comparing the two lists. (A commentary such as the *Daily Study Bible* by William Barclay will provide helpful background information on the various words.) Ask how Paul intends the virtues he mentions to become part of a person's life. What part does the Law play in this process?

and/or

Divide the group into four sections and assign each section one of these passages: Colossians 3:18-4:1; Ephesians 6:10-17; Philippians 4:8, 9; James 1:22; 2:14-26. The sections are to read the assigned Scripture and list on newsprint the ways Christians are to demonstrate their righteousness. These ways should be mentioned or implied in the passages.

When the sections have finished their work have reporters present their results to the whole group. Discuss how the items listed on the newsprint can be translated into present day directives.

CLOSING

1. Invite persons to reflect on what they have learned about Paul's understanding of Law and righteousness. Then ask them to complete this statement.

    If I were Paul I would tell this congregation. . .

2. Read aloud Galatians 5:16-23.

    As you reread verse 22, ask each participant to select one of the fruits of the Spirit as a focus for meditation. Invite each member to repeat, prayerfully and silently, the following phrase:

    "Dear God, I seek _____"

    After a period of silence, display verse 22 on the board or newsprint and invite the group to read it in unison. Then ask the group to listen as you read verse 25 aloud.

    and/or

    Read 1 Corinthians 13:1-7, 13 and sing "They Will Know We Are Christians by Our Love."

Looking Ahead

Item #1 under Exploring the Scripture in the next session suggests that several persons prepare either a summary of 1 Kings 3:16-28 and 4:29-34 or a dramatic reading of 1 Kings 3:16-28. It also suggests that four persons prepare comments on other selected Old Testament texts. See the activity for details.

Item #3 in the same section suggests that two members of the group debate the propriety of including Ecclesiastes in the canon.

GOD'S PEOPLE
LEARN WISDOM

THEME
8

*Wisdom in the
Jewish Scriptures*

PART
1

NOTES FROM THE AUTHOR

Wisdom Literature

This theme seems like a drastic switch after the last theme. There are several reasons. Wisdom Literature is often studied only to give biblical support to moral instruction. Wisdom Literature, moreover, is concentrated in a few books, and the focus of Bible study is usually elsewhere. Thus when Wisdom passages are encountered in other books of Scripture, they are often not recognized as such.

The first task, then, is to distinguish the genre of Wisdom in Scripture. In Theme 7 ethics is connected with Torah. This connection differentiates Israel from her neighbors. In Theme 8 ethics is also related to God (*The fear of the LORD is the beginning of wisdom*), but the emphasis is on God as creator rather than lawgiver. In Wisdom, Israel shared the common knowledge and instruction of the world she lived in (recall Theme 4) but adapted them to her faith.

From a theological viewpoint this is a distinguishing mark of Wisdom Literature. The transcendence of God, which is vital in the religion of Torah, is modified to connect God more intimately with the creation. Here is where the personification of wisdom comes into the picture, and this poses theological difficulties. One is the perception of wisdom as female. The simplest observation is that the Hebrew word for "wisdom" is feminine. Further ramifications had best be left for advanced study.[1]

The matter of intermediaries with a transcendent God has been considered in other themes (for example, Abraham's angel-visitors, Theme 2, Part 1). God's creating and governing activities viewed from human perspective are easier to grasp in the figure of a kind of super-woman than in abstract terms. When philosophical concepts are associated with wisdom in

---

1 Some commentators see an "envelope" (1:20-33 and the *capable wife*, 31:10-31) encompassing the Book of Proverbs in personified wisdom.

The Wisdom of Solomon, the advantage of the personification is in jeopardy. Such considerations are really beyond the scope of our study here.

Solomon

Solomon's role in wisdom is generally familiar through the stories in 1 Kings. His connection with the outside world, and with Egypt in particular, is part of the picture. Apparently he supplemented political and economic relations with cultural exchange. His princess-wives and the Queen of Sheba are hints of such contacts.

Israel was a geographical buffer between Egypt and the powers to the east, and this clearly carried a cultural impact.[2] The prehistory in Genesis had counterparts in the early literature of Mesopotamia.[3] We have some evidence of the Hebrew background in Egypt. The Joseph cycle focuses there, and Joseph's wisdom is specifically noted.[4] We may assume also that Moses was learned in Egyptian wisdom (see the assertion of Stephen in Acts 7:22).

Non-Biblical Parallels

One aspect of biblical Wisdom Literature is its common elements with other near eastern wisdom. In the public library you may find James B. Pritchard, *The Ancient Near East: An Anthology of Texts and Pictures*, or Jack Finegan, *Light from the Ancient Past*. Here are some examples. With Proverbs 23:10 compare this text from the Egyptian sage Amen-em-opet:

> *Do not carry off the landmark at the boundaries of the arable land,*
> *Nor disturb the position of the measuring-cord;*
> *Be not greedy after a cubit of land,*
> *Nor encroach upon the boundaries of a widow.*

Proverbs 15:16, 17 has similarities to these Egyptian proverbs:

> *Better is poverty in the hand of the god*
> *Than riches in a storehouse;*
> *Better is bread, when the heart is happy,*
> *Than riches with sorrow.*

---

2   Refer to Theme 4, Part 1.

3   Recall Theme 3, Part 1.

4   For example, Genesis 41:8, 33, 39-41.

Wisdom Literature is best discussed by reference to the particular books. They provide concentrations of wisdom thought, so those texts are our primary focus. Once they are studied, we are better equipped to spot and understand wisdom references scattered elsewhere in the Bible. They are also an indispensable foil for studying wisdom in the New Testament.

Proverbs

Proverbs is a major emphasis in this part because it is the most broadly representative collection of wisdom in the Jewish Scriptures. The Hebrew word for "proverb" is *mashal*, which also means "comparison." The simplest form may be represented by Proverbs 25:11, *A word fitly spoken is like apples of gold in a setting of silver*.[5] The entire book is in poetic form, principally couplets. Hebrew poetry is considered in more detail when we study the Psalms in Theme 9, Part 2, but some knowledge of poetic parallelism is indispensable now.

The most common couplets give contrasts, that is, they are in antithetical parallelism. Proverbs 10:1-16:2 is loaded with them. See also Proverbs 29:4.[6] There is also synonymous parallelism, e.g., Proverbs 19:5; 22:1; 29:22. Synthetic parallelism builds from one part to another, e.g., Proverbs 15:16, 17; 20:1; 25:21, 22. A few proverbs occur more than once, e.g., Proverbs 20:16 = 27:13.

The last two chapters present special problems. Not only are the identities of Agur and Lemuel quite uncertain; scholars are not agreed about the makeup of the chapters. They are probably collections. The number-sayings in Chapter 30 provide a sort of unity for the chapter. Proverbs 31:10-31 is an acrostic and so is clearly a separate piece. This literary form is mentioned in connection with Psalm 119 in Theme 7, Part 2. (By way of review: The first word of each verse begins with one of the twenty-two letters of the Hebrew alphabet, in order.)

Ecclesiastes

The date of this book is variously assigned from the fifth to the third century B.C., and its connection with Solomon is fictional. There are many catchy sayings in the book, but it has become best known in recent years from a popular song that uses Ecclesiastes 3:1-8. This repetition of *time*, however, probably indicates that the writer finds existence monotonous. Human life is helplessly routine, and the author sees little beyond its inconsistencies and disappointments (see Ecclesiastes 7:15; 8:14). He tries, then, to avoid extremes, even too much wisdom (Ecclesiastes 7:16, 17). If you are a literary buff, you may compare what he

---

5   See also Proverbs 11:22; 26:11; 27:19.

6   In the *Resource Book* references have been kept to a minimum. The references given here are supplementary for your study. Do not try to use them all.

says about *vanity* with its treatment by Bunyan or by Thackeray. Do not miss the little story in Ecclesiastes 9:13-16.

All books of the Bible are not equally edifying, and perhaps this one provides a good contrast for other books. There is some evidence that the rabbis had misgivings about including *Ecclesiastes* in the canon. The book is valuable as a reminder that the people of the Bible lived a real flesh-and-blood existence and that sometimes they shared the doubts and earthy sentiments of their neighbors.

Job and the Song of Solomon

Openness to troubles and doubt is reflected in Job from a different perspective. Job is dealt with in Theme 3, Part 2, so here the emphasis is on the wisdom aspects of the book. Job 28:12-28 should illustrate adequately the formal relation to wisdom. Job 40:7-41:34 declares the wisdom of Yahweh the creator, and the passage also reflects wisdom's concern with nature.

Reading The Song of Solomon without presupposing a religious interpretation may arouse some uneasiness. Its earthy sentiments may even be shocking. It is important to understand that here the beauty of ideal love and sexuality are presented as blessings of the Creator. It may serve as a much-needed corrective to prudish misapprehensions today regarding how the Bible deals with this subject.

Deuterocanonical Wisdom Books

In Theme 1, Part 2, 1 Maccabees was introduced, not only because of its contribution to the theme at that point, but because it sheds light on the two centuries leading into the Christian era. Here two more deuterocanonical books are discussed because they shed light on the Wisdom movement, particularly in the later years of its development. Sirach and The Wisdom of Solomon help to illustrate the range of the Wisdom movement. Since our focus is on the sixty-six book canon, we do not study the rest of the deuterocanonical books. This admittedly represents a value judgment as to what is useful for *Kerygma: The Bible in Depth*. The books are probably not familiar to your group.

Sirach/Ecclesiasticus contains much material that is very similar to Proverbs. In addition to the passages mentioned in the *Resource Book*, note that according to Sirach 39:1 the wise man devotes himself to the law and the prophets. Chapter 38 provides interesting insights into social life in the second century B.C. This is just before the Maccabean revolt.

The Wisdom of Solomon is much more speculative than the other Wisdom books. Members of the group who have little grounding in philosophy will probably have difficulty understanding this difference. Wisdom 7:21-26 is a challenge, even to a person with some knowledge of philosophical terms and history. This difficulty is also a good illustration of how Alexandrian Jews were influenced by the culture around them.

The personification of wisdom is more important in this work than in Proverbs. "Wisdom" is a feminine noun in both Hebrew and Greek, but much more is involved. Wisdom 8 broadly expands the scope of her influence, and in Wisdom 9:13-18 the intermediary function of wisdom is clear. The relationship with God's *holy spirit* (Wisdom 9:17) is part of the development. Note Wisdom 9:18. People are *set right*, they are *taught what pleases* God, and are *saved by wisdom*. The concept of God's spirit should not be pushed here beyond this summary. You may note for your own thinking that this is a possible background for agnostic thought (which we encounter in Part 2). The relationship with pagan religion and female deities should be avoided here.

Supplementary Reading

Bible dictionaries and *Introducing the Old Testament* have brief introductions to Wisdom Literature and the books included in this part. *Understanding the Old Testament* has a more comprehensive chapter on Wisdom.

SESSION PLANS

Learning Objectives

This session is intended to enable participants to:

1. Describe the major types of Wisdom Literature and list their characteristics.

2. Recall the teaching of Proverbs on at least three important subjects.

3. Summarize the message of Ecclesiastes and compare it with that of other Old Testament Wisdom Literature.

4. Describe in a sentence or two the content of the Song of Solomon, Sirach/Ecclesiasticus, and the Wisdom of Solomon.

Resources You May Need

Chalkboard and chalk
Newsprint and markers
Construction paper signs with wisdom sayings
Copies of the quiz on Wisdom Literature
Scripts for the dramatic reading of 1 Kings 3:16-28
Slips of paper with references from Proverbs
Extra copies of a Bible dictionary
Copies of Job 28:12-28 for a responsive reading

Leadership Strategy

SETTING THE STAGE

1. By now the practice of asking the group for questions generated from the previous session or the reading for this part may have become routine. If so, pose some questions which arose as *you* prepared for this session and invite the group to assist *you* in answering them during or at the close of the session.

2. Prepare a series of construction paper signs bearing wisdom sayings similar to those below and place them around the room:

> A wise child makes a glad father (Proverbs 15:20).
> A stitch in time saves nine.
> Pride goes before destruction (Proverbs 16:18).
> A fool and his money are soon parted.
> For everything there is a season (Ecclesiastes 3:1).
> Pretty is as pretty does.
> The race is not to the swift (Ecclesiastes 9:11).
> A penny saved is a penny earned.

As people assemble invite them to read the wise sayings on display and to recall other "words of wisdom" they have heard. Have them write these on construction paper and hang them on the wall.

After the participants have had an opportunity to read all of the wise sayings, ask them to determine:

a. The culture or cultures to which the sayings pertain.

b. The time periods to which the sayings speak.

c. The purpose of the sayings.

d. The persons to whom they are addressed.

e. The value of the sayings.

On the basis of the above exercise ask the group to compile a list of the characteristics of Wisdom Literature. Record these on newsprint or a chalkboard.

or

Distribute copies of the quiz on Wisdom Literature found at the end of the session plans for this part. Emphasize that the purpose of the quiz is not to test people's memories but to indicate the widespread occurrence of such literature. After everyone has completed the quiz review the answers.

and

Give a brief presentation on the development of Wisdom Literature in the Ancient Near East and the unique flavor of Israel's writings. The material cited in Supplementary Reading at the end of "Notes from the Author" provides helpful information for your presentation.

EXPLORING THE SCRIPTURE

1. Have two persons who prepared ahead of time summarize 1 Kings 3:16-28 and 4:29-34. Then lead the group in comparing the kinds of wisdom Solomon demonstrated with the characteristics of wisdom listed in Setting the Stage.

or

Introduce four persons who previously volunteered to present a dramatic reading of 1 Kings 3:16-28. The parts are narrator, King Solomon, first mother, and second mother. After the reading ask participants to list the qualities Solomon displayed in solving the women's dilemma. Compare this list with the characteristics of wisdom and/or wise persons discussed in Setting the Stage.

and/or

Assign the following passages to four individuals ahead of time. Each person is to summarize the content of the passage and indicate the type and characteristics of the wisdom presented there. Then compare these qualities with the ones mentioned above.

Exodus 7:8-13   2 Samuel 14:1-21

Exodus 31:1-11   Daniel 2

2. Introduce the purpose of the book of Proverbs by reading 1:2-7. Then present an outline of the book on newsprint or a chalkboard. Dr. Walther offers a brief outline in the *Resource Book*. Other outlines can be found in most Bible dictionaries and the *Oxford Annotated Bible*.

Select a few examples of the different kinds of parallelism from the references mentioned by Dr. Walther in "Notes from the Author" and read these to the group. (*Understanding the Old Testament* provides additional examples.) Ask for volunteers to read other passages which are their favorites.

Then invite the group to identify topics taken up in Proverbs that are still important today, such as friendship, love, labor, wealth, etc. List them on a chalkboard or newsprint. Divide into small clusters of two or three. Each cluster is to select a topic from the list and compose one or more proverbs on that topic. When the clusters are finished have them share their work with the whole group.

or

Select half a dozen or more of the references to Proverbs found in the *Resource Book*. Write each one of these on a separate slip of paper. Distribute these to members of the group and have them read the scripture verses aloud. From this sampling select several topics mentioned in Proverbs. List them and proceed with the activity of writing modern proverbs, following the directions in the above paragraph.

3. The Book of Ecclesiastes is indeed unique. Make a brief presentation on its background and major themes. *Understanding the Old Testament, Introducing the Old Testament*, and a Bible dictionary will provide useful information. Then have three persons read Ecclesiastes 3:1-8; 9:3, 5, 11; and 12:13-14 aloud. Lead the group in forming summary statements of these three texts. Record them on newsprint. Then have another person read Job 28:12-28. Compare the message of this text with the material from Ecclesiastes.

or

Harper's Bible Dictionary refers to Ecclesiastes as "one of the most mysterious" books in the Hebrew Bible. Its place in the canon was debated by the Jews, and the New Testament never cites it. Have two persons who have prepared ahead of time present brief opposing arguments on the question of whether the book should be included in the canon. Following the debate, lead the group in evaluating passages such as 3:1-8; 9:3, 5, 11; and 12:13-14 in terms of their value to Christians today.

4. Invite everyone to form into three subgroups, according to their interest in either the *Song of Solomon, Sirach/Ecclesiasticus*, or the *Wisdom of Solomon*. The subgroups are to answer these questions and report their answers to the whole group.

   a. What is the central message of the book?

   b. What style does the writer use (poetry, narrative, personal account, etc.)?

   c. What are two or three passages which have meaning for us today?

Members of the subgroups will find the necessary information by reviewing the introduction to their book in a study Bible and by scanning the book itself. You may also want to provide copies of a Bible dictionary for each subgroup.

or

Using material from a Bible dictionary and other supplementary books, make a brief presentation summarizing the background and content of the *Song of Solomon, Sirach/Ecclesiasticus*, and the *Wisdom of Solomon*. Invite members of the group to point out the ways these books are similar to or different from other Old Testament Wisdom Literature.

CLOSING

1. Invite members of the group to express their feelings about wisdom and the part it plays in their lives. What connections, if any, do they find between wisdom and age?

or

Read Job 28:12-28 as a responsive reading, alternating verses between the leader and the group.

Looking Ahead

Item #3 under Exploring the Scripture in the next session suggests that a member of the group summarize the context, purpose and content of the book of James.

Quiz on Wisdom Sayings

Identify the sources of these quotations using the code below:

J—Job	E—Ecclesiastes	WS—Wisdom of Solomon
PS—Psalms	SS—Song of Solomon	NT—New Testament
PR—Proverbs	SIR—Sirach	AS—Ancient Secular
		M—Modern

_____ 1. "A living dog is better than a dead lion."

_____ 2. "The multitude of the wise is the salvation of the world, and a sensible king is the stability of any people."

_____ 3. "As unto the bow the cord is, So unto the man is woman."

_____ 4. "Better is bread, when the heart is happy, than riches with sorrow."

_____ 5. "Brevity is the soul of wit."

_____ 6. "Does a spring pour forth from the same opening both fresh and brackish water?"

_____ 7. "Do not become a beggar by feasting with borrowed money."

_____ 8. "Do not be so confident of forgiveness that you add sin to sin."

_____ 9. "For everything there is a season, and a time for every matter under heaven."

_____ 10. "Go to the ant, you lazybones; consider its ways, and be wise."

_____ 11. "Has the rain a father, or who has begotten the drop of dew?"

_____ 12. "Love is strong as death, passion fierce as the grave."

_____ 13. "Human beings are born to trouble just as sparks fly upward."

_____ 14. "Fools say in their hearts, 'There is no God.'"

_____ 15. "The high mountains are for the wild goats; the rocks are a refuge for the coneys."

_____ 16. "The souls of the righteous are in the hand of God."

_____ 17. "To the pure all things are pure, but to the corrupt and unbelieving nothing is pure."

_____ 18. "Train children in the right way, and when they are old, they will not stray."

_____ 19. "When a strong man, fully armed, guards his castle, his property is safe."

_____ 20. "He who has never hoped can never despair."

KEY

1. Ecclesiastes 9:4
2. Wisdom of Solomon 6:24
3. Longfellow, "Hiawatha's Wooing"
4. Amen-em-opet (ancient Egyptian)
5. Shakespeare, *Hamlet II*, ii, 90
6. James 3:11
7. Sirach 18:33
8. Sirach 5:5
9. Ecclesiastes 3:1
10. Proverbs 6:6
11. Job 38:28
12. Song of Solomon 8:6
13. Job 5:7
14. Psalm 14:1
15. Psalm 104:8
16. Wisdom of Solomon 3:1
17. Titus 1:15
18. Proverbs 22:6
19. Luke 11:21
20. G.B.Shaw, *Caesar & Cleopatra, IV*

GOD'S PEOPLE LEARN WISDOM

Wisdom in the New Testament

NOTES FROM THE AUTHOR

Jesus as a Wise Man

It is important to understand that Jesus was a wise man, not because we are looking at wisdom now but because it tells us a great deal about his public ministry. You may recall that Jeremiah ranked the wise man with the priest and the prophet. Jesus was not a priest, and since prophecy had been so long in eclipse, people debated whether he could be a prophet. Jesus' reputation as a wise man, therefore, was the first level of public recognition that he achieved.

First century rabbis were teachers, purveyors of wisdom, and the Gospels indicate that Jesus was sometimes called "rabbi." The Gospels refer more than sixty times to various aspects of Jesus' teaching. In Mark 12:28-37 Jesus, who is addressed as *Teacher*, is adept at debate with other Jewish experts, and he gains popular attention. The fact that so much of his home-spun wisdom was remembered in the early traditions of his followers suggests that this was a particularly attractive feature of his ministry.

The Parables

Many of Jesus' parables are akin to Wisdom teaching. Consider, for example, the rapid fire of Matthew 13:44-53. (It does not matter if the arrangement is the Evangelist's.) Jesus also uses figures of speech that are like those in Wisdom books; e.g., see Luke 8:16 (*a lamp . . . under a jar, or. . . under a bed*); Luke 13:34 (*a hen gathers her brood under her wings*). In Luke 16:1-8 he tells a story about a dishonest steward and concludes, *the people of this world are much more shrewd in handling their affairs than the people who belong to the light* (TEV). This wisdom of the nonbelieving world, however, is finally the absolute antithesis of what God reveals—*hidden from the wise and . . . revealed . . . to infants* (Matthew 11:25).

The Prologue of John

This is a weighty theological passage. Some interpreters deal with it in philosophical terms because of the word *logos* and possible connections with the writing of Philo, but I think you will find it better to work from Old Testament sources. The passage begins with the first two words of the Greek Old Testament, *in beginning*,[1] and *the Word* is almost immediately associated with creation—*all things came into being through [the Word]*. The emphasis on *light* is also a tie with creation, and it is a recurring theme in Job (about two dozen times). Notice, too, the emphasis upon *truth*.

The *Resource Book* discussion about the difference between the personification of wisdom and the uncreated Word in John is difficult. Proverbs 8:22 says flatly, *The LORD created me at the beginning of his work*. This is fundamentally different from John's presentation of *the Word*. The incarnation—*the Word became flesh*—does not dilute the oneness of God. After twenty-five sessions with your group, you should be ready to wrestle with this piece of wisdom if it proves to be troublesome. It should be interesting to compare your discussion now with what you were able to manage in Theme 3, Part 3. Other passages that you may find useful are Psalm 33:6-9 and Sirach 1:4, 9, 10.

James

The Book of James differs from every other book of the New Testament. It is the closest to true Wisdom Literature. This focus is set at James 1:5. Like the Wisdom writers, James believes that true wisdom is from God. He stresses practical ethics repeatedly, and he illuminates his text with everyday similes and metaphors (see James 1:22-25). Emphasis on the poor (James 2:5, 6) is akin to both Jesus and Paul. James 4:15 is the source of the expression, "God willing"—*deo volente* (D.V.)—that some folks often use. Notice also Research 4.

The *Resource Book* mentions James' affinity with the diatribe, a literary form in the contemporary pagan culture. This is appropriate in the study of a book that is like Old Testament wisdom, which owed something to other cultures. Epictetus lived a generation or so after Paul. Here are examples of his practical philosophy:

> *If then you wish not to be of an angry temper, do not feed the habit:*
> > *throw nothing on it that will increase it:*
> > *at first keep quiet, and count the days on which you have not been angry.*

---

1 There is no definite article (nor is there in the Hebrew). Neither Genesis nor John means <u>the</u> beginning, for God has no beginning. This is <u>a</u> beginning, when God created this world and communicated with it—*and God said = the Word*.

Remember that you are an actor in a play . . .
This is your duty, to act well the part that is given to you;
but to select the part belongs to another.

Paul and Wisdom

On the whole Paul is skeptical of the value of wisdom, but he uses the term flexibly. He is more interested in conveying ideas than in establishing definitions. His references to wisdom may seldom be identified with Old Testament wisdom. This is evident in the Basic References from 1 Corinthians.

In 1 Corinthians 1:18-25 Paul is concerned to show that God's saving action by the Messiah does not meet the expectations of human wisdom. Reason rejects the thought that God would overcome the deathbound tragedy of humankind by allowing the Messiah to be crucified. Paul declares (1 Corinthians 1:19) that Isaiah 29:14 anticipated the frustration of wisdom, and in a striking reversal he calls Christ *the wisdom of God* (1 Corinthians 1:24). Paul is concerned with wisdom, but he wants to be clear that it must be redefined in the light of what God has revealed in Christ.

In 1 Corinthians 2:1-5 Paul insists that his ministry in Corinth had not been *with skillful words of human wisdom* (TEV). Some have interpreted this as a reaction to Paul's recent experience in Athens, where he made a preaching excursion into secular culture. That speech/sermon, however, was hardly a failure (see Acts 17:34), so here we may say that he is ordering priorities. His decision to keep it simple was appropriate for the Corinthians, whose cultural level was not that of the Athenians.

In the rest of 1 Corinthians 2, Paul takes another tack and proposes that he is, after all, speaking a kind of wisdom. Although he calls it *secret and hidden* (1 Corinthians 2:7), it is a kind of open mystery, revealed by God's Spirit (1 Corinthians 2:10). This near-identification of wisdom and the Spirit we have already seen (for example, in The Wisdom of Solomon). Paul finally says that those who have received God's wisdom through God's Spirit *have the mind of Christ* (1 Corinthians 2:16), thus completing a total identification of God with the special wisdom God reveals. After pursuing other ideas Paul returns in 1 Corinthians 3:18-23 to the wisdom theme and summarizes. A good commentary will help you work your way through these passages.[2]

Other references to wisdom in Pauline writings are scattered, but there is support for the ideas surveyed here in 1 Corinthians. In addition to the passages listed in the *Resource Book*, you may study Romans 1:22, 23; Ephesians 1:9, 10, 17, 18; 3:8-10; Colossians 1:9, 10; 2:8.

---

2   Of course I recommend W. F. Orr and J. A. Walther, the *Anchor Bible. First Corinthians* (New York: Doubleday, 1976).

1 John, Revelation, Etc.

The introduction of proto-gnostic thought may seem to you to be off the mark. It was, however, developing in the first century, and so much has been written about it since the discovery of the Nag Hamadi documents, that it seems good to mention it here. The complications of gnostic thought dictate that we not go into any detail. It is enough to know that (a) it rejected orthodox views of the incarnation (see 1 John 4:2, 3a); (b) it taught that one could avoid sin (1 John 1:8); (c) it rejected the apostolic church (1 John 2:19); (d) it did not promote the Christian ethic of love (1 John 3:18, 23); and (e) it rejected the commandments of God (1 John 2:3;5:2).

The use of *wisdom* in Revelation 13:18 and 17:9 may seem strange in the context of this study, but it is not unusual in apocalyptic. You will be well advised not to get into a discussion of this matter until Theme 10, where it is considered in some detail. Since these wisdom puzzles are mentioned, however, they may come up, and you should be prepared to say something introductory about them in order to avoid an appearance of copping out or in order to sustain interest in either wisdom or Revelation or both.

Revelation 17:9, the allusion to *seven hills, on which the woman sits* (TEV) is a clear reference to Rome. You may refer to this as an example of how the author uses symbolic language with *wisdom*. We can be sure the original readers of *Revelation* understood the reference, and in this case we do, too. Do not go further in the passage, for there the problems become nearly insoluble.

Revelation 13:18, *the number of the beast*, probably also could be identified by the first addressees, but here we are somewhat in the dark. Even if the puzzle was ambiguous then, the message was clear that God "had the number of" the wicked figure. The identification was to be made by using letters of the alphabet corresponding to numbers, but whether Greek or Hebrew letters are intended is uncertain. This number-coding was called "gematria." I strongly recommend that you leave the matter at this point until we deal with it in Theme 10.

You may feel that we have been somewhat afield in this theme. Wisdom in New Testament times is a diverse subject. We have studied a significant number of biblical books because it is better to consider them in a group than to nibble at them piecemeal. Our intention is to find their place in the sweep of Scripture. These books and parts of books give us a handle on how to relate biblical truth to truth as it may be found outside Holy Scripture. In a sense this expands the theme GOD'S PEOPLE LIVE IN THE WORLD.

Supplementary Reading

Material on Wisdom in the New Testament may be more difficult to locate than information on Wisdom in the Old Testament. *Understanding the New Testament* has a section on Christ as the Wisdom of God. You may also want to review Jesus' use of metaphor. Introductory material in your study Bible on the Book of James will be helpful, as will the *Anchor Bible* commentaries on John and 1 Corinthians.

SESSION PLANS

Learning Objectives

This session is intended to enable participants to:

1. Recall at least two sayings of Jesus where he uses "folk wisdom" and two that illustrate a more formal kind of wisdom.

2. Describe how John 1:1-18 is linked with the Wisdom tradition of the Old Testament and Apocrypha.

3. Summarize Paul's attitude toward human wisdom and God's wisdom in 1 Corinthians.

4. State at least three of James' teachings for the church.

Resources You May Need

Chalkboard and chalk

Newsprint and markers

Pictures linking Jesus and wisdom

Copy of the *Revised English Bible*

Copies of a hymn for closing

Leadership Strategy

SETTING THE STAGE

1. Review progress you made on the Loose Ends list at the last session. Add any new questions from the group and decide when to take them up. You may also want to ask for volunteers to follow up some of the questions in preparation for the next session.

2. Ask participants to indicate what they consider to be Jesus' wisest saying and to identify reasons for their choices. Record them on newsprint.

or

Display a selection of pictures from your church school files that link Jesus with wisdom. A partial list might include:

• The wise men following the star to Bethlehem.

• Joseph being warned in a dream to flee to Egypt.

• Jesus with the teachers in the Temple at age twelve.

• Jesus teaching during his ministry.

Point out to the group that the first level of public recognition of Jesus in his own day was as a wise man or teacher. Ask participants to what extent the public still thinks of Jesus in this way. Invite them to specify the role or title they most readily associate with Jesus.

EXPLORING THE SCRIPTURE

1. To continue the discussion about Jesus as a wise man list the passages below on a chalkboard or newsprint. Depending on the size of your group, assign the passages to individuals or small clusters:

Matthew 16:1-3	Matthew 11:16-19
Luke 12:54-56	Luke 7:31-35
Mark 3:24, 25	Matthew 11:28-30
Mark 7:15	Mark 7:24-30
Mark 13:28, 29	Mark 12:13-17
	Luke 11:45-52

Each person or cluster is to read the assigned passage and write a paraphrase of it. The paraphrases are then to be shared with the group. Point out that the references in the left hand column are examples of Jesus using "folk wisdom." The references in the second column illustrate a more formal category of wisdom.

or

Divide the group in half and assign each half one of the above columns of references. The two sections should parcel out the Scripture passages among their members. The assignment is to read the passage and to think of an Old Testament passage or book that is similar in style or content. It may not be possible to find parallels for each reference, but the general categories of folk and formal wisdom will be helpful. When the two groups have finished, come together and share results. Conclude the discussion by recalling Jesus' words in Matthew 12:42/Luke 11:31.

and

Although John 1:1-18 was a Basic Bible Reference in Theme 3, Part 3, it will be worthwhile to make a brief presentation summarizing the relationship of this passage to the Wisdom Literature of the Old Testament and Apocrypha. The section on "wisdom" in *Understanding the New Testament* will be helpful. In his *Anchor Bible* commentary on John, Raymond Brown presents a detailed analysis of John's portrait of Jesus as the culmination of the wisdom tradition.

or

Read John 1:1-18 to the group. Then select three persons to read Proverbs 8:22-31; Psalm 33:6-9; Sirach/Ecclesiasticus 1:4, 9, 10. As these references are read ask members of the group to note the parallels with John's Prologue. List these similarities on newsprint. Indicate that John adds this link with wisdom to the portrait in the Synoptic Gospels of Jesus as the fulfillment of the law and the prophets.

2. In his letters Paul speaks of "wisdom" in several different senses. Divide the group into thirds and assign these references:

     Group 1 - 1 Corinthians 1:17-25
     Group 2 - 1 Corinthians 1:26-31
     Group 3 - 1 Corinthians 2:6-13

Each person is to read the Scripture assigned to his or her small group and to summarize Paul's attitude toward wisdom as it is indicated there. Then persons in each small group are to meet together to compare and refine their individual summaries.

Finally, have the small groups share their findings with the whole group. You may need to remind people that Paul is speaking of more than one kind of wisdom.

or

Place the above Scripture references on three separate sheets of newsprint. Under the references write "Paul and Wisdom." Hang the sheets in front of the group. Ask each person to read one of the references and think of a descriptive phrase that summarizes Paul's attitude toward wisdom. Then poll the group members who have read the various texts and record their phrases on the newsprint. Note that Paul's varying attitude indicates he is speaking of different kinds of wisdom.

or

Make a presentation on Paul's understanding of wisdom, using Dr. Walther's comments in "Notes from the Author."

3. Have a member of the group who prepared beforehand summarize the context, purpose and content of James, using a Bible dictionary, *Understanding the New Testament*, or *Introducing the New Testament*.

Then invite participants to read their favorite verses from James which are related to wisdom or wise sayings. As these are read ask what kind of wisdom is implied in the passage and how it compares with other wisdom from the Old and New Testaments.

or

Divide into four groups and assign each group one of the following passages:

James 1:5-8	James 1:22-25
James 1:9-11	James 3:13-18

After they have read their texts the groups are to rephrase them as if James were writing his message to their present congregation. When the group reconvenes have the small groups share their new paragraphs.

CLOSING

1. Each culture produces its own folk wisdom. Brainstorm with the group proverbs and platitudes that are popular today as guidelines for success in such areas as friendship, love, business, and religion. Record them on newsprint. Then compare them with teachings of Jesus, Paul, and James discussed above. What are the similarities and differences between modern secular wisdom and wisdom in the New Testament?

2. Read aloud John 1:1-18 in the *Revised English Bible*.

or

Recite or sing a hymn such as "O Word of God Incarnate," "Break Thou the Bread of Life," or "Be Thou My Vision."

Looking Ahead

Item #2 under Exploring the Scripture in the next session suggests that six persons give brief reports about various items related to Hebrew worship. See the activity for details.

Item #3 of the same section suggests that you arrange for a rabbi or Jewish lay person to speak to your group about Jewish festivals or visit a synagogue. You may also want to organize a celebration of one of the Jewish festivals mentioned in the Bible.

GOD'S PEOPLE WORSHIP

Early Backgrounds and National Rites

NOTES FROM THE AUTHOR

Early Worship Practices

It is very difficult to determine how far post-exodus worship was influenced by traditions from the prehistory and patriarchal times. At least it is clear that offerings were made to Yahweh, usually on altars, which were often erected for a particular occasion. The sacrifice of Isaac and Jacob's experience at Bethel are classic examples. Altars may be connected to the memorial stones that were erected from time to time (see Deuteronomy 27:1-8). An altar and sacrifices became fixed elements of Tabernacle and Temple practice.

The Ark dramatized the presence of Yahweh. (Recall that in Theme 3, Part 1, we asked the question, "Can God be located?") Before the centralization in Jerusalem, special areas for worship were designated. Although Yahweh was not restricted to such sacred places, the tendency to localize the deity was almost irresistible. It must have been difficult for the Israelites to worship a God who was everywhere in general. Related to this was the idea of taboos, well known in most religions. So Yahweh tells Moses from the burning bush, *Come no closer! Remove the sandals from your feet, for the place on which you are standing is holy ground* (Exodus 3:5). And Uzzah died because he touched the Ark (2 Samuel 6:6, 7).

Solomon's Temple had a *molten sea*, a huge reservoir said to hold twelve thousand gallons of water *for the priests to wash in* (1 Kings 7:23-26; compare 2 Chronicles 4:2-6). Cleansing was important in connection with worship. Torah says much about cleanness and uncleanness, and references can be multiplied throughout the Old Testament. Such symbolism of Temple worship continued in Judaism and on into Christianity.

Israel's neighbors had altars, but their sacrifices are regularly denounced in the Old Testament. The contest between Elijah and the priests of Baal is an example; note the antics of the priests of Baal and Elijah's taunts, 1 Kings 18:26-29. Many reference books have pictures of a Canaanite altar uncovered at Megiddo. Egyptian temples had small lakes adjacent for cleansing rituals.

Cultic leaders appear early in Israel's history. The texts show the assignment of times of service for priests and Levites in the wilderness period. The priests did not always act in acceptable ways. Long before the troubles of the sons of Eli, Aaron's sons Nadab and Abihu *offered unholy fire before the LORD* and died for their act (Leviticus 10:1, 2). Cultic practice was subject to abuse and corruption. The prophets do not hesitate to condemn public worship (in addition to the references in the *Resource Book* see Isaiah 43:22-24; Ezekiel 22:26; and Micah 6:6, 7).

The Temple

The effects of centralizing worship in the Jerusalem Temple were far-reaching. The early effect upon the Northern Kingdom may be seen in 1 Kings 12:26-33. The Temple provided a base for combating false worship, but it tended to stereotype true worship.

Consider what was essential and peculiar to Israel's worship. Certainly we should include monotheism, a sense of election, and belief in a divinely appointed destiny. Such things as sacrifice, music, and ablutions are common to other Middle Eastern religions. We learn a little from the somewhat superficial reforms of Joash and Hezekiah. Josiah's reform had more theological impact. The prophets speak about social and national reform, and this sometimes involves cult reform, too.

The Temple provides a bridge from the Old to the New Testament. The steps are: natural places of worship; the Tabernacle; local shrines; Solomon's Temple; the second Temple of Ezra, Nehemiah, and Haggai; and Herod's Temple. At each step the nature of worship was affected by the place(s) where it occurred. The detailed structure of the Temple may prove interesting, but it does not greatly affect our knowledge of Israelite worship.

Elements of Worship

What went on in the Hebrew Temple? The worship there would seem strange to us even though we might grasp some of the symbolism. The ritual slaughter of animals would be offensive to most of us, and the burnt offerings must have produced strong smells. Prophetic utterances were the nearest thing to sermons, but they did not occur regularly. There were prayer-psalms, but the accompaniment was quite unlike our church music. Amos refers to *noise* (Amos 5:23), and perhaps that is just what we would call it. See also 1 Chronicles 15:28. We consider the Psalms further in Part 2. Compare also the description of Babylonian music in Daniel 3:4-7.

Isaiah's experience in 6:1-13 bears repeated study. It occurs in the Temple. There is praise in response to the vision of God's glory. There is confession, both personal and corporate, and assurance of pardon. There is proclamation with a call to service and a response of the worshiper. Finally, there is a message with a promise to God's people.

The Jewish Festivals

The material given in the *Resource Book* is quite elementary. It may be supplemented from a Bible dictionary. Sabbath and Passover are the best known of the festivals. If you can secure a modern Jewish calendar, you can easily relate the annual cycle to our civil year.

It is important to distinguish the varieties of festivals. Sabbath and new moon occur most often. The weekly day of rest is written into the Decalogue. Sabbatical years and the jubilee are based on the seven-unit principle (see Leviticus 25). If you can consult the *Mishnah*, you may quickly see how Sabbath regulations proliferated in later times.[1] Jesus' disputes with religious authorities demonstrate how the day could be turned from a delight into a burden. The relation of the Sabbath to the Christian Lord's Day is considered in Part 3.

New moon is important because it marks the rotation of the months. Lunar years, of course, are not easy to relate to solar calendars. The people of Qumran used a solar calendar, and their festivals did not coincide with the Jerusalem cycle. Amos complains bitterly about people who are impatient for new moon and sabbath to pass so they can take up business as usual. See Amos 5:4-6. Isaiah has a similar problem; see Isaiah 1:12-17.

Trumpets/New Year/Rosh Hashannah presents one difficult detail. The cycle of the months was counted from Nisan. This is in the spring (March-April) when new life comes to the earth. Exodus 12:1, 2 connects this with the original Passover (see also Numbers 28:16). In Numbers 29:1, 2 a special blowing of the trumpets is ordered for the seventh month (Tishri = September-October), and this observance became the new year festival after the exile. This is harvest time, and the Day of Atonement suggests a new beginning.

Booths, Passover, and Weeks were the pilgrimage festivals. It was impossible for all to go to Jerusalem, but there were minimum expectations, perhaps one festival a year. The population of Jerusalem may have quadrupled during some of the festivals. Modern Jews often say at Passover, "Next year in Jerusalem!"[2]

The Day of Atonement is associated with the new year and Booths, and it is not really a festival. Its meaning is at the heart of Jewish faith. The observance includes a one-day fast. It is rigorously observed by Jews today.

---

1 In Danby's edition (London: Oxford University Press, 1933) see pages 100-121, especially § 7.2, page 106.

2 One of the five requirements of Islam is *hajj*, that is, to make a pilgrimage to Mecca once during one's lifetime.

Purim developed late in the Old Testament period. Perhaps the festal celebration influenced the acceptance of the Book of Esther into the canon. The joy and excitement of the original occasion carried over into later times. It is a time for Jews to let off steam.

Hanukkah and 1 Maccabees present a different situation: The festival was accepted, but the book was not. The background is studied in Theme 1, Part 2. The observance is closely associated with religious freedom and so has had intense emotional significance for Jews through the centuries. An early rabbi described how it differs from Purim: "On Purim we were saved from the attempt to destroy the body of the Jew, but on Hanukkah we were rescued from the decree that would have destroyed our soul."

You may want to make a list of New Testament references to the festivals in case such connections arise, but it is best to hold this until Part 3. The references are of two kinds: those that mark certain occurrences (details of Jesus' movements and occasionally those of Paul), and those that make a religious association.[3] Several events in Jesus' career turn on his understanding of how the Sabbath may be kept (note especially Matthew 12:9-14; Mark 2:23-28; John 9:1-16). Paul's words in 1 Corinthians 5:7 are important. See also Hebrews 11:28.

Modern Contact with Judaism

In connection with this theme I have found it particularly helpful to make some direct contact with a Jewish congregation. If it is feasible, arrange for your group to visit a synagogue. Reform and most Conservative congregations will welcome you. If possible, attend a Sabbath service. Of course this will be in addition to the regular group session, but it is a valuable supplement to those plans. In any case, you may arrange to make such a visit yourself.

If such a visit is impractical, you will find it helpful to talk informally about Jewish festivals with a rabbi or other knowledgeable Jew. You will learn how deeply these observances have contributed to the continuity of Jewish faith. You will also observe how Christian worship practices have developed from the same ancient sources that produced modern Judaism. The better we come to know others, the better we shall know ourselves.

One response you may expect from such an exchange is, "Now just what is it that we believe that is different from Judaism at such and such a point?" Practicing Jews usually understand their faith well. They have been uniquely successful in maintaining their religious identity in the midst of indifferent or unsympathetic communities. We can learn from that.

---

3 The attempt to chart the public ministry of Jesus by reference to his festival trips is complicated. The Synoptics mention only one Passover; John makes more references to festivals.

Jesus was a Jew, and this fact is part of Christian tradition. Many Christians hold to a latent Marcionism. Marcion, about the middle of the second century, tried to eliminate everything Jewish from his Bible, a position soon declared heretical. It is nearly impossible to understand Jesus if one ignores his background. There is a danger in divorcing the revelation in Jesus Christ from real history. If Jesus is made into a nonhistorical example, he then is subject to almost any contemporary interpretation. In other words, we make him in our own image.

Supplementary Reading

You will find a great deal of information about the Ark, Tabernacle, Temple, sacrifice, worship and festivals in your Bible dictionary and the *Lion Encyclopedia of the Bible*. *Introducing the Old Testament* also has a chapter on worship.

SESSION PLANS

Learning Objectives

This session is intended to enable participants to:

1. Cite at least three examples of worship practices in the Old Testament.

2. Describe several similarities and differences between worship in the Temple and worship in their present congregation.

3. Formulate working definitions of:

Priests/Levites	The sacrificial system
Tabernacle	The Temple
The Ark of the Covenant	The synagogue

4. List at least five of the Jewish festivals and briefly describe the background and meaning of each.

Resources You May Need

Chalkboard and chalk
Newsprint and markers
Directions for groups working on passages about worship
Bulletins from a recent church service

Opaque projector and pictures of the Temple's design and furnishings

Pictures or slides of altars, worship centers and churches

Bible dictionaries or encyclopedias for groups researching Jewish holidays

A rabbi or Jewish lay person

Your Neighbor Celebrates

Copies of Psalm 137:1-7

Copies of Scavenger Hunt in the Psalms

Leadership Strategy

SETTING THE STAGE

1. If members of the group agreed to do research on questions from the Loose Ends list at the last meeting, decide where to include their reports in the session plans. Ask for other questions arising out of the preparation for this session and determine when to take them up.

2. Invite participants to recall their most meaningful experiences in worship. After several people have volunteered examples, lead the group in reflecting on what made the experiences memorable. (Some typical factors are the physical environment, the music, the spoken word, the people present, the individual's situation or attitude.) List the responses on newsprint.

or

Ask several people to tell what part of the Sunday worship service they find most meaningful. List these on newsprint or a chalkboard. Then lead the group in discussing the reasons for their choices.

EXPLORING THE SCRIPTURE

1. Divide the group into six small groups and assign one of these passages to each group.

Genesis 22:1-14	1 Kings 8:1-13
Genesis 28:10-22	1 Kings 8:22-30
2 Samuel 6:1-19	Ezra 3:1-13

Provide the groups with these instructions, newsprint and markers:

a. Read your text and summarize it.

b. Select two or three phrases to describe the attitudes and actions of the participants in the story.

c. Discuss how important these attitudes and actions were in Hebrew worship, and whether they have any carry-over to worship today.

d. Prepare a report of your findings. You may want to use the newsprint for your report and include pictures as well as words to convey your message.

When the small groups have completed their work, convene the whole group and receive the reports.

or

List the above six Scripture references on a chalkboard or newsprint. Ask everyone to select one reference, read it, and answer these questions:

a. Who is present?

b. Why are they there?

c. What attitudes are displayed by the major participants in the story?

d. What two descriptive phrases would you select to characterize these participants?

e. What aspects of your congregation's worship might be related to the passage?

f. In what way can you identify with this worship experience?

After the work is completed lead the group in discussing the responses to the questions for each passage.

and

Even if the group reviewed Isaiah 6 in Theme 3, Part 3, you may want to examine verses 1-13 again. Read the text aloud. Explain that the passage has often been used as a basis for designing orders of worship. List the following elements of worship on newsprint:

Call to worship
Praise and Adoration
Confession of Sin
Assurance of Pardon
Call to Service
Response
Message

Ask the group to identify the verses in Isaiah 6 which contain these elements and write the biblical references opposite the elements. Distribute copies of a recent bulletin from your church and compare the order of worship with the one from Isaiah. What parts of Isaiah's order have been left out? What features have been added in your worship?

2. Introduce the six persons who agreed to prepare brief reports (two to three minutes) about the following, using the *Resource Book*, the *Lion Encyclopedia of the Bible*, or a Bible dictionary:

   a. Priests and Levites

   b. The Tabernacle

   c. The Ark of the Covenant

   d. The sacrificial system

   e. The Temple (Some comparison of the size of the three temples is probably worth noting.)

   f. The synagogue

or

Make a presentation describing the layout, furnishings, and worship of the Temple. Use an opaque projector and pictures from the supplementary books or your church school picture file. Attempt to capture some of the sights, sounds, and odors that worshippers would experience. Compare these with the sensory perceptions of worshippers in your sanctuary.

and/or

Display around the room pictures of altars, worship centers, shrines, and churches, or make a slide presentation of the same. Then ask members of the group to describe places where they have been particularly aware of the presence of God. Explore the question of "holy ground," using questions such as these:

   a. If God's presence can be with us everywhere, why have there been special places people go to be with God?

   b. What is it that makes certain places holy?

   c. How important is the church building in your experience of worship?

3. Divide members of the group into nine clusters and assign one of the festivals listed below to each cluster. The clusters are to present reports indicating the basis in Scripture, religious significance, and customs of each festival. Brief material is provided in the *Resource Book*. You may want to have a Bible dictionary for each cluster. The *Lion Encyclopedia of the Bible* has a helpful calendar.

Sabbath	Succoth
New Moon	Hanukkah
Rosh Hashannah	Purim
Yom Kippur	Passover
Festival of Weeks	

or

Invite a rabbi or Jewish lay person to talk to your group about Jewish religious festivals and traditions.

and/or

Dr. Walther suggests you take the group to visit a synagogue or temple for a Sabbath service or festival. This experience has proved to be extremely valuable to other groups, and it is certainly worth the additional time and effort required.

or

Plan for the group to organize a celebration of one of the Jewish festivals for the whole church to participate in. The Anti-Defamation League of B'nai B'rith publishes an excellent booklet, *Your Neighbor Celebrates*. It explains all of the celebrations mentioned in the *Resource Book* and the Bar and Bas Mitzvah.

CLOSING

1. Read Psalm 137:1-6 in unison and comment briefly on the longing of the exiles for their beloved city and Temple. Encourage the group to cultivate this attitude toward corporate worship.

and/or

Invite members of the group to write sentence prayers of praise, thanksgiving, and petition and place them in a basket. Pass the basket so several persons have an anonymous prayer to read aloud during the closing time of group prayer.

Looking Ahead

Encourage members of the group to be prepared to share their favorite psalm next week. Distribute copies of the Scavenger Hunt on the following page, which can be completed before the next session.

Item #2 under Exploring the Scripture in the next session suggests that members of the group present information on the use of simile, metaphor, and parallelism in the Psalms.

Item #4 under Exploring the Scripture in the session plans for Part 3 of this theme suggests that you re-create a worship service from the early church. This will take extra planning time. See the description of the activity for details.

Scavenger Hunt in the Psalms

Using the psalms in the Basic Bible References list for Part 2, locate at least one which can be described as having a mood of:

Elation/unbounded joy   _____

Sorrow/grief   _____

Bewilderment/confusion   _____

Confidence/sureness   _____

Adoration/praise   _____

Thanksgiving/gratitude   _____

Confession/repentance   _____

Supplication/entreaty   _____

Select a psalm from the list that might have been used in:

Temple worship   _____

Synagogue worship   _____

Family worship   _____

NOTES FROM THE AUTHOR

Introduction

No one can be biblically literate unless broadly acquainted with the Psalms. They appear rather frequently in other themes because they touch the experience of God's people at so many points. Some attention to other poetry in the Old Testament provides background and breadth to our study of the Psalms, but the Psalter is a unique part of the Bible. It is appropriate that we spend almost all of this part on this one book.

Modern versions print biblical poetry in verses and stanzas, so it is easy to spot. It is important to identify poetry because this literary form should be interpreted by principles that differ from those applied to prose.

The balance of material in this part differs from that in most other parts. Twenty-four Basic References are more than usual, but the *Resource Book* material is shorter. I hope this means more time given to studying the texts. I recommend that you make a chart for your own use, and list the opening line(s) and any other striking phrases or lines in each of the twenty-four psalms. You will quickly see that we have included ones that are most often quoted.

Development of the Psalter

Psalm 72:20 says, *The prayers of David son of Jesse are ended* (at the end of a psalm ascribed *Of Solomon!*). Some scholars see this as one indication of how the whole book developed. First, there were early collections attributed to David. Then psalms of Asaph and the sons of Asaph (1 Chronicles 25:1 and the ascriptions of Psalms 73ff.) and the Korahites (ascriptions of Psalms 84ff.) were added, and other groups were included still later. Certain persons probably became cantors or choirmasters (see the ascriptions of 4, 42, 88, 89).[1]

It is beyond the scope of this study to argue about the dating of the Psalms. If some folks have a problem about separating David from the entire book, the clearly stated setting of Psalm 137 and the ascriptions to Asaph and the Korahites should take care of that. The ascription of Psalm 51 to an event in David's life must be offset by verses 18 and19, which point to a time in the exile. There seem to be three options: (1) The ascription is wrong. (2) Part of the psalm is from an old tradition. (3) The ascription means "what David must have felt when . . ." In Psalm 76:1, 2 the mention of *Judah, Israel*, and *Zion* seems to place it before the division of the monarchy. See also Psalm 68:24-27, where mention of northern tribes may imply the same thing.

Literary Forms and Devices

For your own study, here are additional examples of the kinds of parallelism in Psalms.

> Synonymous: Psalms 2:4; 22:19, 27, 28, 30; 100:2; 139:7.
>
> Synthetic: Psalms 19:7-9; 51:15; 91:5, 6; 100:5; 103:2-5.
>
> Antithetic: Psalms 84:10; 91:7; 139:9, 10.
>
> Climactic: Psalms 8:5, 6; 22:9, 10; 24:7-10.
>
> Combination: Psalm 139:11, 12 (synthetic, antithetic, climactic).

If you have access to a Hebrew Bible, you can demonstrate the acrostic form of Psalm 119. It is not necessary to read Hebrew to see the recurrence of the initial letters. This visual *tour de force* helps one understand the great length of the psalm and emphasizes its theme.

The profusion of figures of speech is important. Rich imagery is a characteristic of most poetry. You will readily find examples of repetition, comparison, and contrast as well as simile and metaphor. There are abrupt changes of structure as well as of the thrust of the sense; Psalms 22 and 137 are examples. Note that attention to all of Psalm 22 offers a commentary on the first verse.

Most of the picture language is drawn from everyday life—a practice common to the prophets (and to Jesus); Psalm 23 is an obvious example. Questions are used effectively (see Psalms 8:3, 4; 90:13; 137:4; 139:7).

---

1 The whole matter of ascriptions becomes very difficult with Psalm 90, *A Prayer of Moses, the man of God*. Perhaps this means "in the spirit of." Moses is mentioned with Aaron in Psalms 99:6, 105:26, and 106:16. See also Psalms 103:7 and 106:23, 32.

Note Research 3 regarding *Selah*. You should, of course, check this out for yourself. Be assured, however, that there is no final certainty about its meaning. It occurs outside the Psalms only in Habakkuk 3:3, 9, 13 in a poetic prayer. It makes sufficient sense to consider *Selah* a rubric to introduce some additional element of liturgy.

Use of the Psalms

Many of the twenty-four psalms emphasized here are commonly used in Christian liturgy. This is in itself a sufficient argument for their importance today. Several—Psalms 2, 22, 110—are significant because of their use in the New Testament.

Many psalms have clues as to their original use. The title of this part indicates one of the great divisions, that between public and personal worship. Personal usage, of course, was always set in the context of the people of God. Psalms composed for state occasions, such as the royal psalms and the celebration of victory, are easy to identify. On the other hand, try to analyze the setting of Psalm 116. It is intensely personal, yet it is set *in the presence of all [the* LORD's*] people*. It might have been sung at Jesus' Last Supper.

Why are so many psalms quoted in the New Testament? Part of the answer lies in the devotional life reflected in the Psalter. This can give us a glimpse of how Jesus and his contemporaries worshiped. We pick this up in the next part. Luke 24:44 mentions *the law of Moses, the prophets, and the psalms*, an indication that the Psalter was the most important book of the Writings in Jesus' day.

Addenda

Here is a hymn from the collection at Qumran:

> I give thanks to you, O Lord,
>> for you have put my soul in the bundle of life
>> and hedged me against all the snares of corruption.
> Because I clung to your covenant,
>> fierce men sought after my life.
> But they—a league of falsehood, a congregation of Belial—
>> they knew not that through you I would stand.
> For you in your mercy save my life;
>> for by you are my footsteps guided . . .

And here is a metrical version of Psalm 1:1, 2 (Sternhold and Hopkins, 1549/1562):

> The man is blest that has not lent
>> To wicked men his ear,
> Nor led his life as sinners do,
>> Nor sat in scorner's chair.
> But in the law of God the Lord
>> Doth set his whole delight,
> And in the same doth exercise
>> Himself both day and night.

Supplementary Reading

The major supplementary books on the Old Testament have sections on Psalms. *Harper's Bible Dictionary* also has a brief article on poetry and parallelism. Most public libraries have a book containing translations of the Dead Sea Scrolls, which will include the psalms and worship texts used by those people. These are often being revised and updated, but older editions will serve for this purpose.

SESSION PLANS

Learning Objectives

This session is intended to enable participants to:

1. Describe at least three major classifications of the Psalms and give an example of each.

2. Summarize the contents of at least five other familiar psalms.

3. Recognize four kinds of parallelism used in the Psalms.

4. Discuss the uses of Psalms in Israel's worship and in the church today.

Resources You May Need

Chalkboard and chalk
Newsprint and markers
Church hymnbooks
Copies of a psalm to be read responsively

Hebrew Bible and opaque projector or transparency and overhead projector

Organist and/or choir director

Recording of a musical version of Psalm 23

Psalms Now by Leslie Brandt (Concordia Publishing House)

Leadership Strategy

SETTING THE STAGE

1. Return to the practice of asking members of the group for questions which arose from the last session or their preparation for this one. Add these to the Loose Ends list and decide when to respond to them.

2. Invite members of the group to name their favorite psalm and tell what they particularly like about it. If some psalms are chosen by several people, have the group turn to them in their Bibles and note the features that have been mentioned.

If you distributed the Scavenger Hunt in the Psalms at the close of the last session, review the group's responses at this time.

or

Read one of the psalms responsively. Psalms 24, 95, and 100 lend themselves well to this. You may find them among the selections in your church's hymnal or decide to distribute copies of a particular translation and have the leader and the group read alternate verses.

and

Invite everyone to turn to the first page of Psalms in their Bibles. Ask them to imagine they are looking at this page for the first time. What do they notice? What are some questions that come to mind?

Present an outline of the five divisions of Psalms on newsprint, using information from the *Resource Book* and the introduction to Psalms in a study Bible. Then lead the group through a guided tour of the book, noting the major divisions and the superscriptions pertaining to authorship, musical directions, tunes, and type of composition. Comment briefly on the development and arrangement of book.

EXPLORING THE SCRIPTURE

1. There are various ways of classifying the psalms. The following categories are mentioned under "Organization of the Psalter" in the *Resource Book*:

psalms for public liturgy	thanksgivings
royal psalms	laments
songs of ascent	historical psalms
praise psalms	nature psalms
hymns	psalms for personal meditation

Divide the group into ten clusters. Assign one of these categories to each cluster. They are to examine at least two of the psalms included in their category in the *Resource Book* and make a list of the characteristics of the selections in this category. Reconvene the group and have the clusters report their findings, perhaps listing them on newsprint.

or

Divide into small groups of three or four. Assign each group one or more of the psalms listed as Basic Bible References for this session.

The task of the groups is to read their psalm(s) and analyze what is revealed there about the devotional life of Israel. Questions to discuss might include:

a. What can you tell about the personality, position, or circumstances of the author?

b. What feelings are expressed in the different parts of the psalm?

c. Does the poet seem to be addressing a personal situation or a community or national event?

d. In what kind of worship setting might this psalm have been used?

Reconvene and have the groups report their findings.

or

Using material from the Supplementary Reading, make a presentation classifying the psalms according to their literary form and setting in worship. Take the group through an analysis of at least one hymn and one lament, indicating the major divisions of the poems. Note also the ways Israel's songs may have been used in her pilgrimage festivals. *Understanding the Old Testament* will be especially helpful for this assignment.

2. Introduce the subject of the literary characteristics of the psalms and give a brief presentation on the use of simile and metaphor and the various kinds of parallelism. The comments and illustrative references under "Literary and Poetic Characteristics" in the Resource Book will be helpful. You will find additional information in "Notes from the Author" and the supplementary reading.

or

Have several persons who prepared ahead of time present the same information, perhaps assigning one the use of simile and metaphor and others the four kinds of parallelism.

and

Even if you noted the acrostic structure of the song of praise to a good wife in Proverbs 31:10-31, you may want to illustrate this literary technique again with Psalm 119. *Understanding the Old Testament* has some helpful comments. If you have a Hebrew Bible use an opaque projector or make a transparency for an overhead projector to illustrate the pattern in the biblical language.

and

Invite members of the group to try their hand at writing poetry in the Hebrew style, using simile or metaphor and parallelism of one kind or another. Possible topics for selection are God ("The LORD is my shepherd," 23:1), one's situation ("I have become like a broken vessel," 31:12), God's activity ("He makes wars cease to the end of the earth," 46:9). Invite volunteers to share their efforts with the group.

3. Distribute copies of your church's hymnbook to members of the group. Instruct them to locate the index to Scripture and scriptural allusions. Have them check to see if their favorite psalm or the ones mentioned in Setting the Stage are used in any of the hymns.

Ask half of the group to count the number of different psalms included in the index. Have the other half count the number of hymns that incorporate references from Psalms in their texts. Select several of the hymns listed and examine them to see how the words of the psalms are used. In some cases they will be repeated almost verbatim; in other cases the references are paraphrased or merely alluded to.

You may also want to see how many of the unison and responsive readings in the hymnbook make use of the Psalms.

and/or

Invite your organist or choir director to make a presentation to the group about the use of the Psalms in worship.

CLOSING

1. Have participants open their Bibles to Acts 1:20; 2:25, 34, 35 and other references to see how the early church used the Psalms.

or

Sing one of the favorite hymns based on the words of a psalm, such as "All People That on Earth Do Dwell" (Psalm 100), "A Mighty Fortress Is Our God"(Psalm 46), "Come, Christians, Join to Sing" (Psalm 95).

or

Listen to a recording of a musical version of Psalm 23.

or

The Psalms have been called "Conversations with Yahweh." To illustrate this comment, read a few favorite psalms aloud from the *New Revised Standard Version*, and then read them aloud in the volume by Leslie Brandt entitled *Psalms Now*, published by Concordia Press.

Looking Ahead

Item #3 under Exploring Scripture in the next session suggests that three persons present reports on the background and meaning of the Lord's Supper, Baptism, and the Lord's Day.

If you are going to re-create a worship service from the early church at the next session, you will need to continue your planning at this meeting.

NOTES FROM THE AUTHOR

Jesus' Attitude toward Temple and Synagogue

Jesus' visit to the Temple, Luke 2:40-52, may be considered our first information about him as an adult. Today we might refer to it as his "Bar Mitzvah," the time when a Jewish boy undertakes the responsibility of Torah. Certainly he was brought up as a practicing Jew.

It is worthwhile to consider Jesus' relationship to Jewish worship under the alternatives "conformity/nonconformity." How did he conform to the practices of his day, and how did he not conform to them? In the Nazareth synagogue it seems to have been what Jesus said, not what he did or did not do, that aroused the opposition of the townspeople. When *those who passed by derided* Jesus on the cross, they quoted (apparently from hearsay) what he had said about destroying the Temple (Matthew 27:40).

The cleansing of the Temple is not directed against Temple worship as such but against peripheral conduct connected with it. Note that business was carried on in the Court of the Gentiles, thus disrupting that area of worship. Mark 11:17 includes (from Isaiah 56:7) the phrase *for all the nations*, which is omitted in Matthew and Luke. Isaiah 56:8 elaborates, *I will gather others to them besides those already gathered*. The universal thrust of Jesus' mission should be included in our understanding of this incident. John's reference in 2:17 to Psalm 69:9, *Zeal for your house will consume me*, is quite relevant.

The chronological problem about the cleansing is a distraction, but you should think it through in case it arises. There are five alternatives for questions raised by the Synoptics vs. John: (1) the Synoptics are right; (2) John is right; (3) it happened twice; (4) theological considerations dictated where it was placed in each Gospel; (5) Alternative 4 may be combined with 1 or 2. As a subordinate problem, note that Mark places the cleansing the day after the triumphal entry rather than just after the entry, as in Matthew and Luke. I won't settle this one for you; there are reasonable arguments for several alternatives.

Besides the theological association of Jesus' visits to Jerusalem, there was a practical importance. At festival times the population of the city swelled dramatically—some sources say quadrupled. Thus Jesus seized the opportunity for the widest exposure of his message.

Baptism

Three problems emerge. One is the question why Jesus felt the need to be baptized. Matthew recognizes the difficulty. The Baptist hesitates, and Jesus says, *Let it be so now; for it is proper for us in this way to fulfill all righteousness* (Matthew 3:14, 15). The suggestion in the *Resource Book* should be sufficient: Jesus identified completely with the people for whom he undertook his ministry. The incident also strengthens continuity with the ministry of John. In any case, Jesus' response must be taken seriously; he was not just going through the motions.

The second problem is the background of baptism. Jewish proselyte baptism and the Essene practice at Qumran are certainly relevant. The question may be pushed back to John's practice. There is some evidence to suggest he may have been influenced by Qumran. Whatever the background, it becomes essential in the Christian communities.

The third matter has to do with how and to whom baptism was administered. Clearly, John immersed in the Jordan River. If we take seriously the figure three thousand on Pentecost, however, the practicality of immersion there comes into question. So also for the story of the Philippian jailer. In this latter connection, the question arises whether children were baptized. Here our data are insufficient to give a certain answer. This latter question has been much debated.

The Lord's Supper

Consider with care the Lord's Supper. Regardless of the chronological problems about the relationship of the Supper and the date of Passover, it is clear that Jesus timed his final week in Jerusalem to coincide with the festival. Details from Part 1 are relevant here. Paul makes an indirect reference that should be noted: *our paschal lamb, Christ, has been sacrificed* (1 Corinthians 5:7). The importance of 1 Corinthians 11:23-25 as a primitive witness to the tradition should be emphasized. If you can get a copy of *The Teaching of the Twelve Apostles*, also known by its Greek title *Didache*, read Chapters 9 and 10, which reflect how sacramental practice was evolving at the beginning of the second century. *Didache* also contains information relative to baptism. (Many libraries have copies of an edition of *The Apostolic Fathers*, which includes the *Didache*.)

In interpreting the sacrament you will be guided, of course, by the doctrine of your church. Regarding the text, in addition to the comments in the *Resource Book*, you should note the text of 1 Corinthians 11:24. The textual variant *is broken for* is not original and must have developed from the analogy of the breaking of the bread. John's Gospel makes a point that Jesus' legs were not broken and connects this with a quotation from Exodus 12:46 (John 19:33-36).

Paul

Paul found the synagogue to be an effective reference point in spreading Christian faith. He turned from it for several reasons. Many of its leaders rejected his message. The newly formed Christian congregations quickly developed their own agendas. The large numbers of Gentile converts made it impractical to continue in the synagogues. Christian groups met at first in homes. We do not know when special buildings became common, but it was not in New Testament times.

As a rabbi Paul's relationship would be closer to the synagogue than to the Temple. He regularly uses Temple vocabulary, however, often in new ways. One of his startling ideas is that the Christian *body* collectively becomes God's temple and *a temple of the Holy Spirit* (1 Corinthians 3:16, 17; 6:19; in each instance the second person pronouns are plural). See also Ephesians 1:22, 23; 4:11-16. He uses *sacrifice* (Romans 12:1), *blood* (Colossians 1:20), *cleansing* (2 Corinthians 7:1), *leaven* (1 Corinthians 5:6-8), *libation, offering* (Philippians 2:17). You may discover other examples.

Some Details

In connection with the Lord's Prayer the "doxology" at the end (Matthew 6:13, footnote) has had a varied history in church usage. NRSV, RSV, REB, TEV, NIV, NJB, and NAB all omit it because the earliest manuscripts do. Tradition from later manuscripts brought it into the earlier English versions. It is composed of phrases from Old Testament Scripture, and it is not improper to use it. The omission is a matter related to the earliest history of the text and takes us back to some matters presented in the Introduction.

Information about early Christian worship after Jesus and aside from Paul is of two sorts: What is mentioned in Acts, and what is implied in some of the other non-Pauline books. The material in the first twelve chapters of Acts has to do with an early period before Christianity had spread widely. The last relevant detail is in Acts 12:12, where *many had gathered and were praying* in the home of Mary, John Mark's mother, in Jerusalem.

The Book of Hebrews contains many passages that bear a connection with worship or its vocabulary. In Hebrews 4:14-16 Jesus' function as *a great high priest* is associated with our approach to *the throne of grace*. See also Hebrews 5:3, 7; 7:11-8:6. This is connected further with Temple imagery in Hebrews 9:1-14, 18-28. *Sacrifices and offerings* are discussed in Hebrews 10:1-22.

Hymns and heavenly worship are introduced from Revelation. This book is treated in more detail in Theme 10, Part 4.

Women in the Early Church

The role of women in the worship of the early church is not easy to separate from the general topic of the place of women in the Christian community. Theme 5, Part 3, page 123, introduces the matter. You should give some thought to the subject in case it arises from the limited remarks in the *Resource Book*.

Paul has often been cast as a misogynist, but he was probably ahead of his time in allowing women to take a significant part in church life. Lydia was prominent in the Philippian church (Acts 16:13-15), and that church included two other women leaders, *Euodia* and *Syntych*, who apparently did not always agree (Philippians 4:2). The limited success of Paul's sermon in Athens included the conversion of *a woman named Damaris* (Acts 17:34). The wife-husband team Prisca and Aquila (Acts calls her Priscilla) are mentioned six times, and four times she is named first (Acts 18:18, 26; Romans 16:3; 2 Timothy 4:19; Aquila is first in Acts 18:2; 1 Corinthians 16:19).[1]

Paul is quite positive about the theological equality of women; *there is no longer male and female* (Galatians 3:28). Social and cultural customs of his time doubtless influence some of his difficult sayings about women. I believe the problem passage in 1 Corinthians 14:33b-36 should be dealt with as I have suggested in the *Resource Book*. Men took the leadership in worship; that was traditional and is not under discussion. Wives are not to create embarrassment or disturbance by talking to their husbands during worship.

It is relevant to look at 1 Corinthians 11:2-16, which deals with contemporary dress customs. In our own time we know that Christian folks can get overwrought about nonconformity in hair styles and clothes worn to church, so we should allow for a comparable problem in Corinth. We must not get distracted by thinking that because this is in Paul's letters—in Scripture—it automatically becomes regulatory for us. What about 1 Corinthians 6:1-8, where Paul writes that the Corinthians should settle their legal problems without recourse to civil courts? The argument in 1 Timothy 2:9-15 gets very sticky.

As a postscript, however, check Ephesians 5:21-33. It begins, *Be subject to one another out of reverence for Christ*. The argument gets more involved when it speaks of a wife's sub-

---

1 1 Corinthians 16:19 *the church in their house sends greetings.*

jection to her husband, but the relationship is in a context of love. It is further elevated by the analogy to the relationship of Christ and the church. This leads to the startling conclusion that although the wife owes the husband this subjection, *husbands should love their wives* even to the point of dying for them.

Supplementary Reading

The *Lion Encyclopedia of the Bible* and *Introducing the New Testament* have sections on worship in the early church. You will find entries on the Word List from the *Resource Book* in *Harper's Bible Dictionary*. The article on women in this volume also has a section on women in the New Testament.

SESSION PLANS

Learning Objectives

This session is intended to enable participants to:

1. Describe Jesus' attitude toward the Temple and synagogue.

2. Illustrate the attitude of the early church to Jewish worship with examples from Peter and John, Stephen, Paul, and the Book of Hebrews.

3. Summarize the background and meaning of Baptism, the Lord's Supper, and the Lord's Day.

4. List several worship practices in the early church and describe their relationship to the synagogue and current worship practices.

Resources You May Need

Chalkboard and chalk
Newsprint and markers
Recording of a segment of worship such as the Lord's Prayer or the Apostles' Creed
Overhead projector and transparencies
Copies of statements about the relationship of the early church to the Temple and synagogue
Copies of directions for researching terms such as blood, Holy of Holies, High Priest
Liturgy for celebrating the Lord's Supper and Baptism in your tradition
Materials for a worship service reflecting practices in the early church

SETTING THE STAGE

1. Add any questions left from the previous session or this week's reading to the Loose Ends list and decide when to take them up.

2. To introduce the subject for this session, play a recording of a segment of a worship service such as the Lord's Prayer, the Apostles' Creed, or the words of institution of the Lord's Supper.

or

Read aloud several of the references to worship in the early church, such as Acts 2:46, 47; 20:7-12; Matthew 18:20.

EXPLORING THE SCRIPTURE

1. Ask the group to recall incidents of Jesus' attendance and participation at the Temple or synagogue. Some of these are his dedication (Luke 2:22-32), his visit to the Temple at age twelve (Luke 2:41 ff.), his sermon at Nazareth (Luke 4:14-30), the "cleansing" of the Temple, his prophecy concerning the Temple's destruction (Mark 13:1, 2).

List these items on a chalkboard or newsprint as they are suggested. In each instance ask the group to evaluate how they think Jesus felt about worship in the Temple or synagogue.

or

Divide the group into thirds. The third on the left is to read Luke 2:22-32, 41-51; the center third is to read Luke 4:14-30; the third on the right is to read John 4:19-24. Each person is to answer as many of these questions about the texts as possible:

a. Who was present?

b. Where were they?

c. Did anything unusual occur? If so, what?

d. Summarize your impression of how Jesus felt about worship in the Temple or synagogue in the references you read.

Review the stories and the answers to the questions in the total group. Invite participants to add other stories they recall about Jesus and worship and to respond to the same questions.

2. Using the same division of the group into thirds, ask each section to research the attitude toward Jewish worship of either Peter and John, Stephen, or Paul. The biblical references under "Early Church Transition" and "Paul" in the *Resource Book* will provide the necessary information. Invite persons from each section of the group to share the results of their review with the whole group.

or

Write these statements on newsprint or a transparency and display them for the group to read. Or, distribute a copy of them to all members of the group.

After Pentecost:

- The apostles met with other believers at the Temple.

- They taught at the Temple.

- Peter healed at the Temple.

- Peter and John were jailed for their activities at the Temple.

- The apostles used every opportunity to preach the good news, even to the Temple rulers.

- Paul preached the gospel in synagogues in many cities.

- His preaching caused listeners to invite him back.

- He held discussions in synagogues with both Jews and Greeks to convince them to accept Jesus as Messiah.

- Because of Paul's preaching in synagogues, many Jews and Gentiles became believers in Christ.

Invite members of the group to add statements of their own about the relationship of the early church to the Temple and synagogue. Then lead the group in attempting to formulate a one or two sentence summary of how the apostles used the Temple and synagogue to further their mission.

and

Ask the group to work individually or in pairs. Read the following directions or distribute them to each person or pair:

The New Testament redefined words used in Temple worship. Read Hebrews 9:1-14. As you read try to determine the Old Testament meanings and the New Testament meanings of these words: "blood," "Holy of Holies," and "High Priest." The paragraphs under "Early Church Transition" in the *Resource Book* provide additional help.

or

Write "blood," "Holy of Holies," and "High Priest" on newsprint. Then ask the group for working definitions of the terms as used in Old Testament worship. Record these definitions beside the words. Read Hebrews 9:1-14 aloud. Discuss how the New Testament writer has redefined the terms.

3. Introduce three group members who are prepared to report on the origin and meaning of the Lord's Supper, Baptism, and the Lord's Day. The information in the *Resource Book*, the *Lion Encyclopedia of the Bible* and a Bible dictionary will be helpful.

or

Invite members of the group to recall their first experiences of participating in the Lord's Supper. Have volunteers share with the group what they remember about their feelings and understanding of the sacrament at that time.

and

Read through the liturgy for the celebration of this sacrament in your denominational tradition. As you read, ask the group to listen for references or allusions to Old Testament events and terminology. Discuss how the sacrament builds upon and reinterprets the message of deliverance conveyed through the celebration of Passover.

and

If persons can recall their own baptism, invite them to share these experiences. Then review the service for baptism in your congregation. Note who the participants are and what promises are made. Lead the group in discussing the meaning of baptism for the person being baptized, the parents, and members of the congregation.

and

Summarize the reasons why the church changed its principal day of worship from the seventh to the first day of the week. The *Resource Book* (The Lord's Day) and a Bible dictionary provide useful information.

4. The Lord's Prayer (Matthew 6:9-13; Luke 11:2-4) was taught to the disciples by Jesus as a model of how they were to formulate their prayers. It parallels in some

respects prayers in use in the synagogue in Jesus' day. Make a brief presentation on the structure and content of the two versions of the prayer. Helpful background for this presentation is found in *Harper's Bible Dictionary* and commentaries on Matthew and Luke.

and/or

Assign the following elements of worship in the early church to small groups or individuals. They are to review the information on these topics in the section entitled "Other Details of New Testament Worship" in the *Resource Book* and read the Scripture references mentioned there. Then they are to summarize their findings for the group.

The breaking of bread	Prophecy
Scripture reading and exposition	Speaking in tongues
Sermons	Hymns
Prayers and benedictions	Creeds or confessions

As the reports are given discuss which of these elements are rooted in worship in the synagogue and which ones have been retained in the present church's worship.

and/or

Design a worship service to reflect the situation of the early church. If the group is small enough you may want to consider holding the session in someone's house and serving a meal as part of it. It will be helpful if you know someone who is a member of a denomination which follows the early church tradition of having a love feast before the communion service. Usually foods such as dates, figs, olives, nuts, cheese, and bread are shared. Some groups also practice foot washing to recall the act of Jesus washing the disciples' feet. You may be more comfortable washing each other's hands. This might be followed by sharing bread and grape juice.

The Bethel Presbyterian Church in Prosperity, Pennsylvania, expanded on this idea and created a worship service from Colossae in the year 62 A.D. Some members of the group even chose identities for themselves based on research about the economic and social customs of the time. Others were assigned specific parts of the service. There were also spontaneous events, including a surprise visit by Onesimus and Tychicus bringing letters to Philemon and the congregation.

CLOSING

1. If you re-create a worship service this will provide an adequate closing for the session.

or

Read in unison a passage of Scripture that reflects worship practices or attitudes of the early church, such as Ephesians 3:14-21; Philippians 2:5-11; or Revelation 4:8b, 11; 5:9b, 10.

or

Christianity is called an "Easter" faith. Discuss how your congregation's worship does or does not illustrate this statement.

and

Have the group say together the apostolic benediction as recorded in 2 Corinthians 13:13.

Looking Ahead

Item #3 under Exploring the Scripture in the next session suggests that a member of the group present a summary of the material on *Sheol* and life after death from the *Resource Book* and a Bible dictionary.

NOTES FROM THE AUTHOR

About this Theme

"Hope" is a somewhat elusive theme, partly because it is so pervasive. It is related to "promise." These two subjects have been present often in the first nine themes.

There is an obvious reason for ending *Kerygma: The Bible in Depth* with "hope": history and experience inevitably lead to the future, and the future must be viewed from the perspective of history and experience. There is another reason, however: in few areas of biblical study and interpretation are there more propaganda and inadequate material than in relation to hope of the future. Persons with narrowly biased views have often made this their province. Therefore you should approach this theme positively and build a solid foundation for the doctrinal teaching of your denomination. Apocalyptic can be a particularly deceptive trap, so we shall devote considerable attention to it.

The four parts of this theme serve at least two purposes. First, this is a good opportunity for review. If your group has established good community, about now a sentimental panic may begin to appear. We are almost done, and there is still so much we want to talk about. Don't fight this; it is a good sign.

This leads naturally to the second purpose. This theme should provide a reference point for relating this program to continuing Bible study and its application to life. This is a kind of last chance to consolidate the hopes you have developed in twenty-nine sessions. Beside the content objectives, you have affective goals. You want to leave the group with a sense of achievement and with determination to make use of *Kerygma: The Bible in Depth* in appropriate ways in future life experience.

Israel's Hopes

It should not seem strange that Israel's earliest hope was centered in progeny and land. This grew out of their understanding of God. Expanding horizons of hope came with broader ideas about God. Their view of hope is also connected with their habit of thinking concretely and their slowness in appropriating abstract reasoning. Thus their universe consisted of *heaven above . . . the earth beneath . . .* and *the water under the earth* (Exodus 20:4; Psalm 135:6). Yahweh is God of what can be observed or inferred directly from observation.

The early Hebrews did not often speak of life after death nor did they long for it. This is quite different from the Greeks, who thought about immortality and treated it in their literature. *The tree of life* in the Garden of Eden did not bear promise of immortal life but *the knowledge of good and evil* (Genesis 3:22). According to the serpent this is what makes one *be like God* (Genesis 3:5). That was a goal for this life, so perpetuity of family and nation became of primary importance. The story of the daughters of Zelophehad (Research 1) and the promise of the Davidic dynasty are pertinent.

The word "hope" does not occur in the Torah. It is most frequent in the poetic writings—fifty times; twenty-one times in the rest of the Old Testament. This is what we should expect. Jeremiah expresses the conventional expectation in 31:17. The Psalms often sing of Yahweh as the foundation of hope, as in Psalms 42:5 and 130:5-8.

Messianic Hope

It is not easy for us, who are accustomed to think of messianic fulfillment in Jesus Christ, to appreciate the situation "B.C." The latest translations have helped by using "messiah" in the Gospels where older translations used "Christ." Note John 1:19-21, where popular expectations are reflected *(the Messiah,* that is, the one to restore David's dynasty; *Elijah,* as in Malachi 4:5; *the prophet,* probably a new Moses, see Deuteronomy 18:15).

Because the people found it difficult to divorce hope from the land, it was hard for Jesus' contemporaries to understand his mission. Political expectation was always close to the surface. The *Resource Book* reference to the Dead Sea Scrolls is from the *Manual of Discipline,* Chapter 9: The members of the community *shall not deviate from the whole counsel of the Torah . . . until a Prophet comes and the Messiahs of Aaron and Israel.*

Prophecy and Prediction of the Future

The prophets regularly related the present to the future, so they were often predictors. The word "prophet" can mean "one who foretells," but it also means "one who tells for" God.

The predictions that Yahweh's prophets made were directly connected with their contemporary message on behalf of Yahweh. They predicted the consequences that would follow *if* the people pursued their present course. The message of the prophets is prominently ethical (Theme 7, Part 2).

The prophets addressed the people in Yahweh's name and conveyed Yahweh's will for the people. What the prophets say will surely affect the future, but the focus is on what Yahweh is now saying. This sets three requisites for understanding the message of the prophets. (1) We must understand that the message had a meaning for those to whom it was first addressed. (2) The first step in understanding the message today is to learn what it meant to those hearers. (3) As we are able to relate our modern situation to the times of the prophets, we shall be able to find a true meaning for today.

The Relation of Prophecy and Apocalyptic

Prophecy and apocalyptic both offer hope, and both speak of judgment. The prophets write of *the day of the* LORD. It is not so much the end of history as judgment that is coming to balance the books of history. Apocalyptic writers look for a new day and describe in vivid language what must take place before that day comes. Classical prophecy deals more directly with the details of history than does apocalyptic. In our canon there are only two books that may properly be called apocalyptic: Daniel and Revelation. Parts of other books, however, are apocalyptic in outlook and literary characteristics. We consider these matters in detail in the next part.

Life after Death

Concern about life after death appears only gradually and not very often in the Old Testament. What happens when the scales of justice are not balanced while one is alive? How does God keep promises not fulfilled in this life? If the day of the Lord brings joy and justice, how does it affect those who are not alive at that time? If God lives above and beyond human history, why should not God's people share in such life? These questions pointed to hope beyond this present life.

Much of our popular thought about the afterlife is conditioned by the imagery of Dante, Milton, and Bunyan, so we must work extra hard to clarify what the Old Testament says and does not say. Here are some statistics that may be useful (the figures are approximate). Sheol occurs sixty-three times in the Old Testament. It is translated "hell" by KJV thirty-one times; "grave" thirty-one times; "pit" three times. NRSV regularly uses "Sheol." The Pentateuch has "Sheol" seven times; Samuel and Kings four times; the Latter Prophets nineteen times; the Writings thirty-three times. It is most frequent in Psalms (fifteen times). Thus it becomes more and more a poetic word.

The ideas of "being with God," "rescue from death," or "rescue from the pit" all occur, but the ideas are not worked out in significant detail. Sheol is most often a word-symbol used to refer to experiences akin to death.

There is no idea of "heaven" as the place of utter felicity after death. The Hebrew word "paradise" occurs three times. In Nehemiah 2:8 it is translated *forest*; in Ecclesiastes 2:5, *parks*; in Song of Solomon 4:13, *orchard*. The word is borrowed from the Persian.[1] "Heavens," the plural, is the top tier in what is sometimes referred to as "the three-storied universe." Sometimes God *is in the heavens* (Psalm 115:3); sometimes *the LORD . . . is above the heavens . . . seated on high* and *looks far down on the heavens and the earth* (Psalm 113:4-6). What might seem to us logical conclusions about being close to God and God being in heaven are never worked out.

Hope in Isaiah

Isaiah has four identifiable parts: Chapters 1-23, 28-39, the prophetic activity of Isaiah ben Amoz; Chapters 24-27, an apocalyptic insert; Chapters 40-55, a collection of prophecies featuring the "servant songs"; Chapters 56-66, a prophetic collection from the postexilic restoration.

Isaiah 7:14 became an important reference in the development of the Christian doctrine of the virgin birth of Jesus. The passage in Isaiah must be studied carefully and without prejudice to reach a clear understanding of what it originally meant. The material in the *Resource Book* should suffice. The technical data are plain. The Hebrew word used here, *'almah*, does not indicate the sexual situation of the *young woman*. Another Hebrew word, *bethulah*, does mean precisely "virgin."

The Greek translation used *parthenos*, a word that regularly means "virgin." On this basis, Matthew 1:22, 23 quotes the prophet. The operative word in Matthew's reference, however, is "fulfill." The Christian doctrine was not produced by the word of the prophet; that word was introduced to add a dimension to something that was already believed. Remember that Luke does not cite this verse. It is instructive to note that the Roman Catholic NJB translates the Hebrew as *young woman*. NAB translates "virgin," but has a lengthy note dealing with the original setting and the later development that gave rise to Catholic doctrine. If discussion becomes necessary, it should deal with the nature of "fulfillment" rather than the specific doctrine.

During Advent, Isaiah 9:2-7 is commonly read, for the words seem particularly appropriate in reference to the infant Jesus. *The throne of David* and his kingdom (Isaiah 9:7) puts the prophecy in the mainstream of Jewish hope during the late monarchy. Beautiful similes in Isaiah 11:1-9 describe circumstances in the ideal kingdom.

---

1 It occurs three times as *paradise* in the New Testament: Luke 23:43; 2 Corinthians 12:4; Revelation 2:7.

The apocalyptic chapters receive minimal attention, for the next part will treat that kind of literature. The apocalyptic view is clear in Isaiah 24:20-23. Many passages from the last two parts of Isaiah are used in other themes. We have suggested (Theme 5, Part 2) that the composite nature of Isaiah can raise difficult, technical questions that lead far afield from our themes.

Supplementary Reading

For some of the key words and topics which are discussed in this part you may want to do more than review articles in a Bible dictionary or the supplementary books. More extensive material will be found in the five volume *Interpreter's Dictionary of the Bible* (Abingdon Press).

SESSION PLANS

Learning Objectives

This session is intended to enable participants to:

1. Describe the hopes of Israel as a people.

2. Summarize the factors that gave rise to the messianic hope in Israel, and describe several characteristics of the ideal ruler.

3. Compare Old Testament perspectives on life after death with their own views.

4. Provide at least two examples of the hopes described in the prophets.

Resources You May Need

Chalkboard and chalk
Newsprint and markers
Writing paper
Dictionary
Construction paper and crayons
Literary or visual portrayals of life after death
Sets of directions for analyzing Isaiah's Servant Songs
Copies of Psalm 136:1, 10-26
Hymnbooks

Leadership Strategy

SETTING THE STAGE

1. Ask members of the group for questions which arose in their preparation for this session. Add them to the Loose Ends list. Since you are nearing the end of the program, this is a good time to emphasize the relationship of the themes to one another. Add a question to the list which asks how the hopes of Israel reviewed in this part are related to God's promises to Abraham and Sarah (Theme 2, Part 1) and Israel's experiences under the monarchy (Theme 6, Part 2).

2. Distribute paper to members of the group and ask them individually to write down five things they hope for. These may be tangible or intangible. Personal, family, national and religious hopes may be included.

   List on newsprint or a chalkboard the following four means by which hopes may be fulfilled:

   a. Personal effort

   b. Family or community effort

   c. National or international effort

   d. God's intervention

   Invite persons to share hopes from their lists that can be accomplished through the various means and record these hopes opposite the appropriate categories. Ask them to discuss their attitudes regarding the fulfillment of their hopes. Which ones do they feel most certain of achieving? Which seem least likely to be realized? What are they doing to help actualize their hopes?

   ### and/or

   Have someone read aloud the definition of hope from a dictionary. Then have the group divide into clusters of two or three and discuss the difference between hope and "wishful thinking." Come together again and share results in the total group.

EXPLORING THE SCRIPTURE

1. Invite the group to suggest the kinds of things they hope for our nation. Record them on a chalkboard or newsprint. Then ask them to recall the things Israel hoped for. (If necessary, refer to pages 213-214 of the *Resource Book*.) Record these items beside the first list. Then lead the group in discussing the similarities and differences between the hopes for our nation and those of early Israel.

or

Divide the group into two sections, using all those on one side of the room or those with last names beginning with A through M as the first section and the rest as the other section. Those in the first section are to read Genesis 17:1-8 and list the things for which Abraham hoped. Those in the second section are to read 2 Samuel 7:8-16 and describe the hopes presented there. Record the findings on newsprint or a chalk-board.

and

Then ask everyone to turn to the Chronology of the Bible in the Appendix of the *Resource Book*. Lead the group in discussing whether or not the various hopes listed above were fulfilled during the major periods of the nation's history.

2. In this activity we pick up one of Israel's hopes we looked at before in Theme 6, Part 2. Divide the group into clusters of five or six people. Each cluster is to discuss these questions:

a. At what time in Israel's history did "messianic hope" become prominent?

b. What other hopes were replaced in this process? Why? (You might suggest the group read Lamentations 5:19-22; Haggai 1:12-2:9, 23, or the introduction to Haggai in *Today's English Version*; and Jeremiah 33:14-16.)

c. What kind of messiah was hoped for? (See Isaiah 9:1-7 and 11:1-10.)

Reconvene the whole group and share responses to the questions.

or

Give a mini-lecture about the origin of the "messianic hope," including the reasons for its rise and the form it took. (Review the final two sections of Theme 6, Part 2 in the *Resource Book*.) Then have two persons read Isaiah 9:1-7 and 11:1-10 aloud. Ask members of the group to note the characteristics that describe the ideal ruler in these passages and list them on newsprint or a chalkboard. Then have a third person read Isaiah 7:10-17. Engage the group in a discussion of the similarities and differences between this passage and the descriptions of the ideal ruler in Isaiah 9 and 11. Use materials from the *Resource Book* and "Notes from the Author" for help in understanding the passage.

3. Ask everyone to write out an answer to the question "What happens to people after they die?" Have construction paper and crayons available and encourage those who wish to depict their conceptions of the afterlife graphically.

or

Read selections from literary works such as *Paradise Lost* or *The Inferno* that describe life after death or display artists' conceptions of heaven and hell.

and

Invite eight persons to read these Scripture references aloud to the group:

1 Samuel 2:6	Isaiah 38:18
Genesis 37:35	Job 17:13-16
Psalm 55:15	Job 19:23-27
Psalm 139:8	Daniel 12:1-3

Discuss the portrayals of life after death found in these texts and compare them with the perceptions indicated above.

or

Have a member of the group who was selected previously summarize the material on *Sheol* and life after death from the *Resource Book* and a Bible dictionary.

and

As Deuteronomy 11:8, 9, 20, 21 implies, perpetuity of family and nation were important to the idea of survival after death in the Old Testament. Ask the group how important it is to them to leave behind children, possessions, accomplishments, or contributions to a cause. Discuss in what ways these desires are similar to the Old Testament hopes.

4. Isaiah and Jeremiah present numerous pictures of hope for Israel. Divide the group into four sections. Assign each section either Isaiah 60:1-3, Isaiah 65:17-25, Jeremiah 23:3-8, or Jeremiah 29:10-14. The sections are to discuss how their passages might bring hope and encouragement to Israel and to the church today. When the group reconvenes, have the sections share the results of their discussions.

and/or

Use the same four sections and assign one of Isaiah's "Servant Songs" to each section (42:1-4; 49:1-6; 50:4-11; 52:13-53:12). Give each section a set of these directions:

a. Read the assigned verses.

b. Decide whether the servant is portrayed as an individual, a nation or a remnant of the nation.

c. Describe the servant's qualities.

d. Describe the servant's task and how this song would have brought hope to Israel.

e. Discuss in what ways these verses might have influenced Jesus' understanding of his mission.

Invite the sections to share their findings with the whole group.

CLOSING

1. Review the hopes of Israel mentioned in this theme. Ask the group what factors kept Israel's hope for land, progeny, and liberation alive through the centuries.

2. Use Psalm 136:1, 10-26 as a responsive reading, with the leader saying the opening phrase of each verse and the group responding with the phrase "for his steadfast love endures forever."

and/or

Sing "O God Our Help in Ages Past, Our Hope for Years to Come."

Looking Ahead

Item #1 under Exploring the Scripture in the next session suggests that three persons present summaries of the backgrounds and messages of Ezekiel, Zechariah and Daniel.

Item #4 in the same section suggests that a member of the group present the evidence for dating Daniel at the time of the Maccabean rebellion.

Item #4 also suggests that four persons summarize Daniel's visions in chapters 7, 8, 9, and 10-12.

Plan a special way to conclude your Kerygma study. Certificates for completing the course are available from the Pittsburgh office. Several groups have had a potluck dinner or a dessert smorgasbord coupled with a recognition ceremony. If you are going to do any of these things you will need to begin preparations now.

NOTES FROM THE AUTHOR

Interpreting Apocalyptic Literature

It is practically impossible to avoid some interpretation in dealing with apocalyptic literature. One cannot just say "read it" and hope for the best. There are at least five ways to interpret such material.

1. *Past historical* a.k.a. *preterit*. The meaning of the writing for the original readers is sought in the context of their times. A preterit interpretation focuses on "what it meant."

2. *Continuing historical*. The meaning is sought in the unfolding of history through the ages since the writing. Prophecy is fulfilled in events up to the present time, which is usually considered to be close to "the end of the age."

3. *Futurist*. Most of the writing applies to the end time. This implies that one thinks that the end time is at hand.

4. *Spiritual*. Ideas and principles are sought from the writing. References to history are quite secondary.

5. *Balanced*. The above approaches are considered, and whatever is valuable in them is used in the effort to find "what it means."

If we take the Bible seriously, we must begin with (1) above. Apocalyptic is a child of prophecy, which spoke first of all to needs of the prophets' contemporaries. To assume that the Bible was written only for our particular time is a kind of spiritual arrogance, but of course it is sterile historicity to stop with an examination of the original meaning. I have found useful a kind of equation:

Situation then: Situation now:: Meaning then: Meaning now

We are looking for *meaning now*. We can solve this equation for "x" (*"meaning now"*) only when we know the other parts of it. None of these elements is simple, which means that serious Bible study is not simple, but it is essential for understanding the Bible.

Apocalyptic differs from prophecy in very important literary characteristics, which occur in varying degree in apocalyptic writings. (1) Apocalyptic is usually pseudonymous, but this does not deceive the original readers. (2) There is secrecy; it is primarily for insiders. (3) History is divided into periods. (4) Apocalyptic is deterministic; everything happens according to a rigidly controlled plan. (5) The end is viewed as near. (6) Much is other-worldly; it is set on a cosmic stage. (7) Apocalyptic is pessimistic about the immediate future. (8) It suggests a temporary dualism. God will finally win, but for now the power of evil challenges God. (9) There is much mythological symbolism.

Ezekiel

The two locales of Ezekiel's ministry are nearly a thousand miles apart. This emphasizes how traumatic the exile was for those who lived through its beginnings. The change of emphasis in the book is notable: While there is time, the threat of doom is a weapon against false hope; once doom has struck, the prophet offers hope because of the faithfulness of God.

Since symbolism is a characteristic, apocalyptic requires that we have help in our study. Commentaries regularly offer information. Ezekiel and others use parts of the human body in symbolic ways. A voice may bring a divine oracle (2:1). The creatures and the wheels in Chapter 1 have human features. Eyes (1:18) symbolize all-seeing knowledge. Some animal features are rather obvious: Lion = majesty; ox = strength; eagle = swift flight (1:10); dragon = evil (29:3). A crown means royalty (21:25, 26). In Chapter 17 there is an elaborate allegory, for which the prophet offers some interpretation. Such details are also frequent in Zechariah.

Ezekiel also employs symbolic actions. The *Resource Book* mentions the barber episode. In Chapter 4 Ezekiel portrays the siege of Jerusalem, and in Chapter 12 he dramatizes the flight of the exiles. When his wife dies, he does not engage in the normal mourning rituals, and this becomes an object lesson for the people (24:15-27). He does not always portray bad news. He joins two sticks to symbolize the future reunion of the Israelite people (37:15-23). Certainly his personality is unusual.

We do not know how much influence Ezekiel had in his time. We are impressed that he continuously locates himself *among the exiles* (1:1; 33:21-33). In later times rabbis had problems about his visions of the Temple. Parts of his book, however, have been treasured through the ages. His oracle about Yahweh as shepherd of the people and the vision of the valley of dry bones challenge interpreters today. Some sixty times he gives the divine declaration, *I am the LORD* (6:7, 14, etc.).

Jewish rabbinic tradition has a saying to cover matters that cannot be explained: "Elijah will make it clear when he comes." Parts of Ezekiel must be left for Elijah's explanation.

Zechariah

The Book of Zechariah contains a fine balance of apocalyptic visions and practical reality. The prophet lives in the time of the restoration. He offers encouragement in *the day of small things* (4:10). There was not much to be hopeful about, but Zechariah is hopeful. Look at 1:16, 17. *The measuring line* is a symbol of protection, and there is *compassion, prosperity, comfort.*

Notice the emphasis on *return* in 1:1-6. The verb is the Old Testament background of the New Testament word "repent." Zechariah offers more moral teaching than Haggai. The high priest needs renewal; he is *dressed with filthy clothes* (3:3). The *scroll* and the *basket* in Chapter 5 warn about evil to be removed. Social concern is expanded in Chapter 7.

The outline in the *Resource Book* emphasizes the visions with their apocalyptic details. The final oracle moves through troubles to victory. Over a dozen times the prophet says, *on that day*. Finally Yahweh will right all the wrongs that have been done to the people. There are many allusions to Zechariah in the New Testament. A study Bible will direct you to some of them. We are concerned here to see that the book announces hope in the future.

Daniel

This book is hard to handle. Stories in the first six chapters are generally well known. Details from the last six chapters are often used by persons who are obsessed with the end time. Some readers will find it hard to accept Daniel as a pseudonym, but the thrust of the stories and visions does not depend upon the identification of that man. The real significance of the book in the history of God's people is not generally well known.

The date of the book as we have given it in the *Resource Book* is considered quite certain by most scholars. Parts of the book may come from other times; for example, the prayer in 9:4-19 is probably an older part. The presence of the long Aramaic section is a problem for linguistic experts. The Aramaic is later than the fifth century B.C., but apart from its significance for dating the book, the overall problem is debated. In the Apocrypha there is a long supplement to Chapter 3 (*Additions to the Greek Book of Daniel*). This material includes "The Song of Azariah in the Furnace" (see 1:7), and "The Song of the Three Young Men" (see NJB). The Septuagint places Daniel between Esther and Ezra.

Daniel became idealized as a wise man. The two other additions to Daniel in the Apocrypha, *Susanna* (Chapter 13) and *Bel and the Dragon* (Chapter 14) are part of this image (and rather good detective stories). Daniel's rise to power presents some parallels to the career of Joseph.

The stories in Daniel 1-6 give moral counsel in the face of crisis—Jews call them *haggadah*. There are several problems with the identification of the rulers who are mentioned. The stories are not intended to be historical records.

In Chapters 7-12 the symbolic figures are intended to be identified with historical periods (7:17). The Babylonian, Median, and Persian empires lead up to the Hellenistic age. Here evil culminates in the arrogant little horn, who is usually identified as Antiochus IV. Details of the defamation of the Temple (9 and 11) are quite precise, but the description of the death of the ruler is not so exact. This is one basis of the generally agreed date for the book, about 165 B.C.

Let me emphasize again that the prophets and apocalyptists were not primarily predictors. If this were the case with Daniel, and if the visions looked forward to the rise of the four kingdoms, the book would be a hodgepodge with little significance for its time. The approach to apocalyptic writing given above should prevent wild, interpretative, end-time adventures. (This becomes even more critical in the New Testament.)

In connection with 12:2 you should remember that the Judeo-Christian hope of resurrection is quite different from the Greek idea of immortality of the soul. Biblical realism did not contrast physical and spiritual existence but came to relate them sequentially.

Supplementary Reading

The usual sources of basic information, such as the introductions to each book included in a study Bible and a Bible dictionary, will provide background for interpreting the three major figures in this part. *Understanding the Old Testament* has a section on Daniel that mentions some of the chief characteristics of apocalyptic literature and discusses the relation of prophecy and apocalyptic.

SESSION PLANS

Learning Objectives

This session is intended to enable participants to:

1. Describe the kinds of settings in which the apocalyptic literature of the Bible arose.

2. Summarize, in a few sentences for each, the historical backgrounds and messages of Ezekiel, Zechariah, and Daniel.

Resources You May Need

Chalkboard and chalk
Newsprint and markers
Copies of several supplementary books
Directions for group study of Ezekiel, Zechariah, and Daniel
Commentary on Zechariah
Chart of the characteristics of apocalyptic literature
Concordance

Leadership Strategy

SETTING THE STAGE

1. Record any questions arising from the last session or the reading for this one on your Loose Ends list. Decide when you will take them up. Where it is appropriate, link questions to previous themes and parts to encourage review.

2. Give a brief presentation on the five ways of interpreting apocalyptic literature that Dr. Walther mentions in "Notes from the Author." Then select a brief passage from Ezekiel, Zechariah, or Daniel and illustrate how a student works to find its meaning using the formula:

   Situation then: Situation now:: Meaning then: Meaning now

   ### and/or

   Use a guided meditation to enable the group to relive the kinds of experiences out of which apocalyptic literature grew.

In such an activity the leader lowers the lights, invites the members of the group to relax, close their eyes, and meditate about the subject matter. The leader then becomes a "guide" through the meditation journey, allowing time for individuals to develop images and recall or experience feelings and emotions.

For this meditation you might say:

I would like you to relax and close your eyes. (*Pause.*)

Now, try to recall some period in your life or some experience when you faced a situation that seemed hopeless or a time when the outcome of a problem was uncertain. (*Pause for at least sixty seconds.*)

What feelings engulfed you? (*Brief pause.*)

Did you feel despair (*pause*), helplessness (*pause*), frustration (*pause*), fear (*pause*)?

Is anything hopeful happening? (*Pause.*)

Would you welcome someone who could offer you assurance that everything will somehow turn out right? (*Pause.*)

The situation has now been resolved. Think about the hopes you experienced during the crisis. How do you feel now? (*Pause for at least sixty seconds.*)

Slowly turn on the lights and ask members of the group to share with one or two others some feelings they experienced during the meditation.

Emphasize that apocalyptic literature grew out of feelings of national despair. Apocalypses were tracts for hard times. They were written when the future was uncertain, and hope for a satisfactory outcome in this world was dim.

EXPLORING THE SCRIPTURE

1. (If you wish to have the group explore all three prophetic books at the same time, use this activity. Otherwise, use activities 2, 3 and 4.)

Divide the group into thirds and assign each section either Ezekiel, Zechariah or Daniel. Or, allow members of the group to select the prophet they wish to study further and divide them accordingly.

If possible, give each section a separate room in which to work. If that is not possible, separate them as much as space permits. Assign one person to be an enabler for each section. Provide newsprint and markers, as many of the Kerygma supplementary books as available, and these directions:

a. Everyone is to reread the material in the *Resource Book* about the assigned prophet. Be sure to cover all of the basic Scripture references and develop a summary of what they say.

b. Decide how you are going to gather the following information. Perhaps assign specific details to members of the section.

   1. Author's name (if known) and a brief biographical sketch

   2. Date and purpose of the book

   3. Historical and political situation

   4. Reason for "hopelessness"

   5. Summary of hope promised

   6. Parts of the books that are apocalyptic

   7. Some of the symbols used and their meanings

   8. Any other pertinent or interesting facts

c. Gather the information.

d. Decide how you will present this to the total group.

e. Prepare your presentation.

Reconvene the whole group, listen to the presentations, and discuss any questions that arise.

or

Have three persons who prepared ahead of time present the information requested above.

or

Prepare handouts with the important information about the three prophets. Review them with the group. A sample sheet for Ezekiel is included at the end of these session plans.

2. Make a brief presentation on the historical background of Ezekiel and outline the contents of the book. Highlight some of his central emphases. A Bible dictionary and *Understanding the Old Testament* provide helpful information.

Then divide the group into seven clusters. The first cluster is to read Ezekiel 1:26-28 and 3:15-21 and prepare a brief report on the prophet's commission and responsibility.

The next three clusters are to read one of the following passages and present Ezekiel's words of doom to the whole group by acting out the passage or designing another form of presentation.

    5:1-4   23:22-26
    16:15-22

The final three clusters are to select one of the following texts and present to the group a word of hope from the prophet.

    34:11-16   47:13-14, 21-23
    37:1-14

3. Zechariah is probably the least known of the three books to be reviewed in the session. You may wish to touch on it only briefly. If so, summarize its background and content. Then have the group read the three passages in the Basic Bible Reference list (Zechariah 1:8-17; 4:1-14; 9:9-17). With the aid of a commentary, provide a brief interpretation of these passages.

or

If you have more time, divide the group into seven clusters. You may want to use the same groupings that worked on Ezekiel. Assign six of the clusters one or more of Zechariah's visions (1:8-17; 1:18-21; 2:1-5; 3:1-10; 4:1-14; 5:1-4; 5:5-11; 6:1-8). The seventh group is to work with the oracle in 9:9-17.

Provide the clusters with newsprint and markers. They are to design a way to communicate the meaning of the visions or the oracle to the group through symbols, a picture story, or some other means. After the clusters complete their work, reconvene the group for reporting.

4. Since Daniel is the one thoroughgoing apocalypse in the Old Testament, single it out for special attention. Begin by displaying a chart with the main characteristics of apocalyptic literature as described in "Notes from the Author." Then show how Daniel illustrates these various characteristics. Include the Basic Bible References in your presentation.

and

Introduce a member of the group who is prepared to make a brief presentation summarizing the evidence for dating Daniel at the time of the Maccabean rebellion. (Note that the Chronology of the Bible in the Appendix of the *Resource Book* dates Daniel several centuries earlier.)

and

Several of the stories in Daniel were mentioned earlier in Theme 5, Part 2, and Theme 6, Part 2. Select one of the stories you have not yet considered, have everyone read it, and show how it illustrates the purpose of Daniel as a "tract for hard times."

and/or

Have four members of the group selected at the previous session summarize Daniel's visions as presented in Chapters 7, 8, 9, and 10-12. Discuss how these visions would have been important to a community undergoing oppression.

CLOSING

1. Using a concordance locate several New Testament references to the prophecies of Ezekiel, Zechariah, and Daniel. Read these passages to the group, noting the Old Testament texts that they reflect.

2. Ask the group to suggest contemporary situations where the church is facing threats. Lead the group in discussing how an apocalyptic message such as a portion of Ezekiel or Daniel might be helpful in this context.

Looking Ahead

Item #2 under Setting the Stage in the next session suggests that members of the group bring articles from recent newspapers and magazines which offer signs of hope.

Ezekiel

The holiness of God permeated all of Ezekiel's life and thought. He was one of the greatest spiritual figures of all time. Although he was overshadowed by Second Isaiah, we owe an emphasis on the Good Shepherd concept to him. He called his hearers to repentance and promised God's mercy to all who sincerely turned to him. Ezekiel emphasized the need for inner renewal of the heart and spirit and the responsibility of each individual for his or her own sins. These concepts place him among the forerunners of Christianity.

Ezekiel the man

- was a Temple priest in Jerusalem

- was taken to Babylon during the first deportation in 597 B.C.

- was God's spokesman from 593-571 B.C.

- was married.

- lived in his own home in Tel Abib in Babylonia by the river Chebar (a canal for the Euphrates).

- was eccentric.

- spoke and acted symbolically.

- delivered the word of the LORD to elders in the exile until 571 B.C.

Ezekiel's Hope

1. Resurrection of the nation (37:1-14)

2. Return to Zion (11:17; 34:11-16; 39:25-29)

3. Reuniting of Israel and Judah (37:15-19, 22; 48:1-29)

4. Reign of God's servant, a descendant of David (34:23-24; 37:24-25)

5. Marvelous fertility of the land (47:1-12)

6. Rebuilding of the Temple and careful observances of its holy rites (40-46)

7. Worship of a holy God by a people indwelt by his Spirit (36:26-28)

Other Facts

Good Shepherd concept – Chapter 34 (see John 10:1-18)

Apocalyptic writing – Chapters 38-39

593-587 B.C. – The message was Doom (see Chapters 4-24 – Jerusalem was still standing)

587-571 B.C. – The message was Hope (see Chapters 33-48 – Jerusalem had been destroyed)

New Hope in Christ

PART 3

NOTES FROM THE AUTHOR

New Testament Hope

The New Testament is a book of fulfillment, essentially fulfillment of Old Testament hope. It is very important, therefore, to discern the similarities that mark the New as fulfilling the Old, and it is equally important to recognize the differences that make the New Testament new. This was also a task for the New Testament writers.

Take messianic hope, for example. Jesus is affirmed to be the Messiah, but he certainly did not fulfill the Old Testament hope in the way it was usually held. The hope was redirected. Nationalistic elements were sublimated when it became clear that the good news is for all the world. Family hope now is expanded to embrace the whole family of God.

People now confront in a person those characteristics that were attributed to God in the Old Testament. In Jesus' person and ministry *the kingdom of God/heaven has come near*. One may now experience the rule of God in human form. (Compare also the striking affirmations of the *I am* sayings in the Fourth Gospel.)

Comparing Mark 9:1 with Matthew 16:28 and Luke 9:27 is instructive. Mark reads literally, "will not taste death until they see that the Kingdom of God has come with power." Jesus expects the Kingdom in the lifetime of his hearers, or perhaps he is saying that it has already come. Unless Jesus is mistaken, this is not "the end of the world." Matthew's verse clearly shows the apocalyptic heightening that is characteristic of that Gospel. Luke has the simplest form and may be interpreted in several ways.

At the least, we can say that Jesus expected his ministry to usher in a new time in the relationship between God and people. Thus the allegory in Matthew 25:31-46 may be taken to mean that today is the day of judgment. This is in line with 2 Corinthians 6:2 and Hebrews 3:7, 15; 4:7.

The Synoptic Apocalypse

When we set these passages among Jesus' other sayings, the apocalyptic elements are not strong enough to demonstrate that he usually spoke in this manner. Jesus did use some apocalyptic language, but there is no evidence that his thought was substantially apocalyptic. As a wise Jew he must have felt very deeply the grave danger that threatened the Holy City. The disaster would create a crisis for his followers. Apocalyptic imagery would be the natural language to describe such an event.

There are at least nine exhortations to preparedness and steadfastness. The Gospel writers tended to bring together similar statements from the sayings of Jesus, and this may have happened here. If so, the apocalyptic concentration in Jesus' teaching is certainly not great. Do not miss the significance of *let the reader understand*. It says a lot about the role of the church in appropriating what had been handed on by the original hearers. It is further evidence that we are dealing with the third layer of the traditions.

Hope in the Gospel of John

John 14-16 is certainly about hope but cannot be considered apocalyptic. The long discourse steps from reference about Jesus to reference about the Spirit. This is a unique approach to the future. It provides a continuity from the career of Jesus to the time of the Spirit in the church. The Spirit will take Jesus' place. Jesus even hints that in one sense this is his coming again. Note the flow from John 14:18 to 14:26, and add John 15:26 and 16:12-14, 19, 20. This does not mean, however, that the church has been wrong in expecting another future climax after the coming of the Spirit at Pentecost (see 2 Thessalonians 2:2).

Paul writes of living *according to the Spirit* (Romans 8:4-6), yet one of his favorite phrases is *in Christ* (over thirty times). Today we speak of the presence of Christ, but of course we do not mean that it is the same as the bodily presence of Jesus of Nazareth. It helps to understand the nature of the Holy Spirit if we identify that Spirit with the presence of Christ, and we must understand this double presence in light of the biblical revelation in Jesus. Moreover, all this is bound up with our belief in one God.

The Centrality of the Resurrection

Theme 1, Part 3, shows how in a sense the gospel actually begins with the resurrection. Hope in the New Testament is inseparably bound to the resurrection. The shift from seventh day to first day as the special day of the week is barely implied in the New Testament, but it is clear in the Apostolic Fathers. This is a far-reaching item that is little emphasized in churches today.

All four Gospels refer to the empty tomb, but Paul and the other New Testament books do not mention it. This implies that the empty tomb was a part of the earliest oral traditions and was therefore entered in the Gospels. The vivid, eyewitness testimonies to the bodily appearances of the resurrected Jesus, however, quickly rendered the tomb detail secondary, and it dropped from the apostolic preaching. This should be sufficient guidance if the matter should come up in group discussion.

Another detail that may call for clarification is the time factor in Jesus' word to the thief, *today you will be with me in Paradise* (Luke 23:43). There are a number of complicated solutions for this issue. I suggest a practical approach. Jesus offered simple hope in response to a simple, desperate plea. The thief's immediate need was for words that would relieve him at once. A tortured conversation on two crosses is hardly the place to treat a theology of the afterlife!

1 Corinthians 15

1 Corinthians 15:3-8 is the earliest written record of the received tradition about the resurrection. *As of first importance* (1 Corinthians 15:3) is rendered *with top priority* in the Anchor Bible. *In accordance with the scriptures* must be taken somewhat loosely. Perhaps Paul had in mind such passages as Psalm 22, Isaiah 53, Lamentations 1:12, 18. The appearance to *Cephas* (as Paul calls Peter) matches the Gospel record except that in the Gospels women are the first witnesses. The explanation in the *Resource Book* is probably adequate. Paul may omit the women's evidence, not because he is a male chauvinist (as is sometimes proposed), but because he is concerned with the effectiveness of the tradition. The political status of women in that society would prompt him to focus on the recognized leadership of the church. The appeal to living eyewitnesses is strong.

Regarding the argument in 1 Corinthians 15:12-19, I once heard a scholar propose that there is no resurrection of the dead, i.e., we do not observe it; therefore Jesus Christ did not rise. Paul's argument is precisely the reverse: Jesus Christ rose, and eyewitnesses observed him afterwards; therefore there is a resurrection of the dead.

Many people are concerned about the Corinthians' question, what's it going to be like in heaven? Paul offers very little to satisfy that curiosity. Probably he is content with the summary in 1 Corinthians 15:28. If the matter arises in the group, direct the inquiry toward theological concerns, as Paul does. There is little apocalyptic language in his writings, and that is usually the language we employ when we attempt to describe heaven.

We really do not know just what Paul means by *baptism on behalf of the dead* (1 Corinthians 15:29). It is not mentioned anywhere else in Scripture. Whatever it may be, it is pointless if there is no resurrection. Someone may comment that Mormons observe this practice. Check a good commentary for more detailed information.

About Preoccupation with the End Time

Hope is not just a collection of expectations for the future; it is a theological foundation for balanced living now. It is important to sublimate apocalyptic stage settings to the deeper principles of faith. So Paul ends the resurrection discourse in 1 Corinthians 15 with the exhortation to vigorous life now.

The reference to Hebrews 9:28 may spark discussion about Christ's return. This is the only place where the ordinal "second" is associated with that return, and it is more than pedantic semantics to insist that "second coming" is not a New Testament term. In the New Testament writings the certainty of God's coming presence in Jesus Christ is not diverted to considerations of "how" and "when." The word translated *will appear* is the future passive of one of the simple Greek verbs meaning *to see*. Hebrews 9:28 concludes a passage in which it is affirmed that the critical event has already taken place (verse 26). God's salvation process will surely be brought to a conclusion, but "second coming" focuses on "when" and "how" rather than on "who," "to whom," and "what."

Predictions about the future fly in the face of warnings in the Gospels: see Matthew 24:36, 44-50; Mark 13:32-37; John 16:16-24. Descriptions of the end are quite diverse. Matthew 24:27 uses one figure; Acts 1:11 is very different. Then there are 1 Thessalonians 4:16, 17 and 5:2-4. Add the confusing figures in 2 Peter 3:10. Which description is the true one? All are simply not possible at once. No one figure can exhaust the significance of the more important message. The Book of Revelation adds to the figures but also helps with pinpointing the message.

Supplementary Reading

The activities in the session plans suggest you have commentaries on Mark and 1 Corinthians. Lamar Williamson has written a recent commentary on Mark in the *Interpretation* series (John Knox Press, 1983), and the volume on 1 Corinthians in the *Anchor Bible* has been recommended before.

SESSION PLANS

Learning Objectives

This session is intended to enable participants to:

1. Indicate how the Old Testament hopes described in Parts 1 and 2 of this theme are taken up or redefined in the New Testament.

2. Summarize the central hopes of the New Testament.

3. Present their own interpretations of the Synoptic apocalypse.

4. Explain why the resurrection was so important to the early church and Paul.

5. Describe at least two ways the church responded to the delay in Christ's return.

Resources You May Need

Chalkboard and chalk
Newsprint and markers
12" x 18" construction paper, scissors, glue
Current newspapers and magazines and directions for making a montage
Paper for the group to write letters
Group directions for items 2, 3, and 5 under Exploring the Scripture
Commentaries and other resources on the Synoptic apocalypse
New Oxford Annotated Bible or *Today's English Version*

Leadership Strategy

SETTING THE STAGE

1. Add any new questions to your Loose Ends list and decide when to consider them. Follow the procedure suggested in the last session for linking questions to previous themes and parts.

2. Divide the group into clusters of three. Each cluster will need a 12" x 18" sheet of construction paper, scissors, glue, a dark marker, and current newspapers and news magazines.

Directions for the clusters:

    a. Make a HOPE montage by cutting out pictures, articles, titles, and headlines that show signs of hope in today's world.

    b. Glue them randomly on the construction paper, covering the whole sheet.

    c. Write HOPE across the completed sheet, or cut out letters from headlines to spell HOPE.

    d. Be prepared to share the montage with the other participants.

Reconvene the group and have the montages presented.

or

At the close of the previous session, it was suggested that you ask members of the group to bring articles that offer signs of hope today from recent newspapers or magazines. Invite the members to describe the articles they have brought and tell why they find hope in them. Come prepared with several articles you have located.

EXPLORING THE SCRIPTURE

1. Hang two sheets of newsprint at the front of the meeting room. Mark one sheet "Old Testament Hopes" and the other "New Testament Hopes." Ask the group to reread the material under "A New Kind of Hope" in the *Resource Book*. Then invite everyone to identify hopes for each Testament and record them on the appropriate sheets. Discuss the similarities and differences between the two lists.

or

List these four categories on a chalkboard or newsprint:

    Hope for the nation
    Hope for the family
    Hope for the individual
    Hope for a messiah

Have members of the group form into pairs and discuss what the Old and New Testaments say about hope in each of these categories. Then reconvene the group and poll the participants for suggestions for the categories.

2. Divide the group into four sections and assign each section one of these Scripture clusters:

Section 1	Section 2
Mark 12:18-27	John 14:15-26
Matthew 25:31-46	John 15:26-16:11
John 11:1-44	John 16:12-16

Section 3	Section 4
Romans 5:1-5	Hebrews 9:23-28
Romans 8:11-39	1 Peter 1:3-21
1 Cor. 15:3-8, 12-28, 50-58	2 Peter 3:1-13
1 Thessalonians 4:13-5:11	

Then give these instructions to each section:

a. Read the assigned passages and describe the hope offered or implied in each.

b. Compare ways the hopes are similar or dissimilar.

c. Summarize the hope contained in these passages by having each person or the whole section write a letter to a "non-Christian friend," sharing the joy one experiences because of the hope that is founded in Jesus.

Reconvene the group, share several letters and discuss any questions that arise.

or

Using the thirteen passages listed above, assign each member of the group one passage. Distribute these directions:

a. Summarize the message of hope found in your passage.

b. Answer these questions:

1. What impact do you think this hope had on the people of the early church?

2. How does this hope relate to your faith?

c. Get into a cluster with two other people who have read different passages. Compare your work under a. and b. above with theirs.

d. Decide on a way to share your findings with the total group. You might write a poem, sing a song, make a poster, do a "TV interview," etc.

Reconvene the whole group and share the findings.

and

Ask the group to revise the original list of New Testament hopes completed in item 1, if necessary.

3. Assemble a collection of commentaries and resource books. Divide the group into four sections. (You may want to keep the same sections that worked together in the previous activity.) Separate the sections so that they can work without disturbing each other and assign the following passages:

Group 1	Mark 13:1-13
Group 2	Mark 13:14-23
Group 3	Mark 13:24-31
Group 4	Mark 13:32-37

Distribute these directions to the sections:

a. Pick one person in your section to read aloud the verses you have been assigned.

b. Using the available commentaries and resource books find out what they have to say about your passage. Note especially details that seem to say that the end of the age is imminent and ones that refer to a more distant or ambiguous future.

c. Summarize your findings.

d. Prepare to share your passage and findings with the other sections.

Reconvene the group. Ask each section to indicate the verses it studied and share its findings.

or

Give a brief presentation on the interpretation of the Synoptic apocalypse in Mark 13 and parallel passages. You will need to supplement the *Resource Book* and other readings with a good commentary.

4. Invite the group to recall experiences that were most significant in restoring hope to the disciples and Jesus' other friends after the crucifixion. List them on newsprint. Note which are related to the resurrection of Jesus.

Then have the group turn to 1 Corinthians 15:35-50. Note that Paul is dealing here with the question of the resurrection of the body. Using a good commentary such as the *Anchor Bible*, lead the group through Paul's reasoning and relate it to the postresurrection appearances of Jesus.

and/or

Have the group turn to 1 Corinthians 15:3-19 and lead them through a summary of Paul's argument for the resurrection. In verses 5-8 he mentions individuals and groups to whom Jesus appeared. List them on newsprint or a chalkboard. In verses 12-19 he engages in a reverse argument or what some commentators have called "negative pragmatism." Using newsprint or a chalkboard show how Paul develops the consequences of beginning with the assumption that there is no resurrection:

> If there is no resurrection of the dead:
> Then Christ has not been raised,
> Our preaching and faith are in vain,
> We are misrepresenting God,
> We are still in our sins,
> We are to be pitied.

Paul believes that the resurrection appearances of Jesus and the experiences of God's grace among the Corinthian Christians provide a sound rebuttal to his critics. Discuss with the group their response to Paul's argument. How important is the resurrection to them? Why?

5. Present a definition of "parousia" to the group, using a Bible dictionary or a word book. Post it on newsprint at the front of the room.

Assign 1 Thessalonians 4:13-5:11 to half of the group and 2 Peter 3:1-13 to the other half. Then give these instructions to both groups:

a. Have one person read the introduction to your book in the *New Oxford Annotated Bible* or *Today's English Version*.

b. Read the passage you have been assigned.

c. As you read, look for answers to:

  1. What problem seems to be bothering the church?

  2. What answer is given to this concern?

  3. What hope is being addressed?

  4. What are believers encouraged to do?

  5. How appropriate is such admonition today?

Reconvene the group and share findings. Invite persons to recall similar passages among those read for this session. List them on newsprint or a chalkboard and briefly review them.

or

After presenting the definition of "parousia," invite members of the group to suggest passages from the reading that refer to the hope of Christ's return. Lead the group in discussing what the early church believed regarding Christ's appearance and the problems that occurred when he did not return. Invite several persons to share their personal beliefs about "parousia." How are their beliefs related to their attitudes and actions in the church today?

CLOSING

1. Ask the group to imagine they are first century Christians who are encountering danger or persecution because of their faith. They are to write a page in an imaginary journal outlining their feelings and reasons for maintaining hope.

and/or

Read aloud Hebrews 11:1. Ask the group to list thoughts they would include in a sermon on hope to their present congregation.

Looking Ahead

Item #1 under Setting the Stage in the next session suggests that the leader or a panel of three or four persons who have prepared ahead of time field questions concerning the origin and purpose of the Book of Revelation.

Item #1 under Exploring the Scripture in the same session suggests that seven persons present reports on the churches in Revelation 2-3. It also suggests that four members of the group prepare to read the script of the interview with John. See the activity for details.

NOTES FROM THE AUTHOR

An Encouraging Word

The Revelation has been largely a closed book, more from negligence than from the real difficulties of the book. It is introduced in Theme 1 because it is quite relevant there, and it has appeared in several other themes. So we should be prepared to accept it here as a fitting conclusion to our study. Review what I wrote about the book in Theme 1, Part 4.

I urge you to try the lines of interpretation I suggest. Have courage that the deep significance of the book will come through. Keep in sharp focus the central, unifying perception: The future is ultimately secure in the hand of the Lord, who is present among the churches, and this is guaranteed by the already-won victory of Jesus Christ.

We live in an age that threatens to become apocalyptic. Honest appraisal renders the imagery of Revelation terribly timely for our world. If our assessment of the book is right, the final hope found here is a pressing need for the church today.

Tackling the Task

The first principle in undertaking such a difficult book is to learn as much as possible about what it meant for its original readers/hearers. This usually saves us from presumptuously applying details of the book to our present time. There is a long, unfortunate history of persons who confidently declared that Revelation contains a secret journal of the history of the church up to their time. The care with which John addresses each of the seven churches makes it clear that he believes his visions are specifically applicable to them. (See the commentaries for details like the illustration about Laodicea in the *Resource Book*)

This is not contradictory to my statement that the book is timely today. To arrive at that timeliness, the meaning for the seven churches must control our interpretation for the churches today. Review the equation on the first page of my notes to Part 2.

The *one like the Son of Man* gives the interpretation of the first vision (Revelation 1:20), and this is very important. It sets at once a direction for understanding what follows. The destiny of the churches is secure because Christ keeps them in his hand. The guardian angels are symbols of this security; see Psalm 91:11-13. Throughout the book the connection between earth and heaven is dramatically repeated. When the scene on earth becomes almost unbearably fearsome, the scene shifts to heaven. There a kaleidoscopic variety of visions affirm that the victory of Christ has already determined the outcome of the earth-drama.

Revelation 4 and 5 stretch the imagination. Note the hymns; they are loaded with Old Testament allusions. The church has used these hymns often in its prayer and praise. Handel's *The Messiah* is a distinguished example; we hear its echo several times in this part.

John desperately wants to know what will happen to the church in the future. The answer is in the scroll. *The Lion of the tribe of Judah* is clearly the Messiah, and he can open up the future. When he takes the scroll, a startling switch occurs: He is not a lion at all but a sacrificed Lamb! The meaning is a dramatic presentation of Jesus' reinterpretation of messiahship.

You will find that Christ, in one guise or another, dominates the whole book.[1] What he has done has already affected the final course of history. Thus the interpretation of the book must be christological throughout.

Highlights

In a somewhat complicated way the rest of Revelation deals with the opening of the seven-sealed scroll. The fate of the martyrs (fifth seal) is noteworthy. *Under the altar* probably refers to the Temple practice of pouring the blood of sacrificed animals at the base of the altar (see Leviticus 4:18). The word for *testimony* in Greek is cognate with our word "martyr"; Christians became martyrs because they were witnesses. Besides receiving white robes, they are told that there will be more martyrs.

Dramatic details pile up in anticipation of the opening of the seventh seal. It should bring the end, but instead there is the double interlude. It presents the earth-heaven change of

---

1 Curiously, Luther declared that "Christ is neither taught in it nor recognized," but he did make use of the book in polemics against the papacy. Calvin did not write a commentary on the book.

scene. Those who are *sealed* on earth are counted; those who finally appear in heaven are beyond counting (recall the spiritual, *Plenty Good Room*). The great moment comes, the seventh seal is opened, but it reveals a new series of seven. These are trumpets, symbols of judgment.

And so goes the book through Chapter 19. Suspense is built to the breaking point, but the successive scenes in heaven show no suspense at all because all is praise of God for the victory of the Lamb. The suggestion that the book is conceived in dramatic forms can be very helpful—the gospel is, after all, dramatic. The theater was prominent in cities influenced by Greek culture. Greek staging sometimes utilized two levels, so John's earth-heaven scenery would not tax the imagination of his hearers.

Do not allow the group session to bog down in one or another text. Make some quick resolution—even if tentative— and move on. The book as a whole really explains the details, not vice versa.

Some Details

Details there are, however, and some can hardly be avoided. The familiar names for the personification of evil, Revelation 12:9, 10, are a helpful way of emphasizing that all evil is one. The beasts of Chapter 13 are a continuation of this, and in Chapter 17 Rome itself is clearly part of this connection. In Revelation 13:18 it is an individual. Probably you cannot escape old *666*. Summaries of the possibilities are in the commentaries. The traditional identification with Nero is easiest to explain. It is also possible that Domitian was thought of as a new Nero. As soon as this epitome of evil is mentioned in the text, there comes a vision in heaven.

The fall of Babylon is declared in Revelation 14:8. This anticipates (literally) Revelation 18:2. Here is one of many examples that the book is not a straightforward narration. (Recall how 7:9-17 anticipates the salvation of the sufferers.)

The outcome of the series of sevens brings a magnificent response in heaven, Revelation 19:6-9. *The marriage of the Lamb* is a consummation of Christ's relationship with the church. There are allusions to such a supper in the Gospels: besides the references in the *Resource Book*, see Matthew 22:1-14; Luke 12:35-38; 22:15-18. There is a parody or caricature of this in the awful banquet of the birds, Revelation 19:17-21. (There are other caricatures in the book; for example the rider on the white horse, compare Revelation 19:11 with 6:2.)

You may have to deal with the *thousand years*, Revelation 20:1-10. The use of symbolism throughout the book and the seer's freedom from rigid sequences of times and events strongly suggests that the thousand years are not to be taken as a literal span of time. The saints are promised in Revelation 5:10 that *they will reign on earth.* Perhaps this is the fulfillment of that promise before the earth is changed. At any rate, do not allow disagreement or controversy over this detail to divert attention from the theological message of the whole book.

Throughout the Revelation faithfulness and works are important. In the last judgment, Revelation 20:11-15, *the dead were judged according to their works.* In the critical times faced by John and the seven churches, there can be no relaxation of conduct and loyalty. In the end, however, it is *the Lamb's book of life* that determines who will enter the New Jerusalem. Deeds are judged, but Christ's grace has the last word.

Final Scenes

The splendid vision of *a new heaven and a new earth* was anticipated by the prophets. The relationship between Yahweh and the wife Israel is now expanded to embrace Christ and the church. The details in Revelation 21:24-27 indicate that these visions are not to be projected totally into the future but are to be seen in the context of the world known to John's addressees.

Let there be no confusion about the warning in Revelation 22:18, 19. It concerns *the words of the prophecy of this book.* While it may seem fitting at the end of the Bible, that is not its first intention. The sixth beatitude, Revelation 22:7, says that these words must be kept. What words? Worship God. Hope in Christ's victory. Endure. Work faithfully. Live cleanly.

This puts the message of the book in the mainstream of early Christian thought. Luther and others have considered the book to be theologically inferior. Perhaps they have been distracted by some of the "stage business." 2 Peter 1:20 warns *that no prophecy of scripture is a matter of one's own interpretation.* The Revelation offers Christ-based hope. God does and will save a people, and the victory of Christ already guarantees it. The assurance that Christ is *coming soon* holds no terror for one who has seen the seven stars *in his right hand* and who has responded to the invitation of *the Spirit and the bride.* We can with complete confidence pray with the very words of Christians in the seven churches, *Come, Lord Jesus!*

Supplementary Reading

Your study Bible, a Bible dictionary and the supplementary books on the New Testament will have introductions to Revelation. The commentary by M. Eugene Boring in the *Interpretation* series is convenient to use and reliable in its interpretations (John Knox Press, 1989).

SESSION PLANS

Learning Objectives

This session is intended to enable participants to:

1. Describe the context and purpose of Revelation.

2. Locate the seven churches of Revelation 1:11; summarize the context and content of John's message to at least three of them.

3. Cite several examples of how the author of Revelation uses symbolism to communicate his message.

4. Discuss how the message of hope in Revelation speaks to the church today.

Resources You May Need

Chalkboard and chalk
Newsprint and markers
Supplementary reading books
Map of Asia Minor
Seven Bible dictionaries
Instructions for groups studying the seven churches
Copies of the dialogue with John
Copies of the outline of Revelation
Seven Commentaries on Revelation
Construction paper and markers
Recording of *The Messiah*

Leadership Strategy

SETTING THE STAGE

1. This is the last time you will use the Loose Ends list. After adding any new questions to the list, think of ways to relate them to earlier themes and parts, as you did at the last session.

2. Ask members of the group to suggest adjectives that come to mind when they think about the Book of Revelation. List them on a chalkboard or newsprint. Then review the characteristics of apocalyptic literature that were discussed in the earlier parts of this theme, illustrating your remarks with examples from Revelation.

and/or

Invite everyone to prepare questions about matters that puzzle or interest them concerning the origin and purpose of Revelation. The questions are to be directed to areas that do not require interpretation of specific texts, such as the author's immediate situation, the political context, and the purpose of the writing.

You or a panel of three or four members of the group who have prepared ahead of time can respond to the questions. Material in the supplementary readings and a Bible dictionary will provide useful background information. If questions are asked that you or the panel cannot answer, invite other participants to assist.

EXPLORING THE SCRIPTURE

1. The following activity is similar to one suggested for Theme 1, Part 4. If you used the activity then, skip to the dialogue suggested below or another activity of your choice.

   Project a map of Asia Minor onto the classroom wall and locate the seven churches of Revelation. Many Bible dictionaries will have maps with the locations clearly indicated.

   Then divide the group into seven sections. Assign each section the role of one of the congregations addressed in Chapters 2-3. Give each section a Bible dictionary and these instructions:

   Prepare a report for the group where you:

       a. Summarize the characteristics of your assigned city and church.

       b. Describe John's message to your church.

       c. Outline your response to his message.

   Gather the whole group and have the seven sections report.

or

   Have seven persons who were selected at the last session present the information suggested above for the seven churches addressed in Revelation. Discuss which of the churches seem most like your congregation. How would your church respond to John's message?

or

Invite four members who volunteered at the previous session to read the following dialogue to the group. The parts are narrator, reporter, pastor, John.

Narrator:	Pretend that you are viewing an interview between a reporter and a pastor who have traveled back in time to talk with John, the author of Revelation. The setting is the Greek island of Patmos, and the date is about 89 A.D. Domitian is the emperor of Rome. The space travelers have found John seated in a small, sunlit courtyard. He appears to be completing a long letter.
	Introductions and explanations are made, and John agrees to an interview, although he seems a little confused as to how this has happened and why anyone from the future would want to interview him.
Reporter:	When I was a kid in Sunday School, I used to think of your writing Revelation on a barren desert island. This is quite a place. It looks like Patmos is a port of call for many of the ships that travel Rome's commerce routes.
John:	You're very observant. It is a very busy island. Nevertheless, this is a penal colony, too. I certainly wouldn't be here if I were free to leave! There are many others besides myself here because we are considered political dissidents for opposing the worship of that scoundrel Domitian as a god.
Pastor:	We'd like to thank you for allowing us to visit you. You don't know how much we have been looking forward to this opportunity to ask you some questions.
	John, you can't imagine all the disagreements that your letter has caused in churches through the centuries. What was your real reason for writing Revelation?
John:	I should think that the purpose is quite clear. Are you aware of the political situation at this time? Things in the recent past have not been pleasant, but under the rule of Domitian I foresee terrible trials and tribulations for the Christians in Ephesus, Smyrna, Pergamum, Thyatira, Sardis, Philadelphia, and Laodicea. If I were free, I would

	go and speak to them. However, this is the best I can do under the circumstances.
Reporter:	So you wrote the letter hoping to warn the churches about the terrible times that are coming.
John:	Yes, but I have some other reasons, also. First, some of the churches are doing very well. For instance, Smyrna is a strong and faithful group. The people are very poor, but they have great spiritual wealth. They will undergo harsh trials. I want them to know that I appreciate their steadfastness, and that I am with them if only in my heart.
Pastor:	How about Laodicea?
John:	Those people! They are blind to the truth. All of the salve that is used in the famous hospital of Laodicea can't cure the kind of spiritual blindness that afflicts them. Their wealth will be their downfall, if they don't become serious about their faith in our Lord Jesus. They suffer from the terrible sin of being only lukewarm.
Reporter:	What is your concern for Pergamum?
John:	Pergamum was the seat of emperor worship long before emperor worship was a law of the state. I fear for the church because the people are weak and easily swayed. The Nicolaitans have influence there. If the believers continue on their present path, they will be destroyed.
Reporter:	Nicolaitans? Who are they?
John:	Perverted persons who were once Christians. They are teaching that it is right to eat food offered to idols. They encourage sexual immorality. They want to form a compromise between the state religion and Christianity. There can be no compromise!
Pastor:	Our time is limited and there are so many other things that we would like to know. Over and over my congregation asks me why you chose to use so many confusing symbols in your writing.
John:	Confusing? They are very clear to me and they were very clear to the congregations that heard the letter. However, they were chosen to confuse the Romans! They are constantly on guard against

	subversive literature. The symbols I've used no doubt allowed my document to survive for the people of the future. It appears the symbols have given you something to ponder. That gives me some satisfaction!
Reporter:	John, could you give me a brief summary of your book? My editor would be very pleased with that.
John:	Summary! All right. What I have tried to tell the churches is this: Trials and tribulations are coming. You must be strong and hold fast to the faith that you have in Christ Jesus. Be firm in your hope that in the future God will prevail. Soon this difficult time will pass and you will be vindicated. The plan may not be clear to us, but God is in charge of the entire world. Evil will be punished. Your reward will be great if you hold tightly to what you know to be the truth.
Reporter:	Thank you.
Pastor:	Thank you very much.
John:	The grace of the Lord Jesus be with all the saints.

or

Compose your own dialogue.

2. Provide the group with an outline of Revelation. Your study Bible or a Bible dictionary will have suggestions. If you prefer a more detailed outline you may want to copy for the group the one included at the end of these session plans.

Then divide the group into seven sections. Give each section a commentary and construction paper and markers. Assign these Scripture passages:

Section 1 - Chapter 4   Section 5 - Chapter 20:11-15
Section 2 - Chapter 5   Section 6 - Chapter 21:1-7
Section 3 - Chapter 12:1-12   Section 7 - Chapter 22:16-21
Section 4 - Chapter 19:6-16

Each section is to read its passage, making note of unusual words or symbols. Using the footnotes and cross references in their Bibles along with the commentary, they are to review other biblical references or allusions to the same words and symbols. Then they are to prepare a summary of their passage in the form of a visual or oral report highlighting the discoveries they have made about the most important words and symbols in their passage. They should also indicate how their passage fits into the outline of the book that you have presented.

Reconvene the group and have the sections share their findings.

or

Select several of the above passages and give a brief presentation indicating how you would interpret them.

and

Dr. Walther believes that the message of hope in Revelation makes it a most timely book for the church to study today. Invite members of the group to share responses to this statement and discuss them. What parallels are there between the situation of the church then and now? How might Revelation speak to the issues facing us today?

CLOSING

1. Invite volunteers to suggest one hope they have for their congregation. Record them on newsprint or a chalkboard. Then lead the group in a prayer into which you weave the various hopes that have been suggested.

and/or

Read Revelation 22:20-21 responsively.

or

Read Revelation 19:6-9 and play a portion of the *Messiah*.

Looking Ahead

Item #1 under Exploring the Scripture in the next session suggests that the answers to the question "What is the Bible?" from Theme 1, Part 1, be displayed. Use your original notes from the earlier session. If they are no longer available, ask several members of the group for the responses they wrote in their *Resource Books* or notebooks.

If you are planning a special celebration to conclude the program, final details should be completed now.

Outline of Revelation

Part 1 *Preface (1:1-3)*

Part 2 *Letter to the Churches (1:4-3:22)*

      a. Covering letter   e. Thyatira
      b. Ephesus   f. Sardis
      c. Smyrna   g. Philadelphia
      d. Pergamum   h. Laodicea

Part 3 *Introductory Visions (4:1-5:14)*

Part 4 *Seven Seal Visions (6:1-8:6)*

      a. White horse   f. Cosmic woes
      b. Red horse   g. Sealing of martyrs
      c. Black horse   h. Glorified martyrs
      d. Pale horse   i. Preparation for trumpets (Interludes)
      e. Lament of martyrs

Part 5 *Seven Trumpet Woes (8:7-11:19)*

      a. Hail and fire
      b. Burning mountain falls into sea
      c. Blazing star falls into sea
      d. Darkening of sun, moon and stars
      e. Eagle's warning
      f. Demonic locusts
      g. Destroying horsemen from Euphrates
      h. John eats doom scroll
      i. Two heavenly witnesses
      j. God's taking of power (Interludes)

Part 6 *Seven Visions of Dragon's Kingdom (12:1-13:18)*

      a. Heavenly mother and birth of Messiah
      b. Michael's victory over dragon
      c. Song of woe and rejoicing
      d. Woman and other children
      e. Beast from sea
      f. Beast's authority
      g. Beast from the earth

Part 7 *Seven Visions of Worshippers of Lamb and of Beast (14:1-20)*

      a. Martyrs and Lamb on Mt. Zion
      b. Angel's advice to worship God
      c. Angel pronounces doom of Babylon
      d. Angel condemns worshippers of beast
      e. Benediction of martyrs
      f. Son of Man and harvest
      g. Angel and vintage

Part 8   *Seven Visions of Bowls of God's Wrath (15:1-16:21)*

      a. Preparation

      b. Plague of ulcers

      c. Sea turned to blood

      d. Rivers and springs turned to blood

      e. Scorching heat of sun

      f. Darkness of beast's kingdom

      g. Kings assemble for Armageddon

      h. Impending destruction of Babylon

Part 9   *Seven Visions of Fall of "Babylon" (or Rome) (17:1-19:10)*

      a. Harlot—Babylon the Great

      b. Interpretation of harlot and beast

      c. Proclamation of Rome's fall

      d. Exultation and mourning over fall of Rome

      e. Millstone thrown into sea and dirge over city

      f. Hymn of praise to God

      g. Marriage hymn to the Lamb and his bride

Part 10   *Seven visions of the End of Satan's Evil Age and the Beginning of God's Righteous Age (19:11-21:8)*

      a. Conquering Christ

      b. Victory of Christ over beast and Anti-Christ

      c. Satan bound and his rule suspended for 1,000 years

      d. Reign of Christ for 1,000 years

      e. Gog and Magog defeated and Satan cast into lake of fire

      f. Disappearance of heaven and earth, 2nd resurrection and general judgement

      g. New Creation and God's Eternal Age

Part 11   *Supplement (21:9-22:5)—Description of New Jerusalem*

      a. External appearance of city

      b. Measurement of city

      c. Composition of city

      d. Divine glory of city

      e. New Garden of Eden with river and Tree of Life

Part 12   *Epilogue (22:6-21)—A collection of the last words of John*

Last Things

NOTES FROM THE AUTHOR

The End as a Fine Beginning

You have completed a major study that touches most of the contents of the Bible. One of the surest marks of the success of your endeavor will be an expression by the group that your work together has been only a beginning. It is a beginning, however, with a difference. You have constructed, as it were, a set of pegs on which the group can continue to attach pieces of study. Or, to change the metaphor, they now have an adequate framework into which they can fit further biblical knowledge.

Upon reflection you will also see that the perspectives of this Bible study provide an entry to legitimate application. By studying the Bible whole you have lessened the temptation to interpret by proof-text. You have reinforced the Reformation principle of interpreting Scripture by Scripture.

Our approach has been founded on a conviction that the divine revelation, which occurred precisely in history and therefore to specific people at specific times, is a unique element of Judeo-Christian religion. Christians affirm that it is an important basis of their hope: God's act at one unique time in one unique way in one unique person is definitive for the people who espouse this faith at all succeeding times.

So you may seriously embrace a somewhat trite declaration: this ending of *Kerygma: The Bible in Depth* is really a commencement. Where it may lead in terms of further biblical study and further understanding of the application of faith to life is a glorious and substantial surprise awaiting every willing learner.

The Bible References

The passage from Psalm 119 conveys more than praise of God's law. In the context of our study it shows how Jews have revered and loved the Hebrew Scriptures. Jesus' disputes with the legalists of his day have given some people an impression that Torah was a grievous burden. It is true that the oral interpretations became onerous, but the Scriptures were fundamentally a delight to the Jews—and are so today.

Most scholars think that the pastoral letters were probably not composed in just the forms we have today. This is a technical matter that need not concern us here. The words about Paul's impending death give evidence of being quite genuine, and problems about the organization of the early church reflected elsewhere in these letters need not affect this.

The passage about inspiration and Scripture must be handled carefully. The placing of the verb *is* does not really settle the interpretation. The important detail—difficult as it may be for people to accept—is that the church, guided by God's Spirit, ultimately decided which books belong in the canon. This process was only in embryo when this passage was written. The point of the passage, then, is the function of Scripture, not its definition. This is surely a point that this Kerygma program has been making.

Finally, remarks about the "apostolic benediction." Note the order of the clauses; it is not the credal order to which we are accustomed. For Paul, *grace* came first. Unless he had experienced *the grace of the Lord Jesus Christ*, he would not have appreciated *the love of God*. The third element is to be clarified by understanding the word communion. Note the NRSV footnote, *the sharing in*. The Greek word is *koinonia*, which indicates having something in common. In Luke 5:10, a cognate word is translated *partners. The Holy Spirit* is how we experience partnership with God, how the *grace of the Lord Jesus Christ* and *the love of God* become contemporary and effective in our lives.

Research and Review

Number 3 in Research includes ten items to focus a review on all of the themes. These points are not intended to be definitive. They are directions that seem to me to deal with the main thrust of each theme.

Now Finally

"In the beginning"—when this Kerygma program first took published form—these "Notes from the Author" were to be on audiocassette so that my relationship with leaders would be as personal as possible. It turned out that they have always been in print. Nevertheless,

I feel close to those who have been leading this program in thousands of churches, and I have reason to believe that many of you have felt some such relationship to me.

One result of teaching *Kerygma: The Bible in Depth* seems to be fairly uniform: the leader learns more than anyone in the group. That is probably as it should be. We have tried to make Kerygma a personal program. We maintain a fat file of letters from people who have been enriched by this study.

The *Resource Book* urges group participants to make this program a launching pad for further learning. That appeal is even more applicable in your case. You have a substantial investment in Bible study. Thirty-four sessions as leader in a demanding program is evidence that you have the ability and background to achieve more in leadership.

The two verses following the 2 Timothy passage read in part: *I solemnly urge you: proclaim* (the verb is the root word of *Kerygma) the message; be persistent whether the time is favorable or unfavorable; convince, rebuke, and encourage, with the utmost patience in teaching* (2 Timothy 4:1, 2). Let these words end our Notes.

Supplementary Reading

If you are not familiar with the other Bible study courses that are offered by The Kerygma Program, now is a good time to contact the office in Pittsburgh for information. Just as a reminder, their toll free number is 800-537-9462. Mail information is included on the acknowledgments page. The momentum from *Kerygma: The Bible in Depth* may then be directed into another study.

SESSION PLANS

Learning Objectives

This session is intended to enable participants to:

1. Name some of their learnings from the course.

2. Describe how their view of Scripture has changed since the beginning of the course.

3. Celebrate arriving at the end (conclusion and goal) of the study.

C

Resources You May Need

Chalkboard and chalk
Newsprint, markers, and masking tape
Newsprint sheets with themes written on them
Sheets of paper for each member of the group
Newsprint sheets with answers to question from Theme 1, Part 1
Overhead projector and transparency of Psalm 119:97-105
Copies of handout of Psalm 119:97-105
Transparency or handout of a hymn on the theme of the Holy Scriptures

Leadership Strategy

REVIEW

1. Write the names of the ten themes on separate sheets of newsprint and place them around the room. As you go through the themes one at a time, invite members of the group to make brief statements about what they have learned. Record these responses in abbreviated form on the newsprint.

or

Invite everyone to turn to page 246 in the *Resource Book* and find the suggestions for review in Research #3. Read these suggestions aloud, allowing ample time after each of them for participants to offer their responses and engage in discussion.

or

Divide the group into ten clusters. Assign each cluster one of the suggestions in Research #3. Allow the clusters time to prepare their responses. Reconvene the group and have the clusters summarize their answers. Encourage the group to discuss the responses and to offer additional insights as appropriate.

EXPLORING THE SCRIPTURE

1. Ask members of the group to suggest responses to the question, "What is the Bible?" List the responses on newsprint or a chalkboard.

or

Distribute paper to participants and ask them to complete the following statement in two or three sentences: "To me the Bible is . . ." Have them read their statements aloud. Record these responses in abbreviated form on newsprint or a chalkboard.

or

Divide the group into three or four sections. Ask each section to answer the question, "What is the Bible?" A scribe from each section can write the answer on newsprint and then report it to the reassembled group.

and

Post the newsprint sheet(s) you have prepared with the answers to this question offered during the session on Theme 1, Part 1. Ask members of the group to compare the responses from this session and the earlier one. Reflect on the significance of both the similarities and the differences between the responses.

and/or

Ask a volunteer to read aloud 2 Timothy 3:14-17 while the rest of the group follows the reading in their own Bibles. Discuss how this passage reinforces and/or augments insights from the previous discussion. (If the group is large, this discussion may begin in the same three or four sections suggested earlier. The group may then be reconvened for reports and a brief discussion.)

Since the "sacred writings" mentioned in verse 15 did not include all of the Bible as we know it today, make a brief presentation on how the canon was formed. Helpful information can be found in the reading for Theme 1, Part 1.

2. Ask the group to name the three ways of "hearing" and "listening" that Dr. Walther describes in the *Resource Book*. Invite participants to give illustrations from their own experience of each of the shades of meaning. Write them on newsprint. Lead the group in reflecting on how these ways of hearing and listening are related and the significance of these relationships for how we study the Bible.

CLOSING

1. Project a transparency or distribute a handout of Psalm 119:97-105. Divide the group into two sections and invite them to read the first eight verses aloud antiphonally and to conclude by reading verse 105 in unison.

and/or

Invite the group to sing a hymn on the theme of the Holy Scriptures.

and/or

As you conclude this study, evaluate the program. One way to do this is to ask members of the group to make four lists: the program's strengths; the program's weaknesses; their personal accomplishments; their personal frustrations. Invite partici-

C

pants to share their lists. Record the suggestions on newsprint and determine the ranking of the most common items. Share this evaluation with the committee or persons who planned *Kerygma: The Bible in Depth* in your church.

and/or

As was suggested earlier, many groups will want to conclude their study experience with a special celebration, awards ceremony, or festive meal.